Talking with My Mouth Full

Talking with My Mouth Full

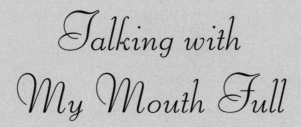

My Life as a Professional Eater

GAIL SIMMONS

HYPERION

New York

B/SIMMONS/[Gail]/Simmons

All photos are courtesy of Gail Simmons and all illustrations are by Julia Rothman, except as noted below:

Page 148: Michael Katz; page 152: devI NC; page 158: © 2011 American Express Publishing Corporation. All Rights Reserved. Photo: Allan Zepeda; page 210: Trademark Logo © 2011 American Express Publishing Corporation. All Rights Reserved; page 216: Tara Donne; page 218: THUSS + FARRELL.

Library of Congress Cataloging-in-Publication Data

Simmons, Gail.
  Talking with my mouth full : my life as a professional eater / Gail Simmons.
    p. cm.
  ISBN 978-1-4013-2450-6
 1. Simmons, Gail. 2. Cooks—Biography. I. Title.
  TX649.S293A3 2012
  641.5092—dc23
  [B]

                                                  2011046485

Book design by Cassandra J. Pappas

FIRST EDITION

10 9 8 7 6 5 4 3 2 1

SUSTAINABLE FORESTRY INITIATIVE

Certified Fiber Sourcing

www.sfiprogram.org

THIS LABEL APPLIES TO TEXT STOCK

For Jer

CONTENTS

Talking with My Mouth Full

Introduction

....

Eat. Write. Travel. Cook.

I LOVE TO eat. Not in a gluttonous way. Not in a pack-it-in-as-much-as-you-can-as-fast-as-you-can sort of way. I love the ritual of eating. How the way you hold your knife and fork (or chopsticks or fingers), and what you choose to put between them, determines so much about who you are, where you are from, how you came to be eating this very meal.

I love how everyone in the world has a different palate, different likes and dislikes, nuanced phobias or aversions, obsessions or cravings, which shape the way we nourish ourselves. I love how, like a thumbprint, no two people's noses and tongues perceive smell and taste the same way. I, for one, have come to realize that I much prefer salty, savory foods in the morning. Runny poached eggs with spicy Sriracha, hearty grain toast and butter, avocado, smoked salmon, bacon.

I am pretty democratic in my love of food and its applications for lunch and dinner. I love vegetables and fruit as much as I love meat. I love fish, seafood, and whole grains. I absolutely love dessert. Not a lot, not every day. But most days certainly, I adore a bite or two of something rich and sweet at the end of the last meal of the day. Or as a midday snack. Ice cream. A simple fruit tart, especially when the fruit caramelizes on the outside but is still a bit juicy within. A chocolate éclair.

I also know I love vinegar and I love chilies: pickles and heat. I love creamy, pungent cheeses. Maple syrup. Fresh corn that you can basically eat raw. Peaches (my favorite white peaches are Opals, and Cal Reds are the juiciest you will ever taste). Spaghetti alla carbonara. I love dark chocolate. So does my father. But I love how it's possible that one of my two older brothers, raised eating largely the same meals as me for the first two decades of their lives, doesn't eat vinegar and the other doesn't eat chocolate.

From an early age, I knew my biggest interest was food, but what could I do with this information? No teacher at school suggested I might be able to make a living as an eater. Back then, our cultural obsession with food wasn't nearly the juggernaut it is today. Reality TV was just in its infancy when I graduated from college in the late 1990s, so the thought of judging professional chefs on national television would have never entered my mind.

On the eve of adulthood, my friends would declare with confidence: "I'm going to medical school." "I'm going to law school." "I'm doing an MBA." "I'm getting a master's in art history." "I'm going to law school." "I'm going to law school, too!"

Nothing against law school, but how did they know? Was I the only person without a clue about the next step? It sure felt that way. My parents and my friends' parents expected great things from their children, and great things usually involved postgraduate degrees. Graduate school is great if you know what you want to do. But I didn't have the foggiest idea. None of the things my friends were doing interested me. *Especially* law school.

I felt at the time like the only one in my crowd—full of so many bright, strong young women—who really didn't know what she wanted to be. So where did that leave me?

Well, after college, it left me back at home, in my parents' basement to be exact, where I spent a month or two feeling sorry for myself and depressed. I was lost. I couldn't believe that not one professor or advisor, in four years of attending one of the best colleges in the country, ever said, "Let's start planning for when you leave here." I couldn't believe I'd never thought about it myself. Then one day at a family dinner, my mother, who was starting to worry, made me sit down with the accomplished daughter of one of her closest friends. She was about ten years my senior. She listened to my dilemma.

Then she handed me a pen and said, "Make a list of what you like to do. Not jobs. Just anything that comes into your mind."

On a random piece of paper, I wrote: "Eat. Write. Travel. Cook."

It seemed like a ridiculous exercise. But this wonderful woman (who now works for the Food Network Canada, of all places) smiled.

"See?" she said, pointing at my paper. "You're not lost. What's your mom so worried about?"

Like an eerie fortune cookie, that scrap became the trajectory of my life.

What do I do for a living? I eat endlessly as a judge on *Top Chef,* write and talk as a food authority in the media, travel the country and beyond for *Food & Wine,* and regularly cook at events, online, and on television. Without a map, I've actually managed to turn my curiosity, enthusiasm, and passion into the life of my dreams. Fifteen years ago, I never could have imagined all that could add up to such a satisfying life.

That's at least in part because the job didn't exist yet. How could any of us have known—even as recently as the 1990s—that a love of good food and the people who make it would spawn an industry so much larger and more layered than just chefs and restaurants?

It hit me more than ever the night of *Top Chef*'s Season 3 finale, which we shot at the top of Aspen Mountain. We ate the final dinner from 4:30 to 8:30 p.m. It was August—hot and beautiful, with zero humidity. There was a three-hour break while the crew reset. In the meantime, Bravo's senior vice president of programming, Andy Cohen, came up and interviewed us for a short video that appeared on the show's website.

The sun went down and it was soon below freezing at the top of the mountain, ten thousand feet above sea level. We had blankets on our laps under the table. It was absurd how cold it was.

The cameras rolled on Judges' Table from 11:33 p.m. to 4:06 a.m. But we could still not agree on the season's winner. Finally our producers sent all but one of the camerapeople home, and for another hour we continued to debate between chefs Hung Huynh and Dale Levitski. They literally forced us to sit in a room together until we all were unanimous in our decision. If there's even one judge holdout, he or she has to relent and be comfortable with the outcome before we can continue.

We agreed that Dale had higher highs and lower lows. But Hung had been more consistent throughout his meal. Two of Dale's dishes, scallops with purslane and grapes and lamb with eggplant, tomatoes, and squash, left a substantial impact on us, but his foie gras mousse and his lobster with gnocchi in curry jus were quite flawed. Hung's were technically precise, beautifully presented, like his pristine shrimp with palm sugar, cucumber salad, and coconut foam, but not always as exciting. They didn't hit us in the face with flavor the way Dale's two dishes did.

Our question came down to this: Would you rather have really exciting food that sometimes misses the mark by a mile, or would you rather have a consistently good, well-crafted meal? Tom and I were down for consistency and Padma and Ted Allen were arguing for excitement.

We were freezing and exhausted. In the end, we decided that the sign of a more mature chef was a consistent experience, and picked Hung.

As the sun rose all around us, we knew we had to walk away. It was six in the morning by the time we headed back down the mountain.

As I watched the sunrise from the gondola, I realized my job was about to change the course of two young chefs' lives.

All because I loved to eat.

....

ONE

My Mother's Kitchen Counter

MY MOTHER BAKES plum tarts every year in late August. The smell fills the house. As they bake, the juicy plums sink into the vanilla cake base. I'm smitten by the smell, the vanillaness of it. My mother's kitchen counter overflows with bowls and vessels. So many that it is often hard to find room to cook. There are ten different kinds of vinegars and oils. A smattering of porcelain teapots. A giant wooden bowl shaped like a carrot, always filled with peanuts in their shells. A little glass cloche containing soft runny cheese. A bowl of dried fruit—pears, apples, prunes, and apricots. A beige ceramic butter dish with soft butter, one of hundreds of ceramic pieces my parents have collected over the years. Clementines in winter. Peaches in summer. Wasabi peas. Spiced pumpkin seeds. Whole walnuts, hazelnuts, and almonds alongside an ornate silver nutcracker. A loaf of zucchini bread with flecks of green.

A MAGNET ON OUR refrigerator read: "A gourmet is just a glutton with brains." It served as the family motto.

I grew up in a four-bedroom redbrick house built in 1948, in the picturesque central Toronto neighborhood of Cedarvale. It was a real *neighborhood,* even though it was in the middle of a bustling metropolis, less than a fifteen-minute drive from downtown. It was an upper-middle-class community, with a large Jewish population. The three sizable synagogues within walking distance of my house made parking on any observed holiday a treacherous task. There was a big apple tree in the backyard, perfect for climbing, and a little door under the stairs with a sign that read PRIVATE: ALAN & ERIC'S HIDEAWAY, belonging to my older brothers. They let me hide out there, too.

My father, Ivor, is from South Africa, and my mother, Renée, is a Montrealer. They moved to Toronto independently and met and married in 1966. They created an adventurous environment for us in that house. Shelves of books, including every last Hardy Boys novel and fairy-tale anthology, lined the tiny passageway between my and my brothers' rooms. They would visit me via this passageway to torment or entertain me, depending on the night.

Like so many Canadian kids, my brothers and their friends played hockey in the streets, throwing me in as goalie when they were down a player or two. We rode our bikes to school. We had lemonade stands every summer, with pink juice thawed from frozen concentrate tins, and annual street-long yard sales. On Halloween the neighborhood dressed itself up, with haunted houses and jack-o'-lanterns, cauldrons bubbling over with dry ice on the neighbors' front lawns, and yards of cotton, subbing in for cobwebs, draping their windowpanes. Not surprisingly, my best costume of all was when I was ten years old and dressed as my favorite Canadian chocolate bar, Mirage. I fashioned it out of a cardboard box painted dark brown and a yellow garbage bag.

Forgive me for assuming you don't know, but for non-Canadians: Toronto is the economic capital of Canada. The Greater Toronto Area is home to more than 5.5 million people, with influences from all over the globe and one of the world's greatest Chinatowns outside of, well, China. It is often cited as the safest large metropolitan area in North America. I am always amazed at how few people know that it is the fifth-largest city on the continent, behind only Mexico City, New York, Los Angeles, and Chicago. The CN (Canadian National) Tower, one of the tallest freestanding structures ever built, dominates the skyline. I often tell friends who have never been to Toronto that it is similar to Chicago in feel. It's also situated on one of the Great Lakes, Lake Ontario, but somehow we screwed up the waterfront by constructing a massive highway that barrels right through it. Americans love to talk about how clean Toronto is, which drives my mother crazy because she feels that it's no longer true.

And yet, our neighborhood was more or less spotless, and the schools were good. I went to Cedarvale Community School. It was small, with about three hundred children, and hosted a huge annual spring fair that, until late into my teens, was my single favorite day of the year. For me, the most important part of that fair was always the Make Your Own Cupcake booth. Go figure.

....

I'VE ALWAYS THOUGHT the way my parents got together was very romantic. They married rather late for the time period. My mother was twenty-seven. My father was twenty-nine. My mom's friends were all married with kids by the time she met my father.

Like me, my mother had two older brothers, Mel and Bernie. Her father was a hardworking and entrepreneurial Polish immigrant who made his fortune in the *schmatta* business (Yiddish for the garment industry). During the Depression and into World War II, he made an impressive living manufacturing inexpensive women's dresses.

This allowed him to buy an architecturally iconic house on auction in a very exclusive part of Montreal called Westmount. The original owner, Emile Berliner—inventor of the disk record gramophone and early versions of the microphone and the helicopter, among other things—died in 1929.

When they moved in, in 1939, the parks had signs that read NO JEWS AND NO DOGS. But here was my mother's family living in the heart of the neighborhood in a beautiful old home.

For a time, they had a Chinese chef named Chang, who taught my mother how to cook and the rituals of eating Chinese food. My grandmother, an excellent cook herself, used to come home at the end of the day to find my four-year-old mother sitting cross-legged on the counter of the kitchen, bowl up to her chin, expertly shoveling rice into her mouth or slurping noodles with chopsticks. Chang also introduced my mother to steamed pork buns, or char siu bao, which somehow became one of my many childhood nicknames, often shortened to Char Siu or "Chash."

My mother's parents were unhappy together for the better part of thirty years and finally divorced when my mother was in her last year of college; she moved into the residence hall at McGill University to get away from all the drama. She had entered college at the age of sixteen, and when she graduated at twenty she pursued a master's degree in European politics at the Collège d'Europe in Bruges, Belgium. Then she traveled through Europe and Israel, meeting up with people along the way, one of whom was Leonard Cohen, my uncle

Bernie's oldest childhood friend. She says they weren't romantically involved, but I'm suspicious. Because, come on, how can you travel abroad with Leonard Cohen and not be enchanted by him?

She stayed in Israel for a brief period, then moved to New York and got a job as a guide at the United Nations, where she had to walk dozens of miles a day giving tours to visitors—in heels. The guides were from dozens of countries and spoke countless languages. By sheer coincidence, one of the other guides at the time was none other than Madhur Jaffrey, now the best-known Indian food authority in the West. She's written the most influential Indian cookbooks in English and since those days has become a notable actor both in India and here.

After less than two years, my mom, in her mid-twenties and still single, moved to Toronto to be near her brother Bernie and her best friend, Linda. She got a job in public relations for the Toronto Symphony and took her work very seriously. At the time Linda was trying to have a baby.

"I bet I can have a baby before you find a husband," Linda dared my mother.

"No way," my mother said. "One hundred bucks on the table."

Well, as luck would have it, just a few months later Linda was pregnant.

"Now I have less than nine months to find a husband," my mother thought.

My father was a South African chemical engineer who studied at the University of Cape Town and three years after graduation saved up just enough for a boat to England, arriving there not knowing a soul. Before he left he got a business degree through the University of South Africa and a job in London designing petroleum refineries, which transferred him to Toronto after just over a year.

Two years after moving to Canada, my father, who was now in market research at Falconbridge Limited, a natural resource and mining company, attended a conference of the American Management Association in Chicago. There he met a man from Cleveland who used to live in Toronto and knew my uncle Bernie.

"You're single and Jewish in Toronto?" he said, getting right down to business. "I know someone whose sister is also single and Jewish in Toronto. We should set you up."

My father called my mother in the middle of the workday to ask her out. When she answered the phone, the first thing he said was, "Am I interrupting you? Is this a bad time?"

My mother stared back at the phone in shock. This was the spring of 1966, and no man had ever thought to ask her that question before. It was destiny.

Linda was by now almost nine months pregnant. The pressure was on.

Charmed by my father's discretion and foreign accent, my mother made a date with him for dinner the following week. While he was on his way to pick her up, Linda went into labor. She called my mother to ask, "Can you pick my parents up at the airport? They're flying in from Montreal. Now."

My mother didn't cancel the date. When he arrived at her door, she said, "We can't go out to dinner, but will you come with me to the airport?" They picked up Linda's parents and took them to the hospital. And that was my parents' first date.

Linda's son Michael was born that night. He's exactly six months older than my parents' marriage. They wed in December of that same year. The bet was a wash.

Once married, my parents had some trouble conceiving. This was well before there was advanced fertility technology. Adoption was much easier, so they adopted my two older brothers, two wonderful baby boys, sixteen months apart.

Five years later, my mother was not feeling well, so she went to her doctor thinking she was coming down with the flu.

The doctor did some tests and reported, "Actually, you're pregnant."

My parents, the newlyweds

My mother was beside herself. The next several months were a bit of a circus. My father called my mom "a moving target." She had just managed to get both her boys off to school and was preparing to get back into the workforce full-time, to be her own person once again. And then I came along—a miracle or a mistake, depending on whom you ask.

She had only one pregnancy craving: she would wake up in the middle of the night demanding chocolate éclairs. I feel like that explains a lot.

The story goes that my parents, feeling blessed to have a healthy baby daughter after having two sons, named me Abigail, meaning: "the father rejoices." My brothers and I joke that we are all first-borns and we are all mistakes. But we found ourselves, through luck and the mysterious power of the universe, in a family where we were all much loved.

My mother had a lot of nicknames for us, because a nursery

school teacher once told her: "A child who is loved has many names." Besides Char Siu Bao, my family and close friends have always called me Snip, short for The Snippet. There was a picture taken of me when I was about two years old, on my stomach and elbows in the grass, with my hair in pigtails. The grass is almost higher than I am, and my father once said I looked like a little snippet of grass. It stuck.

To say I came from a food-loving family is an understatement— both my parents, despite their very different backgrounds, grew up loving food.

My mother was a bombshell when she was younger, with jet-black hair, porcelain skin, and serious cleavage (I may have inherited that last trait from her). To this day, she has the most amazing, insurance-

The Snippet

worthy Tina Turner legs. I feel good about my legs, but my mother's legs, even now in her seventies, are ridiculous.

Our personalities are pretty similar. She's opinionated—sitting across from her at dinner, be prepared to hear in detail her views on the decline of the Paris bistro—and amazingly trustworthy. She's also tough. Growing up we could not get away with anything around her. We really did not want to cross her. She played bad cop and enforced the law, but at the heart of it all, she was a nurturer.

Everyone I knew went to my mother for advice. Our house was a safe haven for everyone in the neighborhood, especially my friends who struggled with their own family issues. She made them all feel comfortable and welcome. And she cooked: poached Arctic char with lemon and herbs, swiss chard, butternut squash soup.

Her kitchen was full of food. Not fussy or orchestrated, just come-as-you-are. That's where we would all hang out. She was loud, casual, and always throwing things together.

We were not a religious family, but my parents cultivated a traditional Jewish home, celebrating the major holidays and observing rites of passage through the years the way their parents had before them, with way too much food and a little prayer. We went to synagogue a few times a year. My brothers and I were bar and bat mitzvahed. I went to Hebrew school three days a week from kindergarten through seventh grade.

Although we ate dinner together around the table almost every night, Shabbat dinner was special, no matter what else we had to do. Every Friday, we said blessings, caught up on our week, and welcomed guests to our family table. I always felt the emphasis wasn't so much on religion as on deeply rooted tradition: family, food, and relaying the oral history of our people.

My mother still likes to say her kids were weaned on leek quiche and pâté. My mother has a thing for pâté. It's always in her house. As children I don't think we liked it much. I can never remember asking for it. My mother made a mean chopped liver, but I wouldn't call it pâté. It was more of a coarse Jewish chopped chicken liver, pureed with onion and seasonings. She kept it in the refrigerator in a green ceramic pot with a lid.

But I can't figure out what it is with my mother and French forced meat. When she would come to visit me in New York, before I was married and was living alone in my first apartment, she loved to take me grocery shopping, as mothers do. Sometimes she still goes shopping with me, and she can't help herself: without fail she buys me pâté—duck, pork, or even veggie versions. Pâté is not something I typically keep in my house. Sure, I like it just fine when it's served to me at a restaurant, but I can't think of a time I've ever served pâté at home. I tell my mother this time and again, but to no avail. There it is in my fridge. I think in her head she sees it as an emblem of luxury. Maybe she thinks it's something she's treating me to. It's a mental block. She's in denial.

But I shouldn't complain. We grew up in a plentiful, healthy eating environment. We ate around the table together every night at six thirty, after my father came home from work, and my mother would call us all downstairs in her booming voice, "ALAN, ERIC, GAIL! SUPPER!" Eating together was an absolute.

There was one exception: my first birthday. For the first few weeks after I was born, my parents had a baby nurse, Heather. She returned from time to time as we grew, to stay with us when our parents were on vacation. We loved it when she visited, because of the food she made and allowed us to eat: milkshakes, chocolate cake with vanilla and chocolate crisscross icing.

My parents' first major vacation after I was born was a trip to Paris that coincided with my first birthday. It's hard to imagine any of my friends in this day and age leaving their kid on such a momentous occasion, but as my mother's birthday actually falls the day after mine, I guess it was her birthday, too, and they were desperate for a getaway. Pictures reveal that I did not seem to mind much.

With my brothers, and cake, on my first birthday

Heather made one of her famous chocolate cakes and I devoured it happily with my brothers.

....

IF MY MOTHER was the voice in the family, my father was the strong, silent type. I liken his looks to a cross between Clint Eastwood and Roger Moore. But his personality is more like my hero, Captain Jean-Luc Picard (Shakespearean actor Patrick Stewart to anyone over sixty and Professor Charles X of *X-Men* to anyone under thirty), serious and stoic.

When I was a little girl, people told me all the time how I looked just like my father. I would cry and run out of the room. I thought they were saying I looked like a boy—an adult boy at that! Now I realize how much my facial features really do mimic his—my eyes, the shape of my face, the dimples on my cheeks when I smile.

Inquisitive and soft-spoken, he's played the recorder for more than forty years, and played the flute for many years before that. He still takes lessons once a week. He's an avid environmentalist and sails often in the summer. He reads a book a week, sometimes more, enjoys bird-watching, scrapbooking, and long walks in nature. If he were single, he could write one hell of a personal ad!

My father rarely raises his voice. When we were growing up, it took a lot to make him angry, but when he was, you did not want to be around for it. There are only a few times I can remember when he was truly furious.

Perhaps most important in describing my father is that he has a parrot named Toby, with whom he has an insanely intense relationship. He (or she; we have no way of knowing Toby's gender without performing surgery) is about twenty-two years old. But parrots can live past sixty, even in captivity. Suffice it to say, Toby's in the will. In the absence of a mate, parrots bond with their caregiver. For life. So my father is the closest thing Toby has to a spouse. It's not completely healthy. I justify it as my father's answer to empty-nest syndrome.

My mother doesn't like Toby much. Neither do my brothers and I. My dad calls it sibling rivalry. I call it downright crazy. Toby tolerates my mother because she feeds him, but he attacks most other people who come near my father. On one occasion, years ago, Toby bit right through my poor uncle Lou's ear. Blood was spilled. A dog could have been put down for such an outburst. Dad, of course, just giggled and checked to make sure Toby was not hurt in the ordeal.

My father still resents the fact that my brother insists Toby has to stay in a cage when my nieces and nephew visit.

"Toby was here first!" is his response when he's asked to put Toby away.

"No, Ivor, *I* was here first" is my mother's rebuttal. Who can argue?

My mother has her own plans for Toby. "I'm teaching him to lie down in a skillet and say, 'coq au vin.'"

My dad is certainly passionate about food, but being from an-

Dad and Toby

other generation, he never learned how to cook. And because my mother was so adept in the kitchen, he soon grew spoiled. Not only was my mom genuinely talented, but also his standards started out pretty low, as his own mother was a terrible cook. She was an incredible woman, a piano teacher and a gifted knitter. I didn't see her or my grandfather much, since they lived in South Africa, and she died when I was twenty-two. In the course of those twenty-two years I only spent about a dozen visits with her.

I'll give my grandma the benefit of the doubt and say perhaps she just didn't care much for food and cooking, as what came out of her kitchen was predictably horrid. I hadn't actually experienced what my mom and dad meant by this firsthand until I was thirteen. My grandparents were getting older and couldn't make the trip to Canada anymore. It was the year of my bat mitzvah, so my father and I went to visit them in South Africa as part of the milestone birthday present. Sadly, it turned out to be the last time I would see my grandfather. He died just a few years later.

They were still living in Bloemfontein, the town where my father had grown up. It's located in the center of the country and is its judicial center and the capital of the Orange Free State—a landlocked town, not far from South Africa's legendary diamond mines. At the time my father grew up, it was a heavily Afrikaans-influenced place, even though my father's family was English-speaking.

On this particular visit, my grandmother made dinner for us. My Jewish guilt compels me to say up front that I love my grandmother dearly and cherish her memory. But, according to my mother, my grandmother would put a chicken in the oven at nine in the morning, go out for the day, and then take it out of the oven at six at night. I had thought she was joking, but she was exactly right. It was the most amazingly dry roast chicken I can remember. So tough that it stuck in my throat. There was no water on the table, and I had just eaten this giant piece of chicken that was impossible to swallow. I worried about choking. It felt like each bite was never going to end. Luckily, that was the only meal of hers I had to endure. On other visits, we ate elsewhere.

When my mother and father first met, she used to make him all sorts of elaborate meals and take him out to Indian and Italian, Chinese and French restaurants. She thought his mother had been an exemplary cook because he had such a sophisticated palate and such enthusiasm for good food. My father told her that, on the contrary, his mother's cooking had barely kept him alive.

As a result, my father would do the dishes and the sewing in the

Produce de Toronto

Grand Vin de Siècle

Chateau Saint Ivor

appellation controlée

Mis en Bouteille

★ | IMS | ★

Au Domaine.

Dad's homemade wine label

house, but rarely the cooking. That said: my father did make four things when I was growing up that I remember fondly.

First of all, he made wine in our basement. Some of it was even pretty good. Lately he's less into wine and more into beer, seeking out microbreweries wherever he goes, but from the time my parents met and into my childhood, he loved wine and made it himself. My mother even had wine labels printed for him as a gift: CHATEAU SAINT IVOR, PRODUCE DE TORONTO, GRAND VIN DE SIÈCLE, APPELLATION CONTROLÉE.

The three foodstuffs my father made consistently when we were growing up bore no relation to one another. They were pickles, applesauce, and chocolate Cream of Wheat.

My dad's full sour pickles are amazing and I now have the recipe. He made them every summer, from a bushel of Kirby cucumbers. He would store them in our cellar all year long. They were made with tons of garlic and dill weed, pickling spices, and salt. They'd sit fermenting for months and are still one of my most favorite snacks.

(Full disclosure: I will eat any kind of pickle I can get my hands on, but it's rare that I can find a pickle as good as my father's. I love how sour they are. He lets them sit so long that they aren't bright and crunchy anymore. Totally fermented. I love pickles in New York, Jewish pickles like Gus's, but I find them a touch salty and not quite sour enough. I love Second Avenue Deli pickles, too, but even their full sours are not quite as good as the Ivor Simmons specials.)

Then there's his applesauce, which he made once a year, in the fall, the recipe for which I published in *Food & Wine* magazine a few years ago. I would come into the kitchen and see a big basket of apples. My father would be at the stove stirring and pureeing the applesauce, which he stored in our extra big freezer in the basement. There's usually still applesauce in that freezer when I come home to visit, and I often smuggle a jar or two back with me to New York.

His applesauce is unlike any other I've had. It's pureed until it's silky smooth, and he adds the skin of Italian prune plums, so it takes on this beautiful deep pink color as it cooks.

We ate his applesauce with everything. On Hanukkah we had it with my mother's famous dill latkes. Sometimes we would drizzle heavy cream into a bowl of it for dessert, or even for breakfast. It was decadent—sweet, tart, and super-smooth all at the same time.

The chocolate Cream of Wheat was something he'd make for my brothers and me on weekend mornings to give my mother a break in the kitchen. Cream of Wheat is the wheat equivalent of what's traditionally called *mieliepap* in South Africa, grits or polenta here, made from cornmeal. My father grew up eating *mieliepap* for breakfast, adding milk or fruit to it. Instant Cream of Wheat became the easiest for him to make us, and he would add cocoa powder to it as a treat—never too much, never too sweet. It was special-occasion food, thick and chocolaty, and something I'll always associate with him.

One of my father's most endearing traits is that he is a certified chocoholic. I say this in all seriousness. He has an addiction. When we were young, he would hoard chocolate, hiding the stuff around the house so his children would not find it. He kept most of it in his dresser drawer, hidden beneath a sea of navy dress socks. We always knew we could sneak chocolate from there when he went out. I would be surprised if he did not still keep it there in case of emergency. He especially loves dark chocolate, the darker the better: 70 percent and up. I have the exact same taste. Milk chocolate is not true chocolate as far as we are concerned. Dark chocolate is so much more pure and nuanced. You can taste the cocoa, the tannins, and the terroir. (Although I can assure you, my father and I never actually use the word "terroir" when we discuss our love for chocolate. We just like the bitter earthiness.)

He's a fit man and very disciplined. At around five feet, eight inches, he weighs, at most, 150 pounds. He's in amazing shape, always has been, and is incredibly regimented in what he eats. My father simply has more willpower than anyone I have ever met.

He eats the same thing every single morning to this day: hot cereal (a mixture of oats, bran, and flax) and two glasses of room-temperature water. He even brings the special hot cereal mixture with him when he travels. He sets everything out the night before.

My mother made his lunch every day of his working life. Although he was trained as a chemical engineer, for more than twenty-five years he had a trucking company that safely disposed of toxic and liquid waste. His office was in an industrial part of town where he could not get decent lunches, so my mother, who was already packing school lunches for us, would pack his as well. As far back as I can remember, my father's lunch consisted of a sandwich of some kind, two pieces of fruit, and again, two glasses of water.

Then he'd have dinner with us, whatever my mother made, and end his day with two pieces of dark chocolate. He only allowed himself two pieces; otherwise, there would be no limit to how much he could consume. He loves hot chocolate, too, even in the summertime.

He travels the world always on the lookout for hot chocolate. He makes himself a cup every single day, and whenever I am home he offers to make some for me, too.

A few years ago, my father had some routine blood work done. His doctor told him his glucose levels were a bit high, that he could be pre-diabetic, and that he couldn't have chocolate or sweets for a year. My heart broke for him. This put him into a serious depression. Thank God he was told he could still have hot chocolate as long as it didn't have too much sugar in it.

With my cup of hot chocolate I would sometimes grab a cookie from the cookie jar on our counter. My parents actually collect ceramics and have some wonderful pottery in their house, including this jar.

My mother keeps it on the counter to this day, as a symbol of plenty, a testimony to her bountiful kitchen. Once in a while my father will ask, "Why do we have this cookie jar? It's just the two of us. These cookies have been in here for a year and a half. Our children aren't here to eat them, and our grandchildren don't eat them either. We should get rid of the cookie jar."

But my mother isn't listening. It's like the pâté she's always buying me. Despite our protests, the cookie jar remains.

....

TWO

Air-Dried Meat in the Glove Compartment

WE'RE ON SOUTH Africa's Garden Route, the popular coastal road, somewhere between Plettenberg Bay and Tsitsikamma National Park. An ostrich runs alongside the car. Klipspringer antelopes sun themselves by the side of the road. The landscape is lush and wet. It's September, the beginning of African spring. We drive down a steep hill and enter a fog so thick that we can't see more than five feet in front of us. We're lost in a cloud hovering above the road. My father slows down the car in case there's another in front of us—or worse, a stray baboon. We are silent, completely focused on the road. I reach into the glove compartment for a little comfort. I pull out a brown paper bag. Concealed inside is our last half pound of my favorite snack. Additional panic sets in as I realize this has to last us the rest of our trip. Sure, there's biltong to be found at other roadside stalls, but this kind, from Joubert and Monty's, is the gold standard of air-dried meat. I rip off a hunk and gnaw on it quietly as my father keeps his eyes on the road. We climb up a hill. Instantly, we emerge from the fog. The sun is shining. We breathe a joint sigh of relief and drive on.

OUR HOUSE WAS always full of noise and life. We had a TV, but my parents only watched the news and *Masterpiece Theatre*. My parents never cared much for pop culture. Fad diets, *Three's Company*, and Michael Jackson were not things they concerned themselves with. It was always up to us kids to discover for ourselves anything current besides world news. My father has only ever listened to baroque music and my mother only to classical (if slightly more modern than the 1400s) and classic jazz.

My father hated how much we children wanted to watch television. He couldn't get us out from in front of it, so he made a rule: no television on weeknights. This drove us crazy. We complained constantly about how all our friends could watch whatever they wanted. To us it seemed sadistic of him to deny us what we, as teenagers, felt was our God-given right.

But it worked. We learned to ignore the fact that we were not in the loop on the latest shows or clothes or toys. We learned to play games or go outside instead. And we read.

I took drama classes and did quite a bit of acting in school, in plays like *Noises Off* and *Blithe Spirit* and musicals like *West Side Story, Sweet Charity,* and *Little Shop of Horrors*.

Every summer from the age of ten I went to sleepaway camp, where we produced and performed large-scale productions of *Damn Yankees*, *A Chorus Line*, and *Hair*. We did an especially elaborate and memorable production of *Cats*, which I directed and choreographed, and which starred forty or so thirteen- and fourteen-year-olds.

I took dance classes, too: jazz, modern, tap, and ballet. I danced at recitals through much of my adolescence, but toward the end of high school the inevitable happened—my boobs grew. Not acceptable for a ballerina. This marked the end of that career path.

My parents were constantly throwing dinner parties. Both my parents chose to make their life away from their respective families. So they created their own family out of their friends in Toronto. Our house was full of interesting people, like my father's first friend in the country, Louis, who is a jazz music fanatic and loves to scat. They remain the best of friends to this day. Uncle Lou's wife, Sue, had a chain of bakeries when we were growing up, and besides my father and his chronic chocolate habit, she is undoubtedly the person most responsible for my love of desserts. Sweet Sue's was the name of her bakery chain and she truly is.

My parents' friends were our aunts and uncles, and their children were our cousins. There was no blood between us, but they were family all the same. They helped raise and nurture us in so many ways. Even my girlfriends still know them as Auntie Sandy, Aunt Sue, Auntie Marilyn, Aunt Rho, and Auntie Linda.

My mother was fiercely independent. Probably because of her parents' divorce, which put my grandmother under immense emotional and financial stress in her later years, my mother felt strongly that she had to be her own woman. She never wanted to be defined by a man, or by anyone at all. Throughout her life, she had several dynamic careers, first as a publicist, then as a food writer and cooking teacher, and later as a manager of classical musicians.

At the same time she found a way to work from home when we

were young. She made sure we were staying out of trouble and, of course, eating well. It's incredible to me that even though she had a busy career, my mother managed to cook an ambitious dinner for us every night. It was a smart thing for her and a great luxury for us.

My mother redesigned and renovated her kitchen in 1982 so she could teach out of it. Here, she held weekly cooking classes for ten to fifteen people. Most of her students were local women, mothers and friends from the neighborhood, who heard about her by word of mouth. She taught kitchen basics, like how to roast a chicken and make soup stock. She offered classes with themes like making the most of offal (sweetbreads, tongue, chicken livers), improvising in the kitchen based on what's in your fridge, winter or summer menus, or the best recipes for brunch.

One year, I even remember her teaching a cooking class for husbands, which felt revolutionary at the time. It culminated in a big

Mom at her crowded kitchen counter, with me as her little helper

dinner that they cooked together. My father even dressed up as a French maid to serve the food—he will probably never live it down!

For all of us, that kitchen was the place to be. When my parents entertain, everyone migrates there. It's a warm, bustling place, full of action and excitement. It has always been the center of our home.

Thirty years later, the kitchen could use another renovation, but it's still very much my mother's domain. When I'm visiting, I don't cook in it much. Her kitchen is her territory and I risk her wrath if I mess with it.

I do try to help my mom with family dinners, especially holiday meals, but it's not easy. She tries to control everything I do. She hovers, hands me Herbes de Provence that have been in her cupboard since 1972, that I don't want to use, and sticks her fingers in my

Mom's cooking class final dinner with Dad serving in drag

vinaigrette. I get that it's her space, but we have different styles. I have professional training, while my mother has instinctive flair. I haven't had her years of practice cooking for a large family.

I admit that I also drive her crazy doing things my way and giving her tips or suggestions that she doesn't want to hear, like how to hold her knife properly, or that her olive oil is past its prime. She'll put me in charge of roasting the vegetables for dinner, and I won't do it until the last second. I can see the steam coming out of her ears because she wants me to be more organized.

Somehow, even though I have a culinary degree and have made my career in the food world, I haven't actually cooked that often for my family. My brothers joke, "You're a famous food personality in New York, but you've never actually made us a meal."

My mother always pushed us to be more adventurous. When I was a little girl, she let me run around in her kitchen. I loved to raid her pantry and her dried spice and herb drawer. I would take out a hundred different ingredients to make soup—ketchup, dried oregano, pink peppercorns, Worcestershire sauce, whole-grain mustard, brown sugar, paprika, tomato paste, powdered garlic, fennel seeds, salt—fill a soup pot with water, and stand next to her on my wooden stool that had a grape scratch-and-sniff sticker on it.

I would stir, sprinkle, and season just like my mother. It was kind of disgusting. But the actions seemed so grown-up and I loved the feeling of cooking. Even if the dish was inedible, I felt the thrill of creating.

When I was six years old, my mother let me make scrambled eggs. I wasn't tall enough to reach the stove, so I stood on that wooden stool; it was about a foot and a half high so I could see into the pot properly. To make it safer, my mother set up a double boiler—a bain-marie. Ours was made of a set of enamel pots, orange on the outside, cream-colored within.

I seasoned the eggs with a cinnamon-sugar mix and raisins. It

seemed right at the time. Then I forced my parents to eat them. I realized at that moment that eggs were so much more complex than their simple form let on—a revelation I maintain to this very day. I had turned them from an inedible viscous fluid into a solid yellow food. I was making magic.

In addition to running her cooking school, my mother wrote about food for the *Globe & Mail*. Through her work, she befriended a man named Garfield who owned one of the great restaurants in Toronto's Chinatown, called Sai Woo. She would often drop by before dinner service started or at the end of the night, when all the cooks and servers would be eating together. My mother noticed they would eat totally different food from what was on the menu. The smells and sight of it would make her drool with envy.

"Why is it that you serve one menu to us," my mother would prod Garfield, "and you guys eat differently?"

"You don't want that food," he would say. "It's not for you."

Finally she convinced him to make her their more authentic dishes. And from then on whenever we went, we got only the good stuff: Singapore chow fun, crackling whole Peking duck, Chinese broccoli, and bok choy in oyster sauce. I remember dark, chewy mushrooms, seafood soup, and deep-fried bean curd. Delicious.

The main reason I adored going was that when I left, they always gave me a little box of rice candies. They didn't really have much flavor. They were just gluten-y and sweet. Each candy was first wrapped in wax paper, which you took off, and then another layer of what looked like cellophane but which was actually edible rice paper. You could just pop one into your mouth and the paper would dissolve instantly. I thought it was the most fantastic candy ever. I would eat the entire box on the way home in the car.

Early on in my career, when family friends learned that I was pursuing work in the food world, they would enthuse, "You're just like your mother!"

It had never occurred to me that I was following in her footsteps. It made me furious, as if destiny was beyond my control. Not to mention: What twenty-two-year-old wants to be told she's just like her mother?

Looking back, I now realize it was the greatest compliment I could have been given. My parents raised us to try all sorts of new things, whether it was in tasting exotic foods, traveling to far-flung locations, reading books about the greater world, or forging our own, independent paths through life.

My mother instilled in me a love of her kitchen and an appreciation of home, but also the courage to leave it. She made it clear that food opens up the world to you. Food can be comforting, but it can also take you far outside your comfort zone. She taught me that a woman in the kitchen isn't a symbol of domesticity, but of empowerment.

....

MY BROTHERS WERE always getting into some kind of trouble together. They were best friends and constant playmates growing up, though they grew to be very different people.

Alan, my elder brother, is a musician and was a huge musical influence on me. He can pick up any instrument and seduce it, from the guitar, piano, or harmonica to the bugle. He introduced me to the Beatles' *White Album*, to Led Zeppelin and their obscure *Lord of the Rings* references, and to Traffic's *John Barleycorn Must Die*. Alan was never in the popular crowd. He was an artist, rebellious and independent and always a bit alternative. He was into drama and theater, but didn't do well academically, either because he couldn't focus or because he didn't care. My parents pulled him out of public school after eleventh grade and put him in a small private school, where, finally, he thrived.

He put my parents through a lot of stress when we were young. My mother now tells me she has guilt about that time, that she worries she neglected my other brother and me. Alan sucked up so much of their energy, and in many ways still does, because he continues to battle his inner demons. Suffice it to say, he was the more difficult child in the family. He was always breaking curfew, getting arrested for shooting BB guns with his friends, stealing from my parents' liquor cabinet.

In contrast, my brother Eric was a straight-A student and the quintessential jock: classically handsome, on the hockey team, and a star tennis player. Both my brothers were rowers in high school, but Eric was the true athlete and always the popular one. Like a scene from an eighties teen movie, my girlfriends used to come over in the summer just to watch him mow the lawn with his shirt off. Eric has always been a hard worker. He has created for himself a wonderful life and family. He married at the age of twenty-six; he and his wife, Kim, had three kids by the time he was thirty-three: Tyler, Elle, and Brooke, my beloved and awe-inspiring nephew and nieces!

Although Alan and Eric remained close, they went separate ways after high school. Their personalities and preferences were black-and-white—the introvert and the extrovert. I always felt that I landed somewhere in between, but I am probably more extroverted than either of them. They both liked to shape me, and since they were significantly older, we never had much to fight about. They teased and bugged me, to be sure, but they were also my greatest confidants and consummate protectors, without ever being overly protective. In many ways they still are.

In an effort to broaden our minds, my parents led us on adventures to faraway lands, especially my father's native South Africa, a complicated and beautiful country with a history as diverse as any on the map. Cape Town is my father's favorite city in the world. He has blinders on when it comes to the crime, poverty, and socioeconomic tensions there. Physically, the city is extraordinary. It feels like it's tumbling down a table-shaped mountain range, crashing into the South Atlantic Ocean. I think he would move back there if my mother would let him.

When I was six, my parents took us there over Christmas holidays for two weeks. It was my first time in the country.

Like the people themselves, the food of South Africa derives from many sources, including India, Malaysia, Britain, Holland, and several native African tribes. There are a few key dishes that are very particular to South Africa, like *bobotie*, a baked egg-and-milk sauce over minced meat, flavored with herbs, raisins, and nuts; pickled herring; *boerewors*, which are mixed meat sausages best cooked on a *braai*, or barbecue; bunny chow, a hollowed-out loaf of bread filled with curry and popular on the coast near Durban; and my favorite, *melktert*, a milk custard tart flavored with orange zest and baked in a delicate flaky dough.

What I remember most from our trips there are the raw ingredients, the country's outrageously delicious and unique fruits and vegetables that you just cannot find (or aren't as good) anywhere else: guava, *naartjies* (native oranges), mangos and apricots, pawpaw (papaya), and *mielie* (corn).

My absolute favorite South African food is biltong: air-dried, salted meat, cut or shaved into bite-sized pieces or sold in large strips that can be sliced up as you desire. It has a very specific savoriness and is not sweet the way American beef jerky is. Sometimes it has a spice rub.

Originally, biltong was made from beef, but now you can get all kinds, including ostrich, kudu (antelope), or buffalo biltong. My favorite is actually chicken biltong. You don't usually want to think about eating raw chicken, but it is dried and salted sufficiently. Ostrich is also outstanding. The flavor is halfway between steak and chicken: the best of both worlds.

Chewiness is the most underrated texture. Biltong is salty and savory, but also chewy. I like gnawing on a larger strip. In Sea Point, where my cousins used to live, there is a shop called Joubert and Monty's that is famous for its biltong. Some people order it sliced or moist, but I like to slice it myself and let it dry out a bit first.

Whenever we go back to South Africa, we buy pounds of the stuff and keep it in the glove compartment to eat as we drive around. Any meat that you can keep for hours on end in the blistering African sun is the perfect road-trip snack, as far as I'm concerned. For ages it was impossible to find in North America. Luckily, a company in North Carolina, called Biltong USA, makes really good biltong and sells it online.

That trip when I was six was the first time I met my extended South African family. We knew my grandparents already, because they had come to visit us in Canada, but we were introduced to a whole new contingent of aunts, uncles, and cousins.

I have a lot of vibrant memories from that trip. We went to Johannesburg for a few days. Then to Kruger National Park, where I went on my first of many safaris. Kruger is the largest safari park in the world. It was an amazing experience as a child to see those wild animals up close: wildebeest, kudu and their young, wild dogs chasing our car, impala, and giraffes, all gathering around a watering hole. Lions!

We also went to Cape Town, and from there we drove through the wine region, to Stellenbosch, about an hour away, where my parents took us wine tasting. Now the area has a booming wine industry, but at the time, it was just budding.

We arrived at our first winery and my parents brought us into the tasting room. They explained that we should taste the wine by dipping our tongues into the glass, just to get the flavor. Well, I

Having lunch at a winery in South Africa in 1982

followed whatever my brothers did, because they were my idols. They were knocking back whole glasses of wine, so I started drinking from a few too. My parents may have noticed us taking a sip, but no one seemed aware of quite how much we were drinking.

We went to a few wineries that day and I kept on slurping glass after glass of wine. Before long, I was having the time of my life. The story goes that I started copying everything everyone said and making my parents crazy. I was running in circles, giggling and jumping up and down. When we returned to our car I promptly passed out cold for eight hours. I woke up with my very first hangover.

I only remember that it tasted bitter and dried out my mouth. I don't remember much else about the experience, but then again, I was six and I was drunk.

Despite my early penchant for Pinotage, I was still a long way from being a sophisticated drinker. It was just seven years later when I had my second encounter with alcohol. I was thirteen, on Christmas vacation in Costa Rica. This was well over twenty years ago, when Costa Rica was not yet an eco-destination. It was still relatively undeveloped. My mother and father had close friends who were working in Peru for a short time, and they had a daughter my brothers' age, so we met them halfway for the holidays.

At the time, I was annoyed by the entire situation. My teenage response to news of the trip was: "Where the hell is Costa Rica?" I was going to be alone with my family when I could have been in Florida, where the rest of Jewish Canada (and America for that matter) migrated for the season, with my friends and my middle school boyfriend. (Yes, I had a serious boyfriend in eighth grade. He was a musician, the first in a long line of musician boyfriends. In the end, I got the music fanatic with the business head, so it all worked out. But that came much later.)

We spent the first week in San José, taking trips to the rain forest and touring the surrounding area. Then, for our second week, we all moved to a small town called Quepos, on the Pacific coast. It is famous for its extensive national park, Playa Manuel Antonio, which was a draw for its quiet, pristine beaches and protected wilderness.

Now, apparently, it's very built up. Ecotourism has thrived in that part of the country, but at the time, there was nothing—no hotels and no resorts. We rented condos for a week, a mile up from the beach, literally *in* the rain forest. We were the only gringos in the tiny town.

Every day we would buy plantains on the side of the road and carry them through the rain forest to the beach. We'd hold them up in the air and the capuchin monkeys would come down from the trees and take them from us for their lunch. We'd wake up in the morning and there would be a toucan in the tree outside of our bedroom window. Other days it might be a sloth or howler monkeys, with their deep, guttural growls at dawn.

On New Year's Eve we all went to what was probably the only fully equipped restaurant in town. My brothers, who were almost twenty, and Lisa, the daughter of our friends, thought it would be fun to get me drunk again. They were doing shots of Jack Daniel's and passing them to me under the table. After maybe two, I was feeling warm and fuzzy.

As with the first time around, I wouldn't shut up. I was talking nonstop, and loudly. At one point, Marilyn, my mother's friend, turned to me and said, "How much do you charge to haunt a house?"

I didn't know what that meant, but I took it as an insult and burst into tears. Then I passed out. Thankfully, once I got out of middle school, I learned to handle my liquor a little better.

I tried to stay miserable in Costa Rica, but it was an amazing trip for a lot of reasons. It took us out of ourselves as children, exposed us to wildlife, to nature, and especially to a culture and way of life so totally different from our own. It was the ideal time in our lives for a trip like this. We were just old enough to appreciate how fortunate we were to have the experience, but still young enough for it to leave a substantial and lasting impression. I look back on it now as one of the most meaningful and idyllic times in my family's history.

Soon afterward, life got more complicated for us. It became more apparent that Alan was struggling—with college, holding down a job, generally finding his way. Several years ago, Alan decided to seek out his biological parents. My parents were remarkably cool about it. My family had always talked openly and inclusively about my brothers' adoption. I am sure they had prepared themselves for this possibility down the road. When he did find his birth mother, she embraced him. She has become a big part of his life and has a good relationship with my mother because of this.

One thing he discovered was that his mother was an artist and his father was a musician. The genes were strong enough that he found his way to music and art and excelled at it, with my parents' support and encouragement.

I could talk about his personal struggles all day, but it's impossible to summarize easily. It's a story that would need a book of its own, and that's his book to write, not mine. I don't want to diminish or label him in any way that doesn't fully explain what an exceptional person he is, and what hell he's gone through.

....

OUR CHILDHOOD DIFFERENCES have manifested themselves in our feelings about food. Alan had food issues connected to his health. He's been a vegan, a vegetarian, and he's been on an all-chopstick diet. He doesn't eat dessert. He has never had any interest in sweets.

And certainly compared to me, Eric could be considered a picky eater. He loves to eat well and is a solid cook, but he has a number of particular food aversions. He *hates* vinegar. He can't stand it on anything, which basically wipes out eating salad or salad dressings of any kind.

I wasn't fussy about food, but as a teenager, I did go through a semivegetarian phase. It's hard to believe now, but for about eight years, I ate no red meat. Vegetarianism was not a moral issue for me. I had stomach issues in my teens, and I thought a vegetarian diet made me feel better. As with so many teenagers, my diet was tied more to what my friends were doing and what I felt would make me healthier based on the accepted knowledge of nutrition at the time (low fat, high carb, less red meat).

In my teens a lot of my girlfriends were vegetarians, too. There wasn't any major activist purpose behind it—it was more about body image, I think. Unlike several girls I knew, I never suffered from an eating disorder, but I wasn't immune to how such disorders were perpetuated at school and at home in so many obvious ways. I even remember some of my friends' parents weighing them, telling them they looked fat, or that they would never get boyfriends, and so would never fit in.

The common message was: if you don't have a boyfriend or aren't skinny enough, you're worthless. It was as though even in high school, people were concerned about girls finding husbands. It infuriates me to think that is actually how the world speaks to young women.

I remember clearly my conflicted feelings at that time in my life, the social pressure that drove me to be a vegetarian, because that's what girls did to show they were feminine. They would "just have a salad." I knew girls who would never eat in front of boys. That to me was so enormously sad and confusing—as if eating were a shameful act, as if you as a woman should be embarrassed for wanting to take pleasure in food. I wondered if I should feel shame that I didn't mind eating in front of people. Many girls I knew counted every calorie they ate, eating only low-fat foods or not eating at all, needing to control that part of their lives in a desperate effort to make adolescence more bearable. At my house the issue was not up for discussion.

I grew up with a comfortable relationship to food, never seeing it as evil or associating it with guilt. It was incredibly healthy, both nutritionally and emotionally.

After college and almost eight years of being a vegetarian, I found myself ravenously hungry and craving steak. My doctor said, "Eat meat. Perhaps you are a bit iron-deficient." So I did. And I never looked back. My stomach is still not perfect; in fact it is quite sensitive and at times a downright hindrance. I'm sure I'm allergic or averse to something, but I don't want to know what it is, and I haven't been tested. My greatest fear is that a doctor will tell me I'm lactose-intolerant or have a gluten allergy, and all of a sudden I'll be out of a job!

Back home, food was always about pleasure, family, tradition— never about excess, junk, or fad dieting. There was never a lot of candy or overprocessed food in our house. We had fast food on rare occasions, as a treat on vacation perhaps, but we ate salad and lots of fresh veggies at every meal, fish, and chicken. Instead of peanut butter and jelly, we ate coquille St. Jacques (the "fancy" name for scallops) and tandoori chicken.

As a consequence, our friends' parents were afraid to invite us over for lunch, intimidated as they were by what they imagined to be our hyperdeveloped palates. Of course, back then we just wanted to eat what our friends ate. We craved hamburgers, hot dogs, and macaroni and cheese. (People still tell me all the time that they are afraid to invite me over for dinner, when in fact I love nothing better than a simple home-cooked meal.)

It was a different story when kids came for dinner at our house, much to the dismay of our young guests. Instead of mashed potatoes or carrots, zucchini was usually the side dish of choice. One night, my brothers' friend was over for dinner. Like a lot of kids, he was a picky eater. When my mother set down a zucchini dish in front of him, he turned up his nose.

"We used to have another child," she explained sadly. "But he died of zucchiniosis, because he ate so much zucchini."

A detour for dinner on a family trip to Seattle

Of course, the boy went home and told his mother about his traumatic experience. His mother called my mother, very upset, exclaiming, "I'm so sorry. I didn't know you lost a child!" My mother was shocked to learn the little boy had believed her.

"What were you thinking?" I asked her years later. "You scared the shit out of that poor kid!"

As silly as it seems, zucchini has become emblematic to me of the way my parents expanded my understanding of the world. As far as vegetables go, zucchini is not first on most young people's lists. It might not be sexy, but it's packed with nutrients and it can be turned into delicious things, like my mother's zucchini bread.

That was so telling of who my mother was: a little more interesting, a little more colorful. Why use a banana when you can use a zucchini? That's what we grew up with as the norm.

Anyone could go to Florida. Anyone could have a puppy. Anyone could make banana bread. But my parents went to Africa and Costa Rica, had a parrot, and cooked zucchini with abandon. They challenged us. They made us look in less obvious places to find ourselves. It gave me a sense of adventure. And to this day there is zucchini in my fridge.

THREE

....

Montreal Bagels

IT'S A FREEZING night in Montreal. I'm on the way back to my apartment from a bar on Rue Saint-Laurent. Back home, my parents have a painting hanging in their kitchen of the Fairmount Bagel Bakery, and that's where I'm headed. I can smell the bagels from a block away—sesame with an underlying sweetness, like burnt toast with honey. The bakery's windows are fogged up as always. The ovens run twenty-four hours a day, fed constantly with wood. Bagels roll down the conveyor belt and fall into their bins. The line moves fast. There's no chitchat. You get your bagels and you move along. Smoked trout salad and cream cheese fill coolers nearby, but I don't want anything but bagels. They're soft and doughy and perfect. I eat one right out of the paper bag while it's still hot. It's like cake, sweet and delicious. It's warmth and comfort on a cold city night. My breath catches as I step back out into the frosty air and continue the walk home.

ONTREAL IS THE second-largest city in Canada, and the second-largest French-speaking city in the world after Paris. Not unlike Manhattan, it's an island, surrounded by the Saint Lawrence River. Montreal is named after Mount Royal, the small mountain that now anchors a park built by Frederick Law Olmsted, who also designed Central Park in New York City. French is the official language, but most people living there are bilingual. There's a wonderful European feel and café culture. The city's residents are stylish and perpetually chic.

I lived in Montreal for four years, attending McGill University, an Anglophone college, often called "the Harvard of Canada."

My degree was in humanistic studies, a specially designed program for people who didn't really know what they wanted to do. You had to choose a concentration as well as a second language (not English or French). I chose Anthropology and Spanish.

My mother and both her brothers had gone to McGill, so it holds special meaning for my family. In fact, my uncle Mel (class of '51) was the first Jewish president of the McGill Student Society. He went on to become one of the most admired judges on Quebec's court of appeal.

I loved going to school in a major city, as opposed to a small college town. Besides the excellent French food, the great thing about Montreal is the extensive array of ethnic cuisines—Chinese, Lebanese, Greek, Thai, Vietnamese. And because those foods are usually inexpensive, that's what you end up eating when you're a student.

Montreal's dedication to affordable ethnic food is best noted by the entire city's allegiance to the traditional Jewish deli. Rue Saint-Laurent, otherwise known as The Main, is the old Jewish drag, where Eastern European immigrants came during World Wars I and II, bringing the flavors of their native countries. What North America has come to know as "Jewish deli" came from Hungary, Romania, and Poland and evolved individually as each population learned to preserve and transport it to where they settled. This is why there are so many subtle regional nuances. In New York, it's pastrami. In Montreal, you have smoked meat—pastrami's slightly fattier cousin, which has been smoked and then steamed. The city's standard since 1928 is Schwartz's Montreal Hebrew Delicatessen. It's the Holy Grail of cured beef.

Montreal also has the best bagels in the world. Every time we go, we bring some back, and I try to convert my fellow New Yorkers. Many of them don't get it.

"What is this?" they say. "It's okay, I guess, but it's not a bagel."

Montreal bagels—and they are bagels—are slightly sweet because there's no salt in them and they're boiled in honeyed water. They're then baked in a wood-burning oven. They're thinner, but dense, not a giant ball of bread like in New York, or the rest of the country for that matter.

I lived in a residence hall that first year, subsisting on bad vegetable jambalaya, frozen stir-fries, chocolate milk, and broccoli cheddar puffs that I'd warm in the toaster oven in my dorm room. I then shared an apartment with three close girlfriends for the next two years, minus a junior semester abroad.

Only in the last year at school did I take control of my food situation. I started looking for better restaurants than the local dives where everyone ate cheap falafels, greasy burgers, and *poutine* (french fries with gravy and cheese curds), one of Quebec's greatest contributions to the global culinary landscape. Cheese curds are a common impulse buy in Montreal and sit on the counter at convenience stores alongside the gum and breath mints.

I realized there was no food coverage in the school paper. Since we were all living on our own and eating at the same five places, I thought it would be helpful if someone was seeking out good, cheap places to eat, so I convinced the editors of the *McGill Tribune* to let me write reviews. In my explorations of the city, I wrote about a local fondue joint ("Eating Fondue Is Worth the Hassle") and a tiny Peruvian restaurant in the Plateau neighborhood, where I tasted ceviche for the first time: slices of raw fish, marinated with chilies, thin slices of onion, lots of lime, then sprinkled with popcorn ("Home Cooking Latin Style").

That year, I also learned to cook properly. Nothing too fancy. Simple things like vegetable lasagne or spinach-and-ricotta-filled pasta with fresh tomato sauce. I'd call my mother, and she'd talk me through the roasting of a chicken. Somehow, I got my hands on Mollie Katzen's *Vegetable Heaven* and cooked from it a lot, especially her root vegetable and lentil soups, perfect for those long, cold Montreal winter nights.

During that year, I lived just off campus, in a section of Montreal affectionately referred to as the "McGill ghetto," with two of my closest girlfriends, Cami and Shana. We paid $900 cumulatively for a three-bedroom tenement apartment on Rue Durocher. It was massive, all things considered. You had to walk through the living room to get to the kitchen, but the kitchen was big enough to hold a huge breakfast table, and that's where I would set up to do my cooking. I made a mess at that table with my mother's extra Cuisinart food processor, which I'd lug from Toronto.

Shana at the time worked a few shifts a week at a restaurant called Grano that served high-concept mix-and-match sandwiches, fries, and all kinds of sauces and seasonings. She smuggled home ingredients for us to incorporate into our concoctions: marinated eggplant, roasted red peppers, thinly sliced Havarti, roast turkey. Cami, meanwhile, subsisted quite happily on candy. Her father was an orthodontist and her mother took health food very seriously growing up, so of course she rebelled by eating industrial-sized containers of sour gummies, red licorice shoelaces, and pink, sugar-coated strawberry marshmallows. She kept it all strategically located under her bed, so she could reach for it at all hours. She liked her candy slightly stale so it would have a chewier texture—sort of like dry-aging. Because of Cami, that's how I now prefer my candy, too.

There was also lots of bad food. I used to make a casserole that my stoner friends went crazy for. It started with a can of cream of broccoli soup and a bag of frozen hash browns. It had tons of chopped garlic, onions, broccoli, cheddar cheese, and sautéed mushrooms. I would mix in sour cream and bake it, with more cheese and bread crumbs on top, for forty-five minutes. It was the perfect hangover food, especially the next morning with a fried egg on top. (I find most things are better with a fried egg on top.)

Montreal winters are abysmal. Some days it felt as if the city were entirely encased in ice. To stock up for the bitter winter months, my roommates and I would make trips to Costco, filling our cart to over-flowing with peanut butter and paper towels.

On those trips I would also buy boxes of Hershey's Cookies'n'Creme candy bars, because it was the only food my boyfriend at the time would eat. It was because of him that I realized I might care about food more than most people. You see, he just didn't eat much, and that made me insane. Looking back, I realize the poor guy was wasting away.

It was unfathomable to me that someone wasn't hungry. All I knew was that he needed to eat. And my instinct was to feed him. I tried with all my might and I failed miserably, except in my ability to procure Hershey's Cookies'n'Creme chocolate bars. The relationship did not last, but interestingly enough he went on to receive a PhD in psychology.

That was around the time that my brother Alan first got sick. He was living in New Mexico after graduating from St. John's College when he went missing. Several months went by with no word at all. My parents alerted the local police and even hired a private investigator to find him. I went through various phases of emotion about it. For months, we all wondered where he was. That summer, while backpacking through Australia with Cami, I found myself on a bus one night, listening to my yellow Sony Sport Walkman, watching the landscape go by, and facing the stark reality that my oldest brother could be dead. I silently said good-bye to him.

My parents were beside themselves with worry. They contacted all his old friends, even his ex-girlfriend, who lived in New Mexico, asking if anyone had heard from him.

Several months later, in January of 1996, just after New Year's, the ex-girlfriend called my parents' house in Toronto and Eric answered the phone. "I saw your brother in the center square," she said. She didn't give many details, but she stressed with some urgency that my parents should come quickly. They flew to Santa Fe and she brought them to him. They found him living on the street.

My parents took him to the hospital in Santa Fe to stabilize him—he was in the grip of a severe mental break. They stayed with him there for about a week, then transferred him back to Toronto, to the Clarke Institute, now part of the Centre for Addiction and Mental Health, where he was admitted for evaluation. I came home from school shortly after he was admitted and saw him, but he wasn't in any state to have a conversation. Over the last fifteen or more years, he's been in and out of hospitals and assisted-living arrangements as he's gone on and off his medication, in what we have learned is a common cycle. But common doesn't make it easy.

Before he was found, I had come to terms with the fact that I might never see my brother again. When he came home, I knew he wouldn't be the same Alan, the brother I remembered from my childhood, my hero. At least it wouldn't be all of him. And I was right. A piece of him had been lost in the desert of New Mexico. Of course, "lost" is a subjective term in the blurred boundaries of mental health. He may see it very differently. Still, sometimes when he's at his most stable, in his best moments, he'll make me laugh. He'll tell an old joke or give me fashion advice or make fun of our parents, smile mischievously with that twinkle in his deep blue eyes, and I'll see my brother's charisma, humor, and kindness shining through.

During this same period when Alan was first hospitalized, Kim, Eric's girlfriend (who later became his wife), found a small lump on the side of Eric's face, which turned out to be a tumor. It was benign, but pushing on his facial nerves. If it grew any larger, it could do serious damage, so he had to have emergency surgery. There was a short period when my mother and father were shuttling between hospitalized sons, one at the Clarke Institute and one at Mount Sinai Hospital in downtown Toronto.

My family's issues were weighing heavily on my mind while I was at school, as you can imagine. It was hard for me to be away at such a difficult time. I felt completely helpless and scared for my siblings. I was trying as hard as I could to keep it together, but the littlest things would set me off. Once I accidentally put a pair of red shorts in with my white laundry. When I took out the wash, I had turned everything pink. I came upstairs and started to cry, and I just could not stop. My roommates didn't know what to do. Eventually, Cami called my mother.

"Do you want me to come to Montreal?" my mother asked. "I'll do whatever you want."

"No," I told her, trying desperately to pull it together, "you can't leave. You have bigger battles to fight right now."

Thankfully, my mother's best friend, Linda—the one who'd made the marriage bet—had moved back to Montreal several years earlier.

Every Friday night, Linda would have me over for dinner. No matter what dramas unfolded in my life, I knew that one day a week I would eat well and be mothered.

Linda lived in Hampstead, a beautiful part of the city filled with old homes. She had a small kitchen with a little wooden breakfast table in a nook and very little counter space. She had a wall-mounted convection oven in addition to a regular oven, but otherwise, she didn't have much in the way of serious gear. It was extraordinary to me that Linda could prepare these intricate and elaborate meals in this tiny kitchen.

In those days I was a bit of a ragamuffin. To Linda I must have been like a Pygmalion project. Linda is a most regal-looking woman, elegant and stylish, with silver hair that she wears either down and long or slicked back in a perfect chignon. She's about five foot nine, rail-thin, and utterly graceful, with the carriage of a ballerina. Her clothes are custom-made. You wouldn't think this woman ate if you saw her. How could she cook? you might wonder. She might break a nail! But she was a force in the kitchen.

My mother cooked intuitively and never had patience for kitchen minutiae. Linda, on the other hand, was all about the details. She followed recipes to the letter and was always poring over cookbooks and magazines. She was methodical about her cooking, which was new for me. She swore by that age-old rule: never serve something for guests that you haven't made before. Unlike my mother, who lived to experiment, Linda would dutifully practice and perfect her dishes.

Every Friday night, Linda's table was full with family and friends. I became a kind of adopted daughter. I usually arrived for dinner in my overalls and secondhand brown cardigan. She never commented, but her younger son would always tease me.

Here, she served an elaborate, multicourse dinner. It was the first time I saw salad served at the end of the meal, or multiple forks and knives, or cloth napkins. It was a very different world, foodwise, from what I was experiencing in college.

There was usually celery remoulade to start, along with Linda's own spicy roasted nut mix. There were always delicate blinis, with perhaps a bit of smoked salmon. The soups were from scratch. She would pour two kinds of soup in the same bowl to make a yin-yang pattern: a yellow pepper and a red pepper soup, garnished with fresh chervil. For the main course: salmon or halibut, served with a lemon wrapped in cheesecloth so you could squeeze it without the seeds falling out. The cheesecloth was always tied with a chive, making a dainty purse.

Her salads were made of tender greens and pomegranate seeds and served with fresh lemony vinaigrette. For dessert, a French apple tart with whipped cream and caramel sauce, cooked to a deep mahogany with a wonderfully smoky, burnt-sugar flavor. By the end of the night, we were eating the sauce by the spoonful out of the bowl.

Linda loved dining in restaurants, too, and took me out on a number of special occasions. She would also take me shopping if I needed anything during the school year, because my mother wasn't around and, to be frank, hated to shop. I never cared about expensive clothes, but Linda wanted to get me out of my ripped jeans and worn T-shirts. Besides, she had incredible taste and loved spending my mother's money on me.

"Renée," she would say to my mother, "I will do these things for you. I will take Gail shopping. I will deal with her messy hair and her corduroys *if* I can pick out the wedding dress when she gets married. That will be my reward." My mother was all too happy to agree.

Suffice it to say, Linda's cooking, fashion, and all-around style had a lasting impact on me. Until Linda, cooking was something my mother did so naturally and organically that I never thought of it as stylish, let alone an art form. I took it for granted. And for all the mediocre food I ate in college, there was Linda, a beacon of light, good manners, and good cooking.

....

FOUR

Heartache and Hard-Boiled Eggs

WE STEP INTO the cider house, a big ancient barn in the Basque country, and pour ourselves hard cider from one of the floor-to-ceiling barrels that line the room. The cider is delicious, like beer but unfiltered and just slightly sweet. It's loud and there's music: a Spanish guitar, the inconsistent rhythm of hands clapping. The floors are dirty and damp. There's conviviality in the room, and in the food. We are served a salty omelet, with *bacalão* (salt cod), whole fish with olive oil and fresh herbs. There is also a steak. I haven't eaten red meat in more than six years, but I know I'll have no choice but to try it anyway. It's char-grilled with a thick salt crust and very rare. They slap it down on the table in rough metal platters. I devour every bite.

*T*AKING A SEMESTER abroad wasn't a common thing to do in Canada when I was in college (unlike in the United States, where many more kids seem to go away for their junior year), but I was desperate to travel and decided to go to Spain with two of my girlfriends, Annaliese and Rachel. Both are super-tall, statuesque blondes. Annaliese, a friend since summer camp, was the life of the party, with a wickedly sharp sense of humor. Rachel was an outdoorsy beauty who, after we graduated, spent several years leading adventure tours through Asia and Europe.

Through the University of Wisconsin we found a school in Seville. For us, this was a massive privilege. We were going to learn Spanish, study art, and explore.

I left for Spain in January of my third year at McGill, but with a heavy heart. My boyfriend, Mr. Hershey's Cookies'n'Creme, was struggling with anxiety and depression. My brother Alan was sick and still in the hospital, and my family was caring for him without me. It was a situation both completely out of my control and still devouring every ounce of my life, and I needed to escape.

Within less than a month of leaving, I discovered said boyfriend was cheating on me. I spent a lot of time feeling sorry for myself that semester, torn between the turmoil at home and the excitement of the foreign culture around me. But thanks to these two girlfriends and a small but close crew of new ones, as well as the lure of late-night tapas bars, I still managed to have a wonderful time.

We were three Canadian girls in a program of about three

hundred American students. We thought it would be a semester of learning the history and being immersed in the culture. What we discovered was that most of the other students were just there to drink. For many of them it was the first place they could drink legally. For us, this was not nearly as exciting, since the drinking age in Canada is eighteen or nineteen (depending on the province).

The food in southern Spain is quite different than in the rest of the country. It's simpler and much more traditional. Seville, in Andalusia, is Spain's historic and cultural capital but hardly an economic hot spot. Due to the proximity of Morocco, there is a strong Moorish influence. In many ways, it feels more North African than European.

Annaliese and I lived with a family. We ate with them five days a week, breakfast, lunch, and dinner. On the weekends we'd fend for ourselves because most of the time, we were traveling. We lived with Remy, a single mother, and her two daughters, Maria Remy and Maria José, who were eight and fourteen. Annaliese and I shared a tiny bedroom, so small that we would crash into each other if we tried to stand up between our beds at the same time.

My most vivid food memories are of what I ate in our Spanish home. Breakfast in Spain is always quick, a café con leche on the go. Waiting for us every morning was a simple thermos of instant coffee with cream, which was completely delicious, and little Magdalena cakes, sort of like French madeleines, but a commercial Spanish version, spongy and sugary.

We had a break for siesta every day from one to four o'clock. This included lunch, the biggest meal of the day, for which we would usually come home. On occasion we'd take our lunch with us to school—a *boccadillo* (a sandwich) perhaps filled with traditional tortilla (Spanish-style omelet with potatoes and onions) and a piece of fruit. But when we came home we ate a much larger and more traditional Spanish meal. Our *"madre"* would prepare a big stew or soup or paella, but it was always quite basic and inexpensive.

She kept us fed well enough, but always seemed to overcook the vegetables. We would drool over enormous globe artichokes on the counter when we left for school in the morning, bowls of garbanzo beans, potatoes, onions, and carrots. When we returned for lunch they had inevitably been turned into a bowl of slop, boiled for hours until they were brown and practically disintegrating.

Thankfully there would always be oranges to finish. Spanish *naranjas* are big and juicy and intensely sweet. They cost about twenty-five cents for one as big as your head. The juice would drip down our chins and arms, all over our shirts. It was heavenly. Annaliese took to calling me "hungry boobs," as there was always something running down the front of my shirt, halted on its way to the napkin in my lap by the shelf my chest created. It wasn't pretty, but it was true.

We'd go back to school from four until seven or eight and then eat dinner quite late. Dinner at our house was always kind of random and on the cheap. A classic meal was spaghetti with ketchup and a fried egg on top. Or the family's version of pizza, with a chewy homemade crust, ketchup, and a can of tuna fish. It was borderline cat food. The ingredients probably cost about forty cents.

All the while, we knew Remy got a stipend from the school for boarding us. We couldn't help but notice that while we lived with her, she bought a new microwave, a new washer-dryer, and a new mini countertop deep fryer. She made good use of it, though, by feeding us an endless stream of fried potatoes. Spaniards love their mini countertop fryers. Every household in Spain has one. They fry everything. Some days I would come home to find Remy even frying little calves' brains for herself for dinner. She never served them to us, though. She knew better.

Because our host family wasn't exactly going out of its way to teach us the pleasures of the Spanish table, we found great meals elsewhere. Southern Spain has the most sublime produce: strawberries and olives and tomatoes. *Pan con tomate* was a staple. It's the simplest thing, garlic and tomatoes rubbed on toast. When we would travel on weekends, we'd go to the local store or market and buy loaves of bread or rolls and tomatoes and cheese, chorizo, *salchichón,* or another Spanish cured meat, and make *boccadillos.* That was what we survived on every weekend for the entire semester.

At this point I was still a semivegetarian, not eating red meat at all, just a bit of *jamón* because it was hard not to, and not even very much of that. It's a shame when I think back on it now. I was living in close proximity to an endless supply of Serrano and Iberico ham and didn't feast on it at every given chance. In a cruel twist of fate, it's now one of my most beloved foods in the world. But back then, I would hold back on the pork and pile on more Manchego instead.

We ate a lot of cheap tapas on our travels, too. A lot of *tortillas españolas,* marinated mushrooms, and tuna in oil. I probably ate my weight in olives and *pan con tomate* that year. Traveling to Lisbon one weekend, we discovered a traditional Portuguese fish stew, with giant prawns and razor clams, mussels, and poached fish in an amazingly rich broth.

Due to our limited student budget, our drink of choice was *tinto de verano,* which translates to "red wine of summer." I call it the poor man's sangria. We drank a lot of sangria too, but when we couldn't get our hands on it, we'd buy a $2 box of wine and a bottle of Fanta and mix them together. Presto magic: the original Four Loko. It was very wrong, yet it always hit the spot.

When the semester ended, Annaliese, Rachel, and I made it up to northern Spain, and that's when I noticed a marked shift in food culture. In Barcelona and San Sebastián, the food is far more diverse. I walked into a bar in San Sebastián and was awestruck by the beautiful *pinchos* we discovered.

Pinchos (*pintxos* in Basque) are basically tapas, small bites, often in open-faced sandwich form, that you eat at the bar while you drink traditional *txakoli* (an effervescent Basque wine). In Basque country they lay the tapas out on display for you to choose, each one like a little jewel box, a perfectly constructed work of art. And here, I fell in love: with little pieces of toast with olives or shrimp or anchovies, tomatoes or cured vegetables, soft, fluffy omelets or fried fish, calamari or lightly grilled clams. Every morsel was carefully presented, colorful, and appetizing.

From there, we spent several weeks backpacking through Europe together, from northern Spain into southern France, through the top of Italy down to Rome, then up into Switzerland, to Germany for a music festival in Nuremberg, and on to the Czech Republic, where I spent the morning of my twenty-first birthday wandering alone through a castle in Prague. From there, we went up to Holland and into Belgium, where in Bruges I visited the school my mother had attended so many years before, and to Paris for several days. I ended my trip in London, staying with family friends. I went to the Royal Ballet Theatre and a performance at the newly opened Globe Theatre. These experiences—not to mention the mountains of crêpes, frites, and cheap beer we consumed along the way— allowed me to get over my breakup and appreciate the larger world outside my door. It forced me to realize I had put so much weight on one relationship, when there was a whole universe of people out there worth getting to know.

....

THIS WASN'T THE first time that travel coincided with heartbreak for me, or that food helped me recover from it.

Upon graduating from high school three years earlier, my then-boyfriend and I decided to spend the summer in Israel. We'd both been before, he with a teen tour the previous summer, me when I was sixteen for a family friend's bar mitzvah. He was fluent in Hebrew. It had all the makings of an idyllic rite of passage before going off to college.

It's amazing that my mother let me go away—to the Middle East no less—with a boy at the age of eighteen. She later explained that I would probably have gone anyway and she trusted I would find my way back. He was smart, but a pretty punky kid at the time (and yes, another musician). We had a very intense teenage romance, because he was a very intense guy. He was a talented guitarist and serious as only eighteen-year-old boys can be. Music defined him, and so music became me, too: we spent endless hours in his basement that year, listening to Soundgarden, Pearl Jam, Nirvana, Jane's Addiction, studying every lyric, every guitar riff.

Ten days into our trip to Israel, he broke up with me. We were sharing a room, living on a kibbutz near the city of Nahariya with six hundred strangers. He just said, out of the blue, "I don't think we should be together anymore." There was no talking about it. And that was the end. I was alone on the other side of the world.

Well, not literally alone. We continued to live and travel together for the next two months of our trip, which is incredible, now that I think back to it. It didn't even occur to me to kick him out of the room for a couple of weeks. Most days I called my mother sobbing. I wrote my best friend, Vanessa, long letters about how devastated I was.

At least kibbutz life was fascinating. Kibbutz is basically a small town: ours had a shoe factory, extensive greenhouses, and farmland. Everyone did the chores that keep the community operating. The concept was founded when Israel first gained independence in 1948, as a way to work the harsh and often inhospitable land.

The tiny village was made up of about six hundred people, living communally. The children from a certain age would all live together in dorms, although their family homes were close by. The first time most of the kids would see the outside world was when they were called to join the Israeli army, which of course is always at war. They rarely went back to the kibbutz when they finished their service, because they had finally discovered the greater world, which is one of the reasons the kibbutz ideology, as it was imagined, is slowly and surely falling apart.

The kibbutz we were on was already starting to show cracks in its surface. We made friends with many of the teenagers who lived there. They were smart and fierce but painfully bored and mostly dysfunctional. Volunteers like us from around the world kept a steady flow of alcohol, drugs, and pop culture dreams flowing in and out of the place, which made the lure of the cities and the larger world even more tempting.

In our first jobs we were assigned to the chicken house, the *lol*, as it is called in Hebrew. They had four massive chicken barns, each the size of an airplane hangar, and each with thousands of chickens. The chickens weren't confined to pens. They were able to run around, and they had little cubicles where they could lay their eggs several times a day.

We were in charge of picking the eggs. Simulated daylight was on them almost twenty-four hours a day to help them produce. We picked eggs four to six times daily, thousands of them, making our way through all four silos again and again.

You had to wear sterile gear so you wouldn't contaminate the *lol*. You also had to shower when you came in and when you left so you didn't bring germs in or out. By the time we left each day, there was just enough time for a swim to cool off and then we would go to dinner.

It was not easy work. The chickens would fight you when you tried to take their eggs. Chickens are not the smartest of animals—there's a reason they're called birdbrains! They attack you. They attack each other. If an egg breaks, chickens rush to eat the fatty, protein-rich yolk and will swarm you, or swarm each other. Make no mistake: they are cannibals. As I write it all down on paper, it occurs to me that this has the makings of a great horror film.

I quickly grew disgusted by the thought of eating chickens. Eating an egg or a chicken at the dining hall was out of the question; it made me gag.

Looking back, I've had my share of bird-related trauma. When I was in kindergarten, we incubated duck eggs and hatched ducklings. We built a big cardboard house for them. The class would care for the ducklings for a month or so, and then they would be sent to a farm.

Each weekend some child in the class got to take the ducklings home to look after until Monday. Finally, my weekend arrived. One of them was the runt of the litter and was always struggling to keep up with the others. On Saturday my family went out for lunch. When we got home, I ran over to the duckling box. The runt was dead. I was devastated. This was the first time I had seen death firsthand.

My mother explained that the duckling wasn't strong enough, that it would have happened anywhere. She placed it in a blue jewelry box and we buried it in the backyard. We had a little ceremony. I was terrified of going to school on Monday morning. How was I going to explain to the teacher that the duckling had died under my care?

And then there was Digger, my pet baby budgie, who somehow escaped from his cage in my room while we were all downstairs eating dinner and mysteriously drowned in the toilet, just a month after we brought him home. Again, I was beside myself.

Come to think of it, there have been a lot of dead birds in my life. But then there's Toby—the one I like the least, who is bound to outlive us all.

So it was only fitting that I developed a strange relationship with these chickens in the *lol*. A funny thing happened a few weeks into my stay on the kibbutz. As my disgust grew to hatred, I started to eat chickens and eggs again, this time out of spite—and with determination. As they bit and pecked each other and me in the *lol*, I would think, "You stupid chickens! I'm going to *eat* you later!"

They weren't raising chickens as meat on our kibbutz, just for their eggs, but on occasion we had to kill one or two if they got sick or injured. So I learned to kill chickens. The veterinarian taught me how to do it painlessly. You grab the chicken by the neck, turn it upside down, stretch it out, and make one sharp snap. It's over in an instant.

I'd be lying if I didn't say I enjoyed it a little. I loathed those chickens. They were such *animals*.

And as awful as it sounds now, I needed to vent. I felt some remorse, but not much, because it wasn't for sport. The birds I was killing were sick or hurt, and it was my job to put them out of their misery.

After about four weeks of this brutish job, where I was the only woman, picking eggs alongside my ex-boyfriend, I'd had enough of the chickens and the heartache and requested to be transferred. I was sent to the fields. It was liberating work, in fresh air—a huge relief from the stench of the chicken coop.

The field was lined with alternating rows of lychee and avocado trees. It was wonderful being in the sunshine, but outrageously hot, well over a hundred degrees. Whenever the heat overwhelmed me, I would seek refuge under an avocado tree with a handful of sweet, ripe lychees.

And every single day for breakfast and dinner, I would eat the same salad. The Israeli kids taught me how to make this kibbutz staple. Dice a tomato and a whole cucumber. Mix them with cottage cheese, salt, and pepper. I also would mix in a little mustard, with a fried or hard-boiled egg.

In the last weeks of our stay, I was transferred to the kitchen, where I worked as a dishwasher. The dining hall served several hundred people three times daily, which made for a lot of pots and pans to be scrubbed by hand. I did so for eight hours a day. After a while, it became a habit and I could completely tune out my brain, listen to music, or have time to just think.

But my last job in the kibbutz kitchen was my very favorite of all, as the "egg girl," on breakfast duty. I began at four in the morning to prep for breakfast at seven. I made giant batches of pancakes, just as

I would make crêpes years later at Le Cirque, and giant batches of scrambled or fried eggs, moving them quickly, methodically over a vast flattop grill, fifty or more at a time. I was basically a short-order cook, invaluable training for what was to come. I could pour myself into it and get lost in the action, temporarily forgetting my teenage angst.

It brought back the same feeling of magic that my childhood egg creations had so many years before. Now I worship eggs. My favorite way to eat them is with what we as children called soldiers: a soft-boiled egg in a little cup, with strips of buttered toast on the side.

Both my time in Israel and in Spain taught me a vital truth about young love: immersing yourself in a totally different world than your own is the perfect way to gain perspective on the troubles that plague you. When you travel, you don't have the option of closing the door and weeping in your bedroom. You're forced to push through it, to be in the moment and appreciate where you are. You're not surrounded by the things that give you comfort. You don't have your friends, your tub of ice cream, your favorite sweatshirt. Instead, you have new experiences; sweet, sour, salty, and serendipitous moments that become new memories, fresher and more powerful than those that came before.

Food is, naturally, an extension of this. Foreign flavors convey so many priceless lessons: discovery, elation, pleasure, nostalgia, comfort, and fear. The food of a new place teaches you so much about its culture. It offers a window into other people's lives, history, and values. It allows you to see that the world is much bigger than you and your broken heart.

FIVE

Finding My Footing— and the Best Back Bacon

LUNCHTIME AT THE Saint Lawrence Market. Hundreds of cheeses are stacked on top of one another—from France, Quebec, Vermont, and Ontario. At my dad's favorite stall, there's elk jerky, with a sign that reads, IT'S NOT PRETTY . . . BUT IT'S GOOD. Maple syrup. Giant ham hocks, slabs of back bacon (known outside Canada as Canadian bacon), and handmade sausages. Russian cabbage rolls. Greek stewed eggplant. Loaves of Italian breads. Wheatgrass. Beeswax candles and local honey. Belgian crêpes deftly poured by young women speaking Japanese. Steaming coffee. Tangy Canadian "triple crunch" mustard. Pickles and olives. Live lobsters. I eat a spicy, saucy Portuguese pulled-chicken sandwich on a roll. Or a huge container of spaghetti with hot peppers and vegetables. I walk the floor of the market, tasting everything, gobbling the noodles. Then I go back to work. By 3 p.m., loaded down with food, I am fast asleep at my desk.

*D*URING MY LAST year of college at McGill, I started to take a more serious interest in eating. I starting writing restaurant reviews for the school paper and reading a lot of food magazines, for the first time feeling like they weren't just for my mother.

Most of all I pored over the U.S.-published magazine *Food & Wine*, scouring the masthead to figure out who was who, trying to guess what each editor's title actually meant, and dreaming about attending the annual *Food & Wine* Classic in Aspen: How awesome does *that* sound? My mother had offered to take me on a trip after graduation and it actually came down to Napa or the *Food & Wine* Classic. For whatever reason, we wound up in California—but the seed was planted to one day make it to Aspen.

Christmas vacation my senior year, a good friend of my parents gave us her New York apartment for a week. I'd been many times before, but this was the first time I was going as a "grown-up," when I could go out alone with friends and navigate the city on my own. Still, my parents were with me, and I certainly let them take me out for nice meals. Our friend made us reservations at some of the city's hottest restaurants. It was 1997.

Over the course of that week I had three meals I will always re-member: The first was lunch at Balthazar. It had just opened and was at the height of its buzz, overflowing with energy. I was con-vinced everyone around me was a model, amazed at how the entire population of a restaurant could be that good-looking. I ate mussels and fries, a towering seafood platter, and profiteroles with chocolate sauce, poured tableside.

Another night we had dinner at Aquavit, which was also new. The young chef, Marcus Samuelsson, must have been only twenty-seven at the time. I sipped black-pepper aquavit and ate cured grav-lax in the romantic room, all dressed up for the holidays.

Then we went to Vong, which had just earned three stars from the New York Times. Hailed as groundbreaking, this was Jean-Georges's initial venture into Asian territory. It was the first high-end restaurant of its kind to demonstrate such an amazingly original mix of Thai and French flavors, and epitomized the 1990s New York dining scene.

It was dark, and the luxurious banquettes were more like private booths, covered in rich quilted fabric. The service was uncannily attentive. They served us a "white plate" with a selection of signature appetizers on it containing several ingredients I didn't know: daikon, galangal, nam prik. There were fried duck spring rolls and delicate Vietnamese summer rolls. I returned from New York for my last semester of school inspired and determined to go back again soon.

Back in Toronto, living at home, I was feeling confused. Although I had learned a lot at McGill, academia didn't prepare me for anything specific. It prepared me in some ways for the adult world: I grew as a person. I learned how to write, how to do research, and how to question. But I did not graduate with a set purpose.

At that fateful meeting with my family friend who helped me realize that "Eat. Write. Travel. Cook." was actually a viable career plan, she also gave me more concrete advice, suggesting I try writing for lifestyle magazines. That made sense, but I had no idea how to go about getting such a job.

By coincidence, at a bridal shower the very next week my mother was seated next to a young woman who worked on the publishing side of *Toronto Life*, the city's award-winning monthly magazine. She told her about me. The woman called my mother a few days later to say I should apply for an editorial internship.

I landed the position and soon realized writing about food was a job people actually had. It wasn't just a pipe dream.

I edited and conducted research for the magazine's listing pages, including theater, art, and restaurants. I spent a lot of time learning about copyediting and immersed myself in fact-checking. It's sort of like being a private investigator, doing reverse research. When an article includes an address, say, 431 Smith Street, in a big brownstone on the north side of the street, it was my job to make sure that was the right address, that it was indeed a brownstone, that it was big, and in fact on the north side of the street. I loved the process, even though some of it was tedious. I liked re-interviewing subjects, finding flaws, and fixing them. It felt rewarding to improve the story or to debate the nuances of the way a sentence read.

Once while spending time in the magazine's archives I found a food article that my mother had written some twenty years earlier. I was officially becoming my mother!

The food editor and the magazine's restaurant critic became my idols. I was like a lost puppy following them around as much as they would let me, picking their brains and hoping they would eventually offer me their scraps. Finally, the magazine let me write. The first thing I published was a sidebar called "Rex Appeal," about a new exhibit of dinosaurs at the Royal Ontario Museum. Eventually the food editor allowed me to do "$25 and Under" restaurant reviews and a feature reviewing the city's best movie theaters, which meant I saw a movie every day for two weeks. Not exactly Pulitzer-worthy, but it was a start.

Not only was I learning about magazines; I was also learning about the Toronto I'd grown up in but never had a chance to explore as an adult. I loved Toronto, but I didn't really come to know its ethnic communities and all it had to offer until I started working. It was invigorating and inspiring.

Even lunch when I was at *Toronto Life* was a thrill for me. The offices were right on Front Street, almost at the lakeshore, just two blocks from Toronto's Saint Lawrence Market. It's a covered market open every day, all year round.

I interned at *Toronto Life* for four months and then freelanced for them for another six, even after I got my next job, at the *National Post*. How I landed that one was total serendipity.

At summer camp, when I was thirteen, I idolized my beautiful camp counselor, Rachel. She was only four years older than me, but when you're thirteen, that's a huge difference—especially where your boobs are concerned. We stayed friends through the years and I always looked up to her.

Flash-forward to the summer of 1998. Shortly after moving home, I met my next boyfriend (this one not a musician, thankfully), and about three months into dating we decided to take a weekend trip to New York. Rachel, who had graduated a few years before, had moved to New York and gotten a job at *Marie Claire*. We had lunch and, again, she enthralled me. She had this wonderful magazine-world life in New York City.

Just a few months later media magnate Conrad Black announced he would launch a new national paper in Canada, aptly named the *National Post*. He poured boatloads of money into it. It was the biggest newspaper launch the country had seen in decades. And it had a glossy, full-color Saturday magazine, with entertainment, fashion, food, and arts coverage.

Black hired the smartest minds in politics, culture, sports, and art from around the country and around the world. Rachel was hired as an editor and moved back to Toronto to work there. She was on staff with her friend from *Marie Claire*, Colleen Curtis (who has come back to my life many times since, in ways I could never have anticipated), and Kate Fillion, a legendary Canadian author and journalist. Rachel tracked me down to tell me they were hiring and I jumped at the chance to work with her. At first I was hired as the Saturday magazine's editorial intern.

Again, I felt drawn to the editor of the food pages. I wrote as much as I could for the section and as much about food as they would allow. The first food-related story I published with them was a sidebar about McDonald's specials all over the world, like the lamb burger in India or the New Zealand "kiwi burger," with an egg on top. Hey, it was a byline, right?

Another story I wrote was about the air service industry, and how much pilots, air traffic controllers, TSA agents, and flight attendants were paid. It showed that you needed very little education to get many of those jobs. Because of it, I got my first piece of hate mail. "How dare you belittle what we do?" They were appalled. "Who is this Gail Simmons?"

I took the letter to my editor. "Do we print a retraction?" I had fact-checked it, but I was still horrified I had upset someone.

"Frame it," he laughed. "It's great! You caused a stir. You provoked an emotion in someone. They read what you wrote and felt forced to respond. You made them think! That's journalism."

I take that advice to heart every day. In my life now I get angry emails and posts on blogs all the time. People go on for pages if they don't like what I said about someone or a decision I made, a dress I wore, a meal I praised. I've read I have abnormally pointy ears, that I'm a witch, mean, racist, a stuck-up food snob, and countless other charming sentiments.

Whenever I read negative responses, I repeat this same mantra to myself: I still win, even if you don't like what I did. You're still watching the show. You're still reading the magazine. You allowed yourself to be provoked and took time to act because of it. That's what I call an attentive audience. It's the ultimate reward: to know that people are listening. It then becomes a dialogue, which is the reason we do it in the first place.

Back then in Canada most of the major food media still came out of the United States. There is still no major food publication in the country, because Canadians read *Food & Wine* and *Bon Appétit*. When I was trying to figure out how to create a career for myself, all the big food jobs in Canada were taken by people in their forties and fifties, who weren't going anywhere, because those jobs were cushy and rare.

After about six months at the *National Post* I was at a loss for what to do next. But I knew I still had so much to learn. So I went to the food editor, wide-eyed and hungry (literally), looking for guidance.

"If you want to write about food, you need to learn about food," he said. "You need to know your beat. If you want to write about politics, you go to Washington. If you want to write about war, you go to the front lines. If you want to write about food, you need to speak the language. You need a point of view, a way to differentiate yourself. Forget about writing for a while. Go learn how to cook and how to eat."

He was right. I researched culinary schools and a plan began to take shape. First I looked at the Culinary Institute of America, in Hyde Park, New York, but their programs all lead to associate or bachelor's degrees. I knew that I didn't want to be a chef in a kitchen, and I had just gotten out of school, so I didn't want to go into a two-year program. That narrowed it down to two major schools in New York: the French Culinary Institute and the Peter Kump New York Cooking School. (Peter Kump was a major culinary figure in New York in the 1970s and 1980s; he was a close friend of James Beard and cofounder, in 1985, of the James Beard Foundation, along with Julia Child.)

A friend of a friend in Toronto had just come back from completing the professional program at Peter Kump's and gave it a rave review. So it was decided. I applied and was accepted for spring admission.

Here was the chance I had been waiting for, the opportunity to realize my dream of living in New York. Sure, there was a good culinary school in Toronto, and several around Canada. But New York was my first and only choice, for the same reasons that it's everyone else's—I wanted to experience the energy, to be at the center of an industry I sensed was far more dynamic than what was available to me at home.

Despite the exciting prospects, I still had guilt about leaving. I was in a relationship of about a year and worried I was not giving it the chance it deserved. But my boyfriend loved New York, too. He was in the advertising industry and threatened to eventually move to New York as well. Then there was my brother Alan, who was still struggling. During the year I'd been home, I had been able to spend so much more time with him and, perhaps, helped ease the stress and worry my parents were carrying. But both my parents had left their childhood homes to pursue their own lives and careers, so they were very supportive of my aspirations. I rationalized that I would just go for the duration of the program—maybe a month or two more if I could get an internship or temporary job to solidify my experience.

New York, I knew, would give me that leg up I needed over my Canadian competition in the industry. Even a year in New York, with a prestigious cooking school degree under my belt and a few months of work at a high-profile publication, would make me a big fish in Toronto's small food-media pond. Like Rachel before me, I could come back and have my pick of opportunities. Or better, perhaps I would gain the respect and knowledge I needed to start something fresh and new, something Toronto had never seen before.

I packed up my room in my parents' basement. Two months from the moment the idea was planted, I was gone.

....

SIX

Coffee, Baguettes, and Borscht in the Culinary School Kitchen

I ARRIVE AT 8:30 a.m. and change into my whites. Someone's making coffee. I never really drank coffee in college, but now I'm on my feet all day and out all night and can't believe it hasn't always been in my life. When morning comes I crave it. I pour in whole milk and a heaping spoonful of sugar. In the kitchen, alongside the day's *mise-en-place*, there are French baguettes from the pastry kitchen and a block of Gruyère cheese set out on the rolling racks. We rip off chunks of the baguette and lop off hunks of nutty, buttery Gruyère, with its slightly crystalline texture. With our chef knives, we make rough sandwiches, and happily gnaw on them as we start the day's lesson.

WE WERE ONE of the first classes at Peter Kump's New York Cooking School's shiny new location on West Twenty-third Street. Our class was fifteen people, representing nine different countries. Welcome to New York.

The first day, I received my knives and tool kit, a briefcase full of all the major items a chef could want. There was an eight-inch chef knife, a boning knife, a paring knife, a serrated bread knife, a tournée knife, spatulas, a lemon zester, wooden spoons, pastry scrapers, a melon baller, a metal spoon, a slotted spoon, and a pair of kitchen shears.

We started with fundamentals: knife skills, food safety, culinary math and equivalences. We learned about seasoning and ingredients. Then we moved on to stocks, soups, and sauces. We learned the five so-called mother sauces, the foundation of French sauce making, like béchamel and hollandaise. Finally, we got to actually cook, to learn about direct heat and indirect heat, dry heat (pan frying, grilling, and roasting) versus wet heat (poaching, braising, stewing, and steaming).

Once we'd been taught the foundations, we moved on to vegetables, grains, and eggs. We did a month-long section on pastry, starting with essentials like dough, bread, custards, fruit-based desserts, and chocolate work. And we learned cake-making, plated desserts, ice cream, and confections.

The theory came easily to me. I loved the academic aspect of it, the why and the how. The hardest lesson for me, which I think is true for many people, was learning timing. Patience was not something that came naturally to me, but in cooking it is the quintessential skill.

Consistency was another attribute I discovered needed work on my part. When I diced vegetables, it was painstaking work to make sure that every single piece looked the same: ¼-inch cubed for small, ¾-inch cubed for large. It's a matter of practice and precision.

My class was a microcosm of politics and opinions. Students from Latvia to Japan. Edward was an ex–postal service employee whose knee injury had taken him off his route. He'd been given a desk job but quit, saying, "I can't sit here. All I want to do is cook."

Anna was from the Philippines, via Hong Kong, a corporate consultant, who took a year sabbatical just to live in New York and learn how to cook. There was a guy from the Dominican Republic and a girl from the Bronx. It was inspiring to learn their backgrounds and reasons for being there, so different from my own.

We started at nine in the morning with a lesson about what we'd be cooking that day. Then we cooked from ten to two, whether it was making bread or pastry or eggs, or learning how to sauté or braise. Between us all, we'd put together a multicourse meal. Then, from two to three, we'd sit down and eat it together.

I took so much pleasure in finding explanations for things I had never taken the time to learn before, things that made cooking so much easier. The biggest revelation was how little I actually knew about food. I loved the jargon, the language of a kitchen, which was all completely foreign: bouquet garni, mirepoix, fumet, forced meat, consommé, gastrique. But most of all, I loved the logic that I found in the details. I learned what kind of shoes to wear (loose, close-toed, and easily removable, in case anything hot or sharp falls on your foot and you have to kick the shoe off quickly). I learned that there are buttons on both sides of a chef jacket so that a chef can get one shirtfront dirty in the kitchen, then rebutton it to present a clean shirtfront to the dining room.

I reveled in the most basic rules and techniques that are the foundation of professional cooking. For example, it is essential to use a sharp knife: the sharper the knife, the more fluid and precise your work and the less likely you are to get hurt. Dull knives are a danger—they slip far more often. Or this: the first step in cutting up any fruit or vegetable is to create a flat surface on it; split your onion in half and put the flat side down so that it doesn't roll around on your cutting board. Eureka! A whole world of knowledge became clear, one lesson at a time. Even the simple act of putting a wet paper towel under the cutting board every morning so it would stay in place made me feel like I was part of a special society. I learned to use a hand towel to create a base for my mixing bowl so it didn't slide around as I whisked sauces, mayonnaise, and vinaigrettes with one hand and poured ingredients in with the other. Cooking, it turned out, was completely rational and scientific! I was in love.

After lunch, from three to five, there would be a workshop. We'd learn about international cuisine—Chinese, Thai, Italian, Spanish— or wine studies, restaurant management, or menu planning. I would practically skip home each night at six, elated. I adored my teachers. I was using my hands and thinking, too, in a new way. It was a relief to not be in front of a computer. And suddenly, for the first time in my life, I was one of those people who had a calling. I wanted to work with food.

One day our teacher suggested we each prepare a dish that represented our heritage. One person made *tres leches* cake. The guy from Japan made tempura. My friend Anna taught us about dim sum. My teacher, a New York Jew, suggested I make something reflecting my East European ancestry. She gave me a book of recipes and I decided to make beet borscht with flanken (pronounced "flunken"), a strip of beef from the chuck end of the short rib.

When I was growing up, my mother made cold borscht with dill and crème fraîche, but this borscht was hot, with turnips, parsnips, and carrots, and far more substantial. I peeled so many beets that I was stained bright pink from head to toe by the end of class. It was hearty and delicious. I made so much that my roommate and I lived on it for days.

With Chef-Instructor Frank Garafolo at my
culinary school graduation

I thought I would be in New York for six to eight months for my
classes and then return, triumphant, to Canada. I could not have
imagined how easily I would fall in love with the city. Perhaps that
in itself was a sign of my naiveté.

I have a theory about Canadians. They're great world travelers,
but they don't tend to move around a lot inside their own country
compared to Americans. That's mostly because there are only a certain number of cities in Canada, only a handful of urban centers
worth living in when you are young, and therefore fewer options for
something new. In the United States, there are countless major cities, endless choices for university or job opportunities.

Like many of my friends, I went away to college but returned
after graduation. This is understandable: if you are going to leave a

city like Toronto for school, you're probably going to go back when school is done, as the city provides the most opportunity. Of all my friends from home, I'm one of about five who aren't still there.

I also imagined I would go back to Toronto because my family was still in a bit of turmoil, mostly connected to Alan's struggles. Everyone's proud of me and they are all very supportive, but because I left, I've missed a lot of what has happened with my brother. Leaving has come with its share of guilt, mostly self-imposed, although my mother has chipped in, whether she has meant to or not.

I guess I don't blame her. For a while, I'm sure she thought I would move back to Toronto and become a lawyer and live next door to her. All my girlfriends in the last several years have had children and moved back to the neighborhood we grew up in. Maybe she believes if I hadn't left, that's what I would have done.

. . . .

MY FIRST APARTMENT in New York was in Murray Hill, on Third Avenue and Thirty-third Street, above La Pizzeria. A friend from summer camp, Jamie, an equities trader, had this tiny apartment with a second room. You could barely call it a bedroom; it was off the living room, roughly eight by nine feet, with one small alley-facing window, through which I would lie in bed spying on the neighbors.

He had been using it as his office, but he was never home. He started work at six in the morning and was asleep by ten each night, five, or sometimes six, days a week. He barely saw anyone. He told me to just pay him a few hundred bucks a month until I found something better. I stayed almost two years.

When I finished my course work, I had to pick an externship, a job in the food industry, to complete my degree. I was convinced I would naturally get a job in the test kitchen for *Gourmet*. My dreams of being a food writer would be realized, as easy as that.

I went to the career services director at school, Steve, to talk about my plan, telling him proudly, "Now I'd like to work at the test kitchen for the Food Network or *Gourmet* magazine."

"That's nice, Gail," he said, "but my advice to you is, don't do it. You've only ever made every dish once. No offense, but you still don't know how to cook. The only way to truly solidify your skills is to work in a restaurant and cook on the line. You just can't get that experience at culinary school."

He was right. Real-world experience is something I lacked. It's the same with any schooling, really. Completing law school isn't the same as working in a law office. Just because you've taken a course in obstetrics as a medical student doesn't mean you know how to deliver a baby. No one is a chef after culinary school. You're barely a cook. You need practical experience. Begrudgingly, I took his advice.

I am a strong, smart woman! I told myself. I refused to fit the stereotype of the girl who can't handle a high-pressure kitchen. I thought I wanted to stick with French food, and when Steve listed restaurant choices, I stopped him at Le Cirque 2000. The name to me was mythical. At the time, it was one of only a handful of restaurants in New York awarded four stars by the *New York Times*. It was an institution. Sirio Maccioni, the owner, is still one of the most renowned front-of-house men in existence.

I went for an interview and handed chef Sottha Khun my résumé. He had been the restaurant's sous chef under Daniel Boulud in its original location at the Mayfair Hotel and had taken over as chef when Daniel left in 1992 to open his eponymous restaurant. He barely glanced at my résumé, but he hired me on the spot.

I would go on to work in two kitchens: Le Cirque for only six weeks and Vong for a few months. In that whole time, I was the only woman in both. It was amazing and disappointing, but not unusual. And I would soon learn why.

....

SEVEN

Working the Line

MY SHIFT AT Le Cirque lasts forever. At midnight, I am soaping down the steel countertops. I feel beaten and exhausted. I steal through the prep areas into the pastry kitchen. There are actual women here, and there is a modicum of calm. They're still putting out dishes, moving methodically. They speak softly. I must look pathetic. They slide me a blackberry soufflé, that night's special. It comes out of the oven stiff and steaming, deep purple, with incredible height. A brisk wind would cause it to collapse, but in front of me at that moment it's still standing. I perch on one of the countertops and pour crème anglaise into it—a traditional whipped French custard of eggs, sugar, vanilla, and hot milk, in a little creamer. The blackberry seeds crunch in my teeth, the tartness mingles with the cream. I finish it and lick my spoon. The night that's just passed suddenly seems bearable. I pack up my knives and head home.

"OW!" I SCREAMED, as I accidentally grabbed a scalding pan barehanded off the counter.

"Take it like a man!" another cook yelled back.

But I'm not a man! And what does that even mean, asshole?

Of course, I knew what he meant, because I had heard variations on the theme as long as I'd been around cooks: "Shake it off." "Get back in the game." "If you cut yourself, cauterize the wound on the stovetop and get back to the business of cooking."

But damn, that burn hurt. Someone had put a metal sizzle platter on top of the stove and said, "Hot! No one touch this," but I wasn't paying attention. Seeing it so close to my station, I instinctively grabbed it to throw it into the sink, scorching each one of my fingertips in the process.

I worked through service with the searing pain. The next morning when I woke up, I had large, gruesome blisters on every single finger of my right hand. I looked like an alien, or a frog, with those crazy finger pads.

That morning I realized: I don't want to work in this world. Not because of the wound, or because of the other cook's gleeful response to my injury, but because I didn't want to work in a place that could not respect me for who I was. I'm never going to be a man. And even if I were, I would want to work around people who, if I screamed in immense pain, would ask, "Are you okay?"

Did that disqualify me from kitchen work? It could not be that simple.

Anthony Bourdain's sadistically delicious bestseller *Kitchen Confidential* would say so.

It was the first book that opened a door into the modern professional kitchen for the world to see. He was dead right about the dark humor and machismo that exist in so many kitchens. He nails the intensity and difficulty of being a young cook, working long, hot, difficult hours for very little pay.

At Le Cirque 2000, I worked six days a week. My day off, if I got one at all, changed all the time. Sometimes it was Wednesday, sometimes Monday. It was certainly never Thursday, Friday, or Saturday.

Le Cirque was at the Palace, a stunning hotel built as a private residence in 1882. There were so many cooks it made my head spin. There were butchers and pasta cooks and prep cooks and vegetable cooks. Dinner service prep started no later than eleven in the morning and usually ended well after midnight.

Let me back up for a moment and explain a bit about professional kitchens. The terminology of a kitchen was adopted by Escoffier from the French military. There's the chef (the chief or boss), and then there's the line. Usually there's a fish line and a meat line. There's the chef de cuisine (chief of the kitchen), who relays the chef's vision and oversees day-to-day kitchen operations. Under him (or her) are the sous-chefs, who manage each line of cooks in the kitchen as the chef's deputies.

You need to become proficient on both sides, at every station, to become a sous-chef. There's the saucier (the much respected sauce cook), the rotisseur and the poissonnier (meat and fish cooks), and the entremetier (who cooks soups and vegetables). The garde-manger handles the cold station. That's usually where a cook starts, with the terrines and pâtés, salads and cold appetizers. Then you work your way up the line.

The term "executive chef" is American. It's usually interchangeable with "chef de cuisine," but many in the industry don't like to use it. I once used that term in conversation with acclaimed American chef

Thomas Keller, who said, "'executive chef' makes this sound like a corporate office. This is a kitchen—not a corporation."

"Got it," I said, only slightly mortified. And I never used the term again.

Surprisingly, Le Cirque didn't start me in the garde-manger job, the usual spot where young cooks enter the kitchen. My theory is that they figured it looked good to have a woman on display. The kitchen was open and elevated from the dining room, almost on a stage, offering diners glimpses into our work area. They positioned me at the hot appetizers, pasta, and risotto station, right out in front, on the hot line, with a clear, front-row view of the extraordinary dining room.

Rest assured it couldn't have been because they thought I was cute: I was in my full cook's garb, with a toque, and big tortoiseshell glasses. I was always disheveled and tired, my hair pulled back in a sweaty bun.

Le Cirque's kitchens were massive. There was an entire second floor of prep space, and an immaculate open-service kitchen. I was the only woman. There were a handful of women in the pastry kitchen, but I rarely saw or heard from them while I was working. They were tucked away. The only reason I knew they existed was that I would sometimes sneak back there for something sweet after the main kitchen had closed and they were still getting dessert out. Like a stray dog begging at the back door.

If I'd had a really terrible night, one of them would take pity on me and slip me a soufflé. There was a soufflé special every day. Blackberry was my favorite. They were miraculous, every time.

Jacques Torres was still the pastry chef then. He is a genius at his craft for many reasons. At the restaurant he created these spectacular desserts that gave the customers a sense of magic, intricate beauty, and a deep sense of emotional satisfaction.

The signature dessert of Le Cirque was a layered opera cake in a perfect rectangular slab, about five inches across. On top was placed a tiny chocolate stove, and on the stovetop were two minute chocolate pots. In one, there was a raspberry or strawberry coulis and in the other was a mango coulis. In front was a tiled floor. It was precious, perfect, and edible!

....

ON SUNDAYS WE started early and usually closed a bit early, too, and every Sunday it was someone else's job to cook breakfast for everyone in the kitchen, as we were usually nursing hangovers. Often they said, "Give the job to the new kid!" It was trial by fire, a fraternity-style hazing, except I was the only one who didn't have balls. Imagine where that puts you in the pecking order.

I had few triumphs from my time at Le Cirque, except this one Sunday morning, when everyone was especially hurting and beaten by the week. Someone said, "It's Gail's turn to make us breakfast!"

I made scrambled eggs with onions, fresh herbs, and cheese on buttered toast for the whole crew. It was the simplest food, but it was for almost forty guys, all of whom were just waiting for me to screw up. Thanks to my days in the chicken house and the kitchen on the Israeli kibbutz, I was certain I could make great eggs for the masses. And I did.

"These aren't bad," one of them said in a shocked tone of voice.

"Nicely done, Simmons!" I put my head down and went back to my work. Victorious. Suddenly, they had a bit of respect for me.

The front of house at Le Cirque was magic to behold. Sirio is probably the most legendary maître d' in New York. He certainly has had the most longevity. Now his sons run the show, but he is still watching closely from the sidelines. When you dined in the grand room, who you were determined where you were seated. Like Michael's or Elaine's, it was one of the most famous power scenes of the time. But unlike those clubhouses, Le Cirque had four stars, so it felt even more like the center of the world.

From my station in the kitchen I could see all the drama unfold. It was the greatest show in town. There were three of us looking out on everyone from Barbara Walters to Sarah Jessica Parker, Rudy Giuliani, the head of every bank. Every major food and fashion magazine editor. Martha Stewart came the day that Martha Stewart Living Omnimedia went public.

The menu was mostly French, with a few Italian accents, but it wasn't so much about what was on the menu as what *wasn't*. Insiders knew we had a secret menu, and all they had to do was ask. One of my favorite items was the restaurant's twice-baked potato. We would bake it once on a bed of salt, then scoop out the inside and mash it with butter, cream, and a heaping spoonful of canned black truffles. We would stuff the filling back into the potato skin, bake it again, and then place a seared piece of foie gras on top. It cost $90.

Another remarkable dish my station was in charge of was a ten-vegetable soup, with carrots and green beans and peppers and celery, that the sultan of Brunei's son would order.

Because it was Le Cirque, the vegetables had to be cut to a perfect *brunoise*, each exactly an eighth of an inch squared. The prince would come in for dinner with no warning and we would have to have this soup ready to go, along with the simplest spaghetti with a very specific, fresh pasta sauce made only with tomato, onion, garlic, and basil. We had to make it fresh every day and have it ready in my lowboy, on the off chance he would show up. If he didn't, we would have to throw it out.

My station was also charged with making a beggar's purse appetizer. It was a crepe, gathered up like a purse, stuffed with leeks and carrots sweated down until tender, resting on a yellow curry sauce. And it had a flash-seared giant prawn on top of it.

Crepe batter needs to rest for a couple of hours after you make it, so it was always the first thing I did in the morning when I arrived at work. There was one specific, seasoned crepe pan that was perfect for it and was passed down to whoever was in charge of the dish.

When making crepes, it is customary to throw out the first crepe made each day, as it usually sticks to the pan and does not cook evenly. From then on you find your rhythm and the crepes come out well. There I would stand with my rested crepe batter, at this insanely hot stove that was barely off before it was fired up again. You get in a groove with it, carefully spooning crepe batter with a small ladle, swirling, cooking, flipping, and spooning again.

There were times when I thought I was never going to be good enough or strong enough or fast enough to keep up. I felt anxious, not knowing what this job would lead to next. On occasion, I would cry out of frustration.

But the oven where we prepped those crepes was so hot that my face was already bright red, and the heat immediately evaporated any tears I shed. Anytime I needed to cry, I would go for the crepe pan and work at that stove. I'm still pretty good at making crepes.

At Le Cirque I could not help feeling that having a woman in the kitchen put the other chefs on edge. No one was outwardly aggressive, but I never quite belonged. When I walked in, I always felt they were annoyed that they needed to adjust the way they were talking or acting. It wasn't like they were on their best behavior or anything around me, but I think they resented me a little for being there, for being in "their" space.

I found the cooks who were the toughest were usually the ones closest to me in age and position. They seemed to have the most to prove. Chef Pierre, the head sous-chef at the time (he later became the chef when Sottha left) and his sous-chefs were always professional. They were past the competitive stage in their lives. I wasn't a threat. Either I could do it or I couldn't. They didn't give me a free pass, nor should they have, but they treated me with respect and took time to teach me what I needed to execute their food. I was always grateful for that.

Part of it may have been cultural—Sottha was Cambodian and didn't speak much English, so he often talked about me and the younger chefs only in the third person. He rarely looked me in the eye the whole time I was there. If he had an order for me, he would tell someone else, like Pierre, and that person would relay the message. We used to call Sottha the Shark. Because it was a four-star restaurant and an open kitchen, we all had to wear classic French white toques. Ours were round and high, but Sottha's toque was different—it came to a point.

He was quite a small man, and in the middle of service, he would weave down the line checking on everyone. All we would see was this pointed toque getting closer and closer. Someone would usually whisper the *Jaws* theme, da-dum-da-dum.

What I loved about Sottha was that he always made us taste things. This was a great lesson and one I hold dear to this day. It allowed me to experience so many flavors I would otherwise never know, like fragrant white truffles from Alba, bright pink lobster coral, and perfectly crispy Peking duck.

The guy barely even knew my name, but he would come over to our station and throw down in front of us this huge platter of beautiful, lacquered Peking duck that he had made for a private party. He would rip off a piece and put it in my mouth with his own hands.

It was nothing like the duck dishes we had prepared in culinary school. The skin was paper thin. The fat had been completely rendered and had dripped over the meat. It was salty-sweet. It had a delicious dark, almost caramelized glaze. The meat was tender and moist. It was exquisite.

Still, despite those rare moments of discovery, after only six weeks I felt defeated. I now understood why there were so few women in four-star kitchens. There was no overt harassment, nor was I ill-treated compared to anyone else, but I was definitely unhappy. I was in an inhospitable environment and I was a manual laborer, sort of like working in mining or construction—fields where there will probably never be an equal number of men and women.

Around the same time, my brother was hospitalized again. It was coming up on Thanksgiving. I knew I wouldn't get a vacation.

Rather than suffer any longer or risk ridicule if I asked to go home to see my family at the busiest time of the year, I quit. If becoming a four-star chef was my goal, that training would have made sense, but ultimately I wanted to be a writer, and I could learn the same thing in a smaller, friendlier kitchen.

I went to Sottha in his office and said I had to leave because of family issues and because it wasn't a good fit. He took out my résumé. I hadn't even known that he'd looked at it, much less kept it. And then he said to me, "I don't think I know another food writer in this town, except for maybe Molly O'Neill, who's spent any time cooking in a four-star kitchen. Few have even spent a night on the line, much less several weeks. If what you want is to be a food writer, you're doing it right."

I was blown away. He said he respected that I'd put in that time, in a way paying tribute to the industry and learning firsthand how hard it all really was.

Not that he remembers. Many years later, I met him again in the prep kitchen at Daniel, where he was helping cook for a large summer event. I reintroduced myself as having been a young commis in his kitchen several years before. He smiled and bowed politely, then went back to his *mise-en-place*.

. . . .

I STILL NEEDED to finish the hours for my culinary school externship, so when I came back to New York from visiting my family, I decided to find a different kitchen. I went back to my school career services department and was given a list of places looking to hire. The most appealing was Vong—partly because I welcomed the opportunity to cook food that was edgier than classical Italian or French. And also because I'd had one of the best meals of my life there two years earlier. And here I was cooking in the kitchen! How could I have imagined I would one day be in charge of making the duck rolls I'd savored two years before? It was an amazing feeling, like joining the cast of my favorite Broadway play.

As garde-manger, I made hundreds of tiny lobster rolls a day. I would peel countless large white daikon radishes and slice them long and paper thin on the mandolin. Then I would stick my hands in a big bucket of pickled ginger and scoop out a pile of it, placing it on the steel counter beside my workstation cutting board. Throughout my tenure at Vong I reeked of pickled ginger, which is why I now have an aversion to it. I always taste it when I'm at Japanese restaurants just to be sure, and each time I am unpleasantly reminded of being immersed in that massive bucket of acrid ginger juice.

The fish prep guys would boil dozens of lobsters and break down the knuckle and claw meat for me. The tails and shells would be used separately later for a main course prepared by the fish station. I would pick through the big pile and take out all the bits of shell, then wash and gently dry a large bunch of baby pea shoots. I would lay out the slices of daikon radish on the steel countertop, adding to each slice one piece of lobster meat about the size of my thumb, one slice of pickled ginger, and one pea shoot. Then I would roll them all up.

They were the size of a slender cigar and were served as one part of the "white plate" appetizer I had eaten on my first visit. They had a great crunch because of the daikon. The pea shoots made them herbaceous and fresh, and they were luxurious to eat because they had a piece of briny, buttery lobster in them.

Twelve years later, I was at a Jean-Georges restaurant in the Bahamas, shooting the finale of *Top Chef All-Stars*, and I saw that these rolls were still on the menu. I had a flashback to that vat of pickled ginger, shuddered, and ordered something else.

At Vong, I had the cushiest kitchen schedule in the world. I am still suspicious as to how I got away with it. I was on the lunch team, which was pure luck. I worked the Monday-to-Thursday lunch service, starting at seven in the morning and usually finishing by six at night. My days off were Friday and Saturday! It was unheard of. Then I worked dinner service on Sunday nights, starting only at one in the afternoon!

There, too, I was the only woman in the back of the house, including the pastry kitchen. There was a young Mexican cook positioned next to me, working prep and the dessert station. He didn't speak much English, but I spoke decent Spanish from living in Spain and studying it at school, and I had picked up some kitchen Spanish along the way. He always helped out when I was "in the weeds," or "in the shit," as they say in a kitchen when you're falling behind.

Everyone on the line was pretty generous, all things considered. The saucier was this gorgeous Dominican guy. The chef was Pierre Schutz, Jean-Georges's right hand. He wasn't around much at lunch, but when he was, he always gave me feedback and asked how I was doing. It wasn't an open kitchen and we didn't have to wear toques.

In some ways the kitchen was rougher around the edges. These were more of the hard-core hoodlum types, not as snooty as the ones with the CIA pedigrees. They were calmer and much less competitive, though. It was an easier place to ask questions. The guys had more fun, so I had more fun, too.

It was still hard physical work. Believe it or not, the only time in my life I've ever lost a substantial amount of weight was working in a kitchen. If you do eat a meal, it's standing up at your station. You never really sit down, and you expend so many calories on your feet all day. At least I was a woman, and I could sit down for thirty seconds or so to pee twice a day. The thing about being a young line cook is you don't use your mind much. You're taking orders. You're not thinking or creating—you're executing. I never thought—ever, ever, ever—that I wanted to be a chef. But after some time there, I realized I needed to go back to using my head.

One day, the cute saucier asked if, on a day off, I would like to go to Jean-Georges with him for lunch. We trekked over to the four-star restaurant on Central Park West, widely believed to be one of the best restaurants in the United States, if not the world.

I had been out for fancy meals before, but this was the first time I was treated differently because I was an insider. They gave us champagne and extra courses. We ate a nine-course meal. One of the standouts was this checkerboard of *hamachi* and bluefin tuna, criss-crossed to make a perfect block of pale pink and deep fuchsia, with herbs, oil, and coarse sea salt on top.

I was drunk on the experience. I got home from lunch at 5 p.m., in shock over how good the food was, and that I'd just spent $111. For lunch! And that included an employee discount. I would have to eat spaghetti for a few weeks because of it. And yet I knew it was worth every penny.

At the time, no one except Jean-Georges at Vong was really doing Southeast Asian–inspired food at that high a level. Spending time in that kitchen, I was exposed to so many new and unusual ingredients. There were bright green sheets of paper made from pea shoots that we used to make duck rolls. We garnished plates with sea beans—salty, crunchy little sprouts from the sea.

And it was there where I first tasted *calamansi*. The small Asian citrus look like limes but are often orange inside. In Singapore, Vietnam, and Thailand, they're everywhere. You don't sit down without *calamansi* at your table to squeeze onto your meal. Some stalls on the street have *calamansi* trees in pots right there.

You still can't get the actual fruit in the United States, probably because of rules about importing citrus into the country. But you can get frozen *calamansi* juice. There's a company called Les Vergers Boiron from France that sells frozen tropical fruit juice, and we would order it by the case for the restaurant. It has a subtle taste, somewhere between a lime and a clementine, bright, lovely, and balanced.

But there usually isn't time to savor such things. Most days working in a kitchen, you taste as you go. You feel like you're eating, but
you're not. You reek of food. It's in your hair, your skin, your clothes.
When I got home, I didn't want to eat much. Of course you can't go
to sleep when you finish working a shift, because you're still hyped
up from all the adrenaline. So what would I do? I read. Food books,
mostly. Anything I could get my hands on.

One of the books recommended to me was *The Man Who Ate
Everything* by Jeffrey Steingarten, *Vogue*'s famed food critic of over
thirty years. Little did I know it would change my life.

In the book, Steingarten often mentions his assistant: one day
she's on the hunt for a rare ingredient in Chinatown, the next she's
running off to the library, the next she's testing recipes from his
latest exotic trip.

I blew through chapter after glorious chapter, and each time his
assistant appeared I would think, *This is it. This is the job I want. The
job I have been trying to articulate for years but didn't even know existed.* I realized it was the perfect way to keep my hands dirty but still use my
brain.

So I went back to my culinary school and spoke to the career
services director, Steve, again. With the book in my hand for dra-
matic emphasis I explained: "This man Jeffrey Steingarten has an
assistant who gets to do everything I want to do. Can you find me a
job like this?"

I had never read *Vogue* in my life. I knew nothing about fashion.
I just knew this was my calling.

Steve burst out laughing. "This is crazy," he said, "but I just saw
Jeffrey last week, and he's looking for a new assistant."

The sun burst through the clouds. I swear somewhere culinary
angels started singing. Steve sent over my résumé that Friday. I
spoke with Jeffrey directly on Monday and set up an interview for
Wednesday evening. When we spoke briefly over the phone, Jeffrey

told me to come over after my shift at Vong, around six. And in his cryptic way, he said, "Don't they have some kind of fried duck roll at Vong?"

I understood that to be a take-out order. So before I left the kitchen I made an extra order of duck rolls and smuggled them out in my backpack.

EIGHT

Alone with Rotting Meat: The Vogue Years

I'M TWENTY-FOUR. On my boss's advice, I'm eating at Pierre Gagnaire in Paris, one of the best restaurants in the world. We're at one of eleven tables in the main dining room. There's a blue Miró-esque glass screen on one wall. Each course seems to arrive with countless components, in an endless parade of tiny plates. Delicate gnocchi in red pepper sauce. Flavors of autumn: wild mushrooms with seaweed and figs. And then: tomato sorbet *en gelée*; *ris de veau en pappiotte*; risotto with white truffles and butter; turbot on braised leeks and herbs; baked pear with cherries and shallots; venison wrapped in seaweed with endive, ginger, and candied passion fruit; chocolate with orange blossom sorbet *en gelée*; veal fillets on a slice of veal liver; kidney on foccacia; beetroot; braised lettuce and spinach juice. . . . And the cheese! Epoisse, Livarot, Rocquefort emulsion; celery crème; chevre; and a hard cheese whose name gets lost in the flurry of it all. To finish, the Grand Dessert Pierre Gagnaire: fraise de bois on short-bread; marshmallows made with rose water; fruit tartlets; three different chocolates stuffed with *eau de vie*; citrus; passion fruit *feuittes*; a shotglass of raspberry mousse; a slice of pineapple over aquavit sorbet; stewed pear with cherry compote; a quivering mousse on poached apple, papaya, and pomegranate; hazelnut and artichoke on pastry with crème fraîche; caramelized plum in raspberry puree with black tea caramel . . . I can't help but weep from pure joy.

IT WAS MORE than a decade ago now, but I can still taste that meal. My parents and I were attending a friend's wedding in London and decided we'd take a week to visit Paris, too. Jeffrey Steingarten had armed me with a list of the best bread bakery (Poilâne), the best cheese shop (Barthélemy), and the best patisserie (Pierre Hermé). He also instructed me to strong-arm my parents into taking me to my first French three-star Michelin restaurant, Pierre Gagnaire.

At most upscale restaurants where tasting menus are common, the standard multicourse meal can be anywhere from five to twelve courses, depending on where you are. Of course, they're not full portions. If a main course consists of a six- to eight-ounce piece of meat and an appetizer is four ounces, a tasting portion is more like two ounces.

The courses usually proceed from light to heavy. Sometimes there's also a savory *amuse-bouche* to get your mouth in the mood. Then typically the meal follows the same general order, give or take a few:

1. Seafood appetizer (usually raw or very light)
2. Vegetable course (such as a composed salad)
3. Pâté (foie gras or another meat that has been pureed, placed in a mold, and poached in a terrine of fat; served with a sweet or acidic wine or fruit to cut the fat)
4. Seafood course (perhaps a seared scallop)
5. Cooked fish course (like roasted sea bass)
6. Poultry course (maybe pheasant or duck)
7. Pork or veal or offal course (read: belly or innards, the good stuff)
8. Meat course (such as beef, lamb, or venison)
9. Cheese course (a selection of three to five, or sometimes just one in a specific preparation, with accompaniments)
10. Palate cleanser or fruit dessert course
11. Chocolate dessert course
12. Petits fours or *mignardises*

At my urging, my father made us a lunch reservation at Pierre Gagnaire. I didn't realize what I was getting him into. This place was as holy as a temple, as quiet as a library. It was the first time anyone gave me a stool for my purse. They even offered me a cashmere pashmina to keep my bare arms warm in the cool dining room.

My father's menu was the only one with prices on it. He quickly grew pale as my mother and I happily ordered away, choosing the season's specials instead of the multicourse tasting menu, which would allow us more choice, and more dessert. It was October, truffle season, so there was a separate truffle menu in addition to the regular offerings. For my appetizer, I chose a bowl of loose, creamy risotto. The waiter grated white truffles over it. It could have cost $400. My father swallowed hard and focused on his breathing.

I had venison for my main course. Pierre Gagnaire's signature style is that every course has many accompaniments, plated individually. With my venison, there were four or five different plates, each with another bite or taste that played off the meat. It had a deep fuchsia-colored, savory sauce made of wine and chocolate. Rich, earthy, divine.

Then came dessert. I did not hesitate to order the famous Grande Dessert Pierre Gagnaire, still a staple at his restaurants. It included a dozen or so different plates, each more exquisite than the last. When it came to our table, I inspected it thoroughly, then I looked up at my father and burst into tears.

Well, it was more of a half giggle, half cry. My father could not help but laugh along with me. My senses were so overwhelmed that tears rolled freely down my face as I sat there. It was all so painstakingly beautiful. Someone had thought up all of these combinations, then carefully, meticulously brought them to life. The artistry of our meal had far surpassed satisfying our expectations and our stomachs—it had struck a deep emotional chord.

We walked around all day burning off that meal. And no, we couldn't bear the thought of eating dinner, even six hours later. We ate a simple salad and called it a night.

....

I COULD NEVER have imagined that an assistant job would expose me to such extraordinary food.

The job description of Jeffrey Steingarten's assistant was legendary in the industry, but it wasn't a joke:

Interviews have begun for the incredibly sought-after job of assistant to Jeffrey Steingarten, the feared and acclaimed food critic for *Vogue* magazine.... The ideal candidate is equally skilled at library and Internet research, cooking and shopping, repairing

Xerox machines, *mise-en-place*, keeping office and kitchen organized, writing clearly, doing errands, eating in fabulous restaurants and possibly traveling.... The ideal candidate does not
exist, but Jeffrey is looking for someone who comes close.

Translation: "You will spend two years alone in a house with a
food obsessive, making goose, after goose, after pizza, after goose."

I smuggled those duck spring rolls out of Vong and showed up at
Jeffrey's house at six thirty in the evening. I didn't quite understand
how important he was in the food industry, having only read his first
book and having never read *Vogue*. Jeffrey lives in an enormous loft
on Union Square. The elevator opens on the third floor right into his
apartment. I got off the elevator and came face-to-face with never-
ending shelves, stacked floor to ceiling with books. And clutter everywhere.

There were three sections to the apartment: the office, the kitchen
and dining area, and Jeffrey's giant bedroom in the back. There was a
harpsichord that Jeffrey built himself. There was a never-used tread-
mill. A printer, a fax machine, and—at the dawn of the twenty-first
century—an *answering machine*. Stacks of books everywhere. A huge
collection of Roto-Broils—a 1950s tabletop spit-roaster, perfect for fitting one chicken or two little poussins for lunch. Ice-cream machines.
Piles of chocolate. Mountains of wine bottles. Filing cabinets. Dust.

We sat down at his dining room table together and talked for
more than three hours. I lost track of time.

He read my résumé and asked, "You speak French and Spanish?"
He pulled books off his shelf in both languages and had me sight-
translate recipes and text. He wasn't joking around.

I fought my way through it.

He opened a bottle of wine and poured me a glass. "What kind
of grape is that?" he asked me. "Give me your tasting notes."

I stumbled and guessed.

He was making Brazilian ribs. He pulled them out of the oven and said, "What do you think? What did I do wrong?"

I suggested they were a little tough and could stand to be braised instead.

Then he asked, "What are your favorite restaurants in New York?"

I had no money. I was a lowly line cook, living in my friend's closet. I was certainly not eating like I do now. But I had just eaten at a tiny sushi place in the Village called Tomoe for the first time just a few weeks before. The fish had seemed impeccably fresh. I had never eaten sushi like that in Toronto, and I had splurged on it. So I mentioned Tomoe, and that I had tried bluefin tuna belly (*toro*) for the first time.

He burst out laughing. "You must not read *Vogue*."

"Why?" I asked, knowing he was right.

"Because," he said, "I just wrote a column about how much I hate Tomoe sushi."

I shrank a little but kept going.

Then we talked about Mexico. He had just come back from judging a tamale competition. I didn't know much about Mexican food. My experience with it in Canada didn't include much more than fajitas. I thought a tamale was a plant, perhaps? Or a vegetable? I certainly didn't know it was masa (a cornmeal mixture) baked in a corn husk. Whatever I said, he realized I had no idea what he was talking about.

"Have you cooked with Szechuan peppercorns?" he asked at another point in the conversation. By now I had completely lost my senses.

"Yes!" I said, happy to finally have a right answer. "We cook with them at Vong."

"Real ones?" he asked.

"I suppose so?" I answered, not totally sure.

He had recently been to China and returned with a small bag of genuine Szechuan peppercorns. He handed one to me. It didn't look at all like what we cooked with at Vong.

I put it in my mouth.

My tongue went numb. My lips were now made of pins and needles. My sense of taste was totally wiped out. It wasn't an unpleasant feeling, but it was one I had never experienced before.

"*That's* a real Szechuan peppercorn," Jeffrey said. "They're why Szechuan food is so spicy."

The next day, I did in fact go to the spice rack at work and put one of their peppercorns in my mouth. The effect was totally different. I faxed Jeffrey a thank-you note for the interview, admitting he was right about the peppercorns.

I remember saying to myself as I left his house that night, sometime after nine: *Well, I blew that.* But I just got three hours with Jeffrey Steingarten. That's my New York moment. I can go back to Canada and die happy. He ridiculed me for an entire evening, and I was thrilled about it. Talk about foreshadowing.

If nothing else, it confirmed how much I had to learn and what a genius he already was. I had learned about tamales and Szechuan peppercorns. Brazilian ribs and where not to eat sushi in New York. It was worth the price of admission.

A couple of days later, Jeffrey called and hired me. I was speechless.

Later on, I realized that by the time I went in for that interview, he was desperate. He goes through a classic cycle. After about two years, his assistant gets exasperated and quits. At first, he won't let her leave, even though he always knows it's coming and, to be frank, is exasperated, too. He makes such a fuss that she sticks it out a little longer.

Then she gets truly incensed and walks out, never to return. Despite the myriad of résumés that he receives, he cannot make a decision on whom to hire next. No one is perfect enough. He fumbles along for a little while and his life starts falling apart. There's no one to get the mail, check his answering machine, or return his calls. No one to pick up his made-to-measure shirts from the cleaners or do his extensive recipe testing. So, in a last-ditch effort before he expires, he hires someone very quickly. At least that is how it all looks from the outside.

On closer examination, I learned that the women he hires in a fit of despair are actually very specific. He gets hundreds of applications. People send him homemade bread and desserts, wine and chocolate truffles. He is quick to judge them, but ultimately right. It's all about chemistry, and he knows in an instant. Over the last fifteen years or so, Jeffrey has amassed a small army of loyal and feisty female assistants. The women who came before and after me, who helped me navigate the darkest corners of his apartment and his mind, served as my first group of trusted, bold, foodcentric girlfriends in New York.

Over the years, our little crew has grown, and we have all moved on to completely different jobs. But we remain closely connected, getting together regularly to celebrate milestones or misery, over cocktails and, always, good food, passing our wisdom and our sympathy down to the next girl in line. It's no coincidence that each one of the women who has lasted with Jeffrey for their tenure has also fit beautifully into the fold of our friendship. It's also no coincidence that each and every one of us has come out of the position with the help of another, more grounded male relationship in our personal lives (an equally impressive small army of very patient husbands and boyfriends), as well as an even stronger sense of self. It makes me think this is all part of Jeffrey's master plan: to create these wonderful friendships for his former assistants. I call us Jeffrey's Angels.

....

SPEAKING OF BOYFRIENDS, it was around this time that I came to know my future husband, Jeremy.

When we met, I was still with my Toronto boyfriend. We were dating long-distance, even though it was quickly becoming clear that I had no intention of leaving New York and he had no plans to move.

The great irony, of course, is that Jeremy and I grew up in the same small corner of the world, in Canada, with dozens of mutual friends, and didn't meet until we both found ourselves hundreds of miles from home, in New York City. How we had not met to this point is a mystery to me. Canada basically has seven people in it. Two of them are Jews. Jeremy and I had led parallel lives.

The high school boyfriend with whom I went to Israel had a friend, Seth, who lived in LA. They met at summer camp in northern Ontario. Through the boyfriend, Seth and I became good friends. During college, Seth would come up to McGill to visit a group of us from time to time. Among the group of friends Seth came to see was a guy named Brandon, whom I had known for years, in high school and college, but never well. He had also attended that same summer camp. Through Seth, Brandon and I became fast friends.

Seth and Brandon both ended up in New York around the same time I did. The three of us were part of a small group of Canadian expats, which also included my roommate, Jamie, and a third guy from this same summer camp posse: Jeremy.

He had grown up in Montreal but attended college in a town just outside of Toronto, so our lives had crisscrossed. He had moved to New York about three months after me, for graduate school, a master's degree in music and entertainment business at NYU. One day, Jeremy came by my apartment to visit my roommate. He claims to remember the first moment he saw me: I was wearing my thick tortoiseshell glasses and my usual culinary school ponytail and was poring over a stack of books. He remembers thinking I was cute, if a bit of a nerd. True.

The next summer, by which point I had been working for Jeffrey for about four months, eight of us Canadians decided to rent a summer share house together in the Hamptons. We found a five-bedroom fixer-upper with a pool in Southampton on Craigslist and rented it every other weekend. The summer was great. We were in our early twenties and more or less single, not a care in the world.

Up to this point I had never seen Jeremy as anything but a friend. It was all perfectly platonic. But then one weekend toward the end of the summer, I came into the kitchen one morning and looked at him differently. Suddenly, I noticed how cute and sweet he was, how funny and easy to talk to, and I found myself attracted to him. We started flirting.

In early September, I ended up at his apartment very late one night. We sat talking until three in the morning.

Is he going to kiss me? I kept wondering.

I thought there was something between us, but maybe I was reading it wrong. I got up to leave. I walked into the kitchen to put my water glass in the sink. I turned around in the dark and he was there.

We kissed briefly, and I left.

The next morning I woke up thinking: *What I have I done?* I wondered if I'd screwed up our friendship and if it would be awkward within our little group.

But I also liked him—a lot.

When I'd broken up with my Toronto boyfriend, I'd promised myself the next guy I dated would be a Man. When life got serious, none of the others could commit. I was only twenty-four, but still, I remember thinking: *The next guy I date is going to have direction. He's going to know what he wants to do with his life. He will be a real live adult.*

Jeremy was not that guy. He was in grad school. He'd never had a long-term relationship before. He was a year *younger* than me. Plus, like I said, he thought I was a nerd.

For the first few weeks we dated, we did a lot of making out on the couch. Finally we had "the talk"—that "What is this?" conversation every man dreads and every woman wants to have immediately, or so they tell us in romantic comedies.

"What if I want to be with someone else?" he asked. "We're not committed, right?"

I was surprisingly bothered by the notion of this. Still, we agreed that we weren't fully together. We discussed how it would affect our group of friends if we broke up.

This went on for a few more months.

That winter, he went to Kenya with his family, and I remember missing him desperately. He called me when he stopped in Amsterdam on his way home. That's when I realized: this was serious.

From the moment we met, he was so easy to get along with and made me feel so comfortable. All the men I'd been with before I'd gotten to know through the dating process. But Jeremy and I were already friends.

There was a lot of common ground. We were both Jewish Canadians with close-knit families. Both our mothers were the Woman in the Kitchen. They were both passionate and accomplished cooks. They both loved coming to New York to eat. They raised us in similar ways, with similar values. He also lived a block from where I was working, at Jeffrey's, which was very convenient.

I'd left home, only to meet another Canadian.

Of course, my parents loved him. After all, how could they not love a man with such passion for old Jewish food? His favorites are kasha and knishes, the beiger the better. He also happens to love British food, which is, of course, also beige. Give him a pudding or a meat pie, and he's happy. In London a few years back, he ate so many meat pies he got the sweats. He would eat bangers and mash every day if he could.

Still, my mother called him "cute but useless," because he couldn't help me procure a green card. "Couldn't you at least find a *New York*

Jew?" she asked. (Those visa issues would continue to haunt both of us for years.)

....

MEANWHILE, THE REALITY of my job with Jeffrey was both more and less glamorous than I imagined. Jeffrey walked around the apartment eating chocolate a lot of the day. I spent countless hours cleaning up wrappers and half-eaten chocolate bars, which he scattered everywhere (Valrhona 61% Le Noire Gastronomie was his preference).

But most days I would focus on learning everything there was to know about a specific food, like the story he once did on Medjool dates, for which I blended date shakes all day long. When we did an article on pizza, we tested pizza dough for months on end. We were tweaking the master recipe constantly. He got a Raytek laser thermometer that let him point at an oven from several feet away and read its internal temperature. He took me to every pizza place in the city. Most of the guys working the ovens were Mexican, not Italian. So it was up to me to translate our interviews about oven temperature and pizza-cooking methods. When he needed a reservation at El Bulli, my Spanish worked, too.

When Jeffrey wanted to translate a chocolate recipe by Pierre Hermé or a vegetable terrine from L'Arpège in Paris, my Canadian French education also came in handy.

The first article of Jeffrey's I worked on was about the coveted (and overfished) bluefin tuna, the history and lore of *tunny*, as it's known in Latin. The next was on U.S. cheese pasteurization laws. I learned about FDA food policy and food-borne illnesses like listeriosis. Pasteurization, heating milk to over 161 degrees, or aging it for more than sixty days, takes away some of the authentic and unique flavor of the cheese, but it also kills any possibility for food-borne illness, which is why the FDA insists all cheese in the United States is either pasteurized or aged.

We discovered that serious illness from raw-milk cheese is actually extremely rare in the United States. Most food-borne illness, like listeriosis, in this country comes from meat, especially deli meat and hot dogs. Listeriosis can be fatal. It attacks those with compromised immune systems, children, pregnant women, and the elderly.

We also learned in the course of our research that we Americans are probably too reliant on those "best by" dates. Packaged food has an expiration date stamped on it, and people think it's like a clock: if it says February 17, then at midnight on that very day it instantly goes from good to bad. But experienced cooks know that judging by smell, taste, and sight is more important. I deplore neuroticism in the kitchen; as Jeffrey often preached, people have so many irrational phobias of food because they just do not understand the science behind it. With Jeffrey, fear of eating is not an option.

About a year into the job, Jeffrey traveled to Thailand for an article. When he returned, he brought me back a selection of insects from the night market in Bangkok and made me try them in front of him. One was an assortment of fried larvae. They were white, each about the size of an Advil, fried in peanut oil with salt. I'll try anything once. They tasted like popcorn—crunchy, salty, and greasy. Not bad.

The larvae were not my first foray into the world of edible insects. When I was nineteen, I spent the summer in Australia with my roommate, Cami. On a small island off the northeast coast, I ate ants that the Aborigines revere. The last section of this kind of ant is bright green and contains vitamin C. That's how the Aborigines avoided scurvy. Our guide encouraged us to eat some of those ants, and we did. No one got scurvy.

After Jeffrey's Thailand trip, he made me search for weeks for the perfect mortar and pestle for his homemade Thai curry blends. I had to go to Chinatown about sixteen times. He sent me to Mexican restaurants, too. Nowhere in New York did the right one exist.

When Jeffrey returned from Palermo, in Sicily, he re-created a velvety pasta dish made with sea urchins that melted and became the sauce, served with chili flakes. It tasted like the sea—so good, in fact, that he decided to go diving for his own sea urchins off the coast of California.

Surprisingly, what you're actually eating is the reproductive organ of the sea urchin. It's orange and looks a bit like a tiny tongue. It's best not to think of this, especially because it can be so delicious. At Nobu just weeks earlier, Jeffrey had introduced me to another amazing sea urchin dish, wrapped in shiso leaf, battered in tempura, and deep-fried.

For all I was learning, I was constantly on edge. Jeffrey believed in negative reinforcement. It's so counterintuitive to the way most of us want to treat our children, our students. My generation has been taught that you reward good behavior—you make it hard to do the wrong thing and easy to do the right thing. Jeffrey believed you make a point of letting people know only when they do something wrong. That way, the reasoning goes, the mistake will be branded into their brain and they will not do it again. It's like Pavlov's dog, or mouse-zapping experiments. I hate to admit it, but it was effective.

Jeffrey's motto was "Precision in word and thought." Not that he was precise himself, which is the irony of it all. His house was a mess. He always had food on his shirt. Some days he subsisted on caffeine-free Diet Coke and dark chocolate. And yet he was constantly correcting others, especially their speech.

You could never say, "No problem."

"Of course it's no problem," he would say. "You work for me." Instead I had to say, "You're welcome."

"Frankly" was poor grammar. You had to say, "to be frank."

When I wasn't being scolded, I was shopping and cooking. Jeffrey's favorite lunch was to buy little chickens, poussin, from the Union Square green market and spit-roast them in one of his Roto-Broils. He liked Bread Alone's levant bread with it. I would go to the market at least twice a week for these and whatever else was on our grocery list. And I would treat myself to chocolate milk from Ronnybrook Farms.

"Chocolate milk?" Jeffrey would ask. "What's the occasion?"

"You don't need an occasion for chocolate milk!" I would insist.

He found my love of chocolate milk absurd, even though he would drink caffeine-free Diet Coke all day, alternating with espressos from his bright green Francis Francis machine.

He always corrected people on the subject of New York's "N. Moore Street." He swears it's not North Moore. It's Nathaniel Moore, named after a revolutionary war hero. Recently, I corrected a girlfriend of mine who called it North Moore, and she sent me the link to an article about how the street used to be Nathaniel Moore and is now North Moore. But I take no pleasure in correcting Jeffrey. I have an allegiance to him. I always want to believe everything he says.

Often we would work on articles around the clock, and it would get him very stressed, as he was constantly scrambling to make his deadlines. We had our first and only true argument while working on an espresso article for *Vogue*. We had called in seventeen espresso machines from around the world, of various sizes and prices. I had to assemble them all and figure out which made the best espresso and why (always why). I had to test for various attributes, including power, water pressure, and packing of the grounds (tamping). (For the record, the key is in the pressure of the water moving through the coffee grounds. The more pressure shooting through the ground beans, the better the espresso. That's why most cheap espresso machines don't make great espresso; they aren't powerful enough to create the necessary pressure.)

Jeffrey insisted on keeping me there testing espresso nonstop for days on end. He made me cancel my travel plans for Labor Day weekend. And after all of it, Jeffrey decided that it was basically impossible to make a good espresso unless you had a $10,000 professional upright Italian espresso maker with a brass eagle on top.

Jeffrey never makes anything easy, but he always leads you to the answer somehow. He always wants you to succeed, as long as he can first watch you stumble your way through it. Sometimes I felt like he knew the answers but had me do the research anyway, just so I would learn. A valuable lesson indeed.

When I was first working for Jeffrey, he had a local television show with Ed Levine called *New York Eats*. Ed is a fellow food writer who has also published a number of bestselling cookbooks and founded the blog Serious Eats, among other things. If Jeffrey was Charlie in *Charlie's Angels*, Ed was Bosley. Besides Jeffrey's wife, Caron, Ed was the only person who really understood Jeffrey and who was helpful and empathetic to his exasperated assistants.

Their show was innovative for its time; exploring three pieces of culinary news each episode, including a New York restaurant review, a guest chef cooking demonstration, and a product taste test. I spent countless hours hanging out with the two of them, calling in products or chefs for the show, and doing various bits of research. I particularly loved when once in a while Jeffrey would let me tag along for their restaurant reviews. They once took me for handmade soba noodles at the legendary and deeply missed Honmura An, where I learned that you were actually supposed to slurp, because it showed you were enjoying your meal. We ate hand-pulled soba in broth, made by a man sitting in a small glass room in the back, tempura, tea, sake, and Japanese pickles. The flavor of the soba was nutty. The noodles were soft but didn't fall apart when I chewed them. The dashi (seaweed) broth was mildly salty and fragrant.

Ed was always the perfect foil, as I knew Jeffrey would scrutinize anything I said. Having Ed there allowed me to relax and not feel like I was under a microscope. I always knew Ed would come to my defense or defuse any tension.

Jeffrey also did an article about salt. We all need a certain amount of sodium to survive, and we need the iodine that's often added to it. His question was: "Does each kind of salt have a specific taste, or does all salt taste the same?" A chemistry professor and *Washington Post* columnist named Dr. Robert L. Wolke, who wrote *What Einstein Told His Cook: Kitchen Science Explained*, believed that salt is salt.

Minerals, he said, that are added to salt may change the flavor, but whether it's coarse, fine, or sea salt, it all tastes the same no matter the shape or place of origin. All salt has the same saltiness. The only difference you taste is determined by the size of the grain and therefore the rate at which it melts on your tongue. A teaspoon of fine salt is saltier than a teaspoon of coarse salt, because there's less air in it, more grains.

Jeffrey conducted a study to try to prove Wolke wrong, but it didn't really work. I said, "I hate to tell you, but I'm siding with Wolke on this one." I'm not sure he ever forgave me for that.

The worst piece we worked on, at least as far as my wardrobe was concerned, was one on goose. Roasting a goose is an arduous process, as they are sizable animals. I was charged with cooking goose in various ways for a month, using methods and recipes from Escoffier to Alice Waters. I would brine each with cloves and anise, mark its skin, and then roast it.

Geese are fatty animals. In the cooking process you render more than a quart container of fat per goose. Jeffrey had a poor ventilation system in the apartment, and for articles like this I was in his home kitchen every day. The smell of roast goose penetrated my skin and hair, the way food used to when I worked on the line. Every night when I got into bed with Jeremy, even after I'd taken a shower, he would complain, "You reek of goose." And I did.

To this day, I'm sure I'm the only person ever to attend a *Vogue* meeting with Anna Wintour with goose fat running down my Old Navy T-shirt and onto my Levi's. Luckily, she never actually looked at me.

Jeffrey's aged-meat story was pretty stinky, too. Rotting meat? Not appetizing. Lobel's, a family-owned shop known at the time to be the best butcher in New York, would send down custom-cut porterhouse steaks for us to try to age ourselves, never successfully. I learned the hard way about butchering and dry- versus wet-aging.

Aging meat properly intensifies the flavor and tenderizes the texture. But it's not an easy process. Jeffrey left town during this experiment, which meant there were steaks rotting on the kitchen counter while I was working in the loft. He insisted I should endure the smell in the name of science.

When the flies began to circle, I tried to cover the meat with a China cap (a conical mesh sieve) so it would still have access to air. It didn't work.

Jeffrey called to check in.

"There are maggots in the meat!" I reported.

"So what?" Jeffrey said with a laugh. He thought it was funny.

"Maggots, Jeffrey!" I said. "I'm throwing it away. This was not in my job description."

"Don't be a Jewish princess," he said. "This is vital research!" (I was the first Jew who had worked for him, and because he was Jewish, too, he loved calling me a Jewish American princess.)

Despite his over-the-phone protests, once the maggots took over, I threw that fetid meat away.

It was during the dry-aging meat story that I first met Tom Colicchio. His restaurant Craft had recently opened just around the corner. He was dry-aging his meat for twenty-eight days or more, which was rare for a chef to do himself in-house. Lucky for us, he agreed to age a few special cuts to various stages and hold taste tests at the restaurant for the article. Most people only age meat up to twenty-one days, if they dry-age it at all, because of various FDA regulations and the cost and space needed to do so.

When you dry-age for that long, the meat loses water, so you lose product. For every ten-pound piece of meat, you lose a pound or so of weight. It's an expensive process. This doesn't happen when you wet-age meat, as the meat is sealed in an airtight bag or container; it retains the moisture but you definitely sacrifice flavor. Through the course of our research we discovered that twenty-eight days of dry-aging is optimal and delicious. The meat's flavor is intensified and the texture is still silky smooth. But past that stage and it starts to taste "high," slightly rotted and past its prime.

Dry-aged steak wasn't our only indulgence. Jeffrey was proud of being an elitist. And working for him, you could not help but become somewhat of an elitist, too. At least it was hard not to get used to very expensive food.

One month, Jeffrey and I worked on a story about caviar. Until then, I had known little about caviar, except that it was expensive. I certainly had never had the chance to sit with twenty different brands of caviar and one big spoon! As Jeffrey and I worked on his caviar story, I learned about the politics of the Caspian Sea, about overfishing and why caviar was so expensive and desired. (Now you can get good American-raised caviar, but for centuries all good caviar was Russian or Iranian.)

Caviar is traditionally served as part of a service, with parsley, chopped egg, and shallots, on a toast point of some sort. But Jeffrey made me a purist. I came to understand that you don't need or want anything to interfere with the flavor and texture of really good caviar. Why would you put all that stuff with it? The texture of caviar is the most sublime part. You want to feel every perfect round sphere, taste the saline and fat pop in your mouth.

What you put it on matters, too. You don't want a dry, hard cracker, because it will overwhelm the texture of the fish eggs and ruin the experience. That's why blinis are their most popular accompaniment. They're soft and pillowy.

Best is to indulge in it simply with a mother of pearl spoon (metal reacts with caviar and turns it bitter). At the end of the article, Jeffrey gave me dozens of jars of caviar to take home, as he had eaten his fill and needed a break.

I didn't. Jeremy and I gorged ourselves every night for a week.

I never burned out on caviar, like I did with goose. But for reasons more complex than extended research for a *Vogue* article, I did completely go off black beans.

....

TWICE WHEN I was in college, I had black bean soup and got sick. Once on a date I ordered it and thought I liked it, but the next day I was rolling around in bed, ill. Maybe it was food poisoning, but at the time all I could think was that black beans just did not agree with me. I felt achy and feverish. A year or two later, I had black bean soup at another restaurant. The next day, again, I was nauseous.

Then just over ten years ago, on Labor Day weekend, Jeremy and I were on our way home from the Hamptons and stopped to grab some food. We ended up at a Cuban restaurant downtown. I had a grilled chicken sandwich with black beans. The next day I woke up incredibly sick. I lived on saltines for what seemed like forever. The first day that I felt like myself was Tuesday, a full week later.

My father called around eight in the morning from South Africa, where he had been visiting family. He had some time to kill at the airport before his flight took off. We chatted away, and I lost track of time. Finally, I looked at the clock. "Dad! I'm late for work! Sorry, I have to go." We said good-bye, and I jumped in the shower and flew out of the house. It was around eight forty-five, and I knew I would be a few minutes late.

I started running north on Seventh Avenue, and at some point I noticed that everyone was milling around in the streets, looking confused and staring south. I hadn't put my glasses on yet and was more or less blind without them. I asked a stranger, "What's going on?" He pointed south with a blank look on his face. A plane had hit one of the World Trade Center towers.

What a crazy accident, I thought. *I have to get to work.*

I ran east on Eleventh Street to Sixth Avenue and suddenly

heard screaming. A second plane had hit the second tower. A woman standing next to me on the street started to vomit.

I continued running. I barged into Jeffrey's, four minutes late. I was hoping that he would still be asleep when I got there, as was often the case, but that morning he was not there. He had left the TV on, showing the news.

I picked up the phone and called my mother. Two minutes later I wouldn't have gotten through, because the phone lines in New York City were overloaded and about to go down, but she picked right up.

"Mom!" I said. "Something is happening. Planes just hit the World Trade Center."

"What's the weather like?" she asked, instinctively.

"What do you mean?" I replied, thinking she wasn't taking this seriously. "It's a beautiful, clear day."

"Terrorism," she responded immediately. "It's a terrorist attack."

That was the first time such a thing even occurred to me. As it turned out, Jeffrey had gone to the corner to watch the events of the morning unfold.

I don't eat black beans anymore. I know it's not rational, but I associate black beans with getting sick, and then with September 11, the day New York City fell apart.

We had been testing coq au vin for Jeffrey's November 2001 column. Coq au vin, I discovered at the start of our research, was first created to make the best use of old roosters. Wine is used in the marinade, as well as the cooking process, to tenderize and then braise the tough bird so it is edible.

We needed a lot of roosters, and I set up a good system for managing them. I found a chicken purveyor in Brooklyn who could deliver a steady stream of freshly slaughtered roosters to Jeffrey's apartment. There are several stages to making coq au vin. I had roosters coming in every day, and I would prepare them to marinate overnight in wine, vegetables, and herbs, and make stock from any unused parts. (We only braised and ate the dark meat, as the breast would dry out, which Jeffrey did not find suitable.)

Meanwhile, I would braise a second batch and finish the sauce, vegetables, and noodles to serve with it, for a third. The birds were in constant rotation as we tweaked and worked out the perfect recipe. We were well into this process on September 11.

My impulse that day was to be with my family. But Jeffrey's reaction, I assume because he was afraid and anxious, was: "We're not going anywhere." The world was crumbling around us, and we were stuck in his apartment, cooking roosters.

Jeremy was still in graduate school at NYU at the time, and asleep at his apartment a block away when I got to work. I spent what felt like hours trying to call before I was finally able to wake him up. We met on the corner for five minutes. I could not leave for much longer. I could not check on my friends. Jeffrey didn't want to be alone. And he had a stoicism about him: "We will stay here and cook these fucking roosters!"

Finally, at around seven that evening I declared, "I'm going home." I went to Jeremy's house and gave my own apartment to Brandon, the close friend who had introduced us, and his family, who had been evacuated from their Tribeca home. I couldn't leave the country, because my visa was about to expire. Jeremy had a car and was going to drive up to Montreal to be with his family, as it was just before the Jewish high holidays. On the way, he dropped me off at my cousin's in Katonah, New York. I needed desperately to get out of the city for a while, to try and make sense of what I had witnessed.

I came back a few days later and continued cooking those roosters. We cooked them right through the search and recovery. We poured ourselves into the project, partially to distract ourselves from the terrifying reality that was unfolding around us. Old roosters are tough. You need to do a lot of work, marinating and braising them to make them tender, but once you do they are delicious.

We hadn't thought about what to do with the copious amounts

of coq au vin and separately roasted breasts that were left over when we were done. Even with our commendable appetites, and the help of a friend or two who would come by for a snack, we could barely make a dent.

Fortunately, around that time, the chefs from Balthazar organized a truck that picked up food from local restaurants to bring to the recovery workers at Ground Zero. And so, at the end of each day, I would lug over our vats of coq au vin for delivery. Suddenly all the work we put into cooking those roosters felt worthwhile again. The smell of the red wine and the taste of the meat and vegetables nestled in their cooking liquid are burned into my memory of that period, too, only in this instance, as a source of comfort and solidarity.

....

GOING TO WORK for Jeffrey was a substantial trade up from the kitchen. It kept my hands dirty and immersed, it allowed me to stretch my mental skills as well as my knife skills. But shortly after the coq au vin experience, I realized it was time for me to move on.

Jeffrey resisted my efforts to leave him, as he does with all his assistants, but ultimately relented and even gave me a good reference. Over the two years of our work together he had exposed me to so much great food and to the most talented people who make it. For this I am forever in his debt.

When I was working for Jeffrey, people were outrageously generous to me. They took pity on all the girls who worked for him. They knew it was a trying and intense position, and most of all isolating, as it was just the two of us alone in his home for hours every day, much of which he spent writing. They also knew that if we had worked for Jeffrey and survived, we had to have half a brain in our heads. The roster of chefs and top food authorities he worked with and in turn introduced me to was staggering—from acclaimed French chef Paul Bocuse to culinary scientist and author Harold McGee and beyond.

I didn't lack for interviews once I started looking for a new job. But the publishing industry was unsettled after 9/11, and the economy was rocky, to say the least.

I made it through three rounds of interviews at *Martha Stewart Living*. I even cooked for the senior food editors in their test kitchen for a day, but I didn't get the job. I was offered a position editing the *Eat Out* guides for *Time Out New York*, but they couldn't help with my much-needed work visa, and besides the pay was miserable, even by magazine publishing standards. I met with then-editor-in-chief of *Bon Appétit*, Barbara Fairchild, whom I'd worked with a few times on projects for Jeffrey and who had once mentioned in passing, "Call if you ever need anything."

I took her up on it. I took everyone up on it! We went out for drinks and she read all my clips, but *Bon Appétit* had no jobs either, especially not for a kid from Canada without a green card. I interviewed with Joe Bastianich, a famed restaurateur and Mario Batali's business partner, who offered me a job as his assistant and PR manager, but he was hesitant to deal with my visa issues as well. Who could blame him?

The red tape involved with getting a work visa in the United States when the country felt so vulnerable, even for Canadians, was more than a little intimidating to people at the time, and not worth most companies' efforts, especially for a junior position.

Through Jeffrey, I had also come to know Daniel Boulud, the iconic French chef who ruled the Upper East Side. We'd worked on a couple of stories with him, and Jeffrey dined at Daniel as often as possible. So I paid him a visit to see if he could offer any advice.

Daniel Boulud is charming and larger than life. The few times I had been in a room with him, I was mesmerized by his charisma. His marketing director, Georgette Farkas, was always generous with me, too. She seemed to appreciate the job I did keeping Jeffrey on track.

I wanted to meet with Daniel and Georgette, if only to pick their brains. After all, they were infinitely connected and the food world worshipped them. Georgette said, "I wish we could hire you. I'm drowning. We have three book projects in the works. I need help on our restaurant openings, public relations, marketing and special events, Daniel's travel . . . But we can't afford to hire anyone right now."

They put me in touch with Dorie Greenspan, a contributing editor at *Bon Appétit* and esteemed cookbook author. Among her many accomplishments: she had written Daniel's *Café Boulud Cookbook* and the English version of *Chocolate Desserts* by Pierre Hermé, a man viewed by many as the single greatest pastry chef in the world. She gave me great advice and put me in touch with a cookbook editor at Simon & Schuster, who offered me a job as an assistant editor. But still no visa. It just wasn't working.

Frustrated and tired of my dismal prospects in New York, I decided to take a ten-day vacation to visit friends in Los Angeles and San Francisco and catch my breath. It was the first vacation I'd taken on my own in many years. On the last few days of my trip I noticed that my glands were swollen and my throat was extremely sore. I flew back to New York on Christmas Eve. When I got out of bed on Christmas Day, Jeremy gasped, "What's wrong with you?"

My body was covered in small red dots. I had a fever. We called my doctor, but no one was around. We had to go to the ER. It was a virus, but no one knew what it was. I was sick. My visa was expiring. I had no job. I flew home to Toronto. It took six weeks to get better. It turned out I had Epstein-Barr virus—the Jewish cousin of mononucleosis, but angrier.

This was another living-in-my-parents'-basement moment.

Meanwhile, I had left Jeremy in New York, finishing his master's degree and working part-time at a record label.

Toward the end of my recovery in Canada, I got a call from Jeffrey saying he'd received a message on his answering machine. He liked to screen his calls. He never deleted the messages, and his machine was always full. Somehow, Georgette from Daniel's office had gotten through saying she was trying to contact me. I called her back immediately.

"We're ready to hire now. Are you free?"

The sky opened up and the culinary angels started singing. Again.

"I am so free," I said. "You have no idea how free I am. But . . . I need a visa." I dropped the V bomb and held my breath.

"Oh, that's no problem," she said casually.

A substantial portion of Daniel's kitchen was in the United States on a visa as well. Many employees were Mexican or Somali. Many were European: French, Swiss, Austrian, or Belgian. There were a few Japanese and one or two Americans thrown in for good measure. They had an immigration lawyer on retainer.

I was going back to New York.

NINE

....

Champagne on Arrival

THE SMELL FROM the baker's oven next door wafts into my office, and I walk over for another butter roll. Each one is a little bigger than a golf ball, with a perfect cube of butter and a pinch of flaky gray sea salt buried deep in the center. I bite into the warm dough, and find the salty, buttery core. It's made from the most humble ingredients of all: flour, water, butter, salt. But in a master's hands, they become the most exquisite, most luxurious midday snack in the world.

$\mathcal{T}$HE ENTIRE FRONT-OF-HOUSE staff at Daniel's restaurant would assemble in the dining room every night, six days a week, at 5 p.m., before dinner service. At this meeting, Daniel Boulud or his chef de cuisine would talk about the night's specials. It was the calm before the storm.

Standing around were up to fifty people, including the runners and busboys, the maître d's, captains, assistant captains, and reservationists—an army, perfect in their uniforms. Daniel has 110 seats in the dining room, so the ratio is close to two to one, diners to service staff.

Michael Lawrence, the then general manager, would read through the list of reservations: "Bruno, in your section you have Howard Stern at table 25 and Bill Cosby at table 19."

The reservation chart was tagged with levels of VIP. On these kinds of lists, importance is usually designated by X's: "PX," "PXX." Some names may have the term "COA" beside them; this stands for "champagne on arrival."

Michael would end every meeting by looking out at the room. "People, remember: this is a ballet, not a rodeo."

And every night it was. It was theater at its highest level. Watching the calculated choreography between the customer, the captain, the sommelier was such a wondrous experience. I now use Michael's phrase all the time, whenever I feel myself becoming unmoored. It reminds me to stay focused. Be graceful. Know that this is not a brutish sport. This is a dance.

For almost three years, I worked in the line of fire, so to speak, managing special events and projects in-house for Daniel, Café Boulud (New York and Palm Beach), and DB Bistro Moderne. All are temples of haute cuisine, among the most sophisticated and creative restaurants in the country.

Daniel, the East Side flagship, has been named one of the top ten restaurants in the world; it earned four stars in the *New York Times* (the highest rating the paper bestows) and has landed the number one ranking in New York's famous Zagat survey.

Everything about Daniel is decadent. The main dining room at the time resembled an Italian palazzo filled with thousands of fresh flowers. You entered from a grand foyer on Sixty-fifth Street. To the right was an intimate lounge with lushly upholstered chairs and low tables. Beyond it was a private dining room. Just past the lounge was the restaurant's bar. Then, past the maître d' and reservation desk was the entrance to the main dining room.

There were two seating levels. We called them the "pool" and the "balcony." The ceiling of the foyer, lounge, and bar was made of hand-painted wood in the most luxurious colors: deep rust, cobalt blue, blood red. The velvet furniture matched. The huge floral arrangement at the front of the restaurant was always evocative of the season. It changed every week and always took my breath away. The small bouquets on each table echoed the large one.

The front-of-house (industry-speak for everyone who works in the dining room with guests, from coat check to general manager) is a brigade the same way the kitchen is. If you're coming up as part of the front-of-house staff, you start as a busboy, setting and clearing the tables, pouring the water, serving the bread. Then you become a runner. Runners deliver food from the kitchen to the table, keeping in mind the positions of every seat in the room. Assistant captains, also known as waiters, do the actual serving of food and drinks.

Captains take the guests' orders, as if the positions at each table were numbers on a clock. They make recommendations and oversee

RESTAURANT KITCHEN & DINING ROOM POSITIONS

Chef

Chef de cuisine

Sous Chef

Chef de partie

Saucier   Rotisseur   Grillardin

Poissonnier   Entremetier   Tournant

Chef de Patissier

Boulanger

Pastry Sous Chef

Patissier

Garde-Manger

Steward

Boucher

Commis

Dishwasher

General Manager

Maitre D'

Head Captain/Head Waiter

Sommelier

Captain

Expediter   Assistant Captain (Waiter)

Runner

Busboy

Bartender   Host/Hostess

Reservationist   Coat Check

all the other service staff in their designated section of the dining room to make sure the meal flows perfectly for their guests. At Daniel, the assistant captains set down the plates at the table and lift off their cloches simultaneously so that everyone's food is served at the same time and the right temperature. Above the captains are the maître d's. The head maître d' handles the reservation service. He makes sure that everyone is seated at the right place and VIPs are treated appropriately, that every occasion is timed correctly and celebrated, and everyone leaves with a smile. When I worked there, the head maître d' was a charming young Austrian with perfectly styled hair and suit, and a knack for charming even the most jaded of guests in the room.

To ensure perfect timing, an expediter stands at the pass (the counter where the food is picked up that divides the kitchen chaos from the waitstaff). As soon as you start your third course, the expediter knows to fire the fourth. Guests are at various stages of their meals, so it can be an incredibly complex orchestration.

The waiters at Daniel were real professionals, and I was in awe of them. I had never spent time in the front-of-house before. The kitchen is one thing, I was perfectly comfortable there, but the front-of-house was a different universe altogether. The chefs train and toil. They hone their craft. And the servers do, too. There is often an animosity between the front and back of the house. The front gets the tips, and they have to answer for any mistakes made in the kitchen. The chefs don't, and they live in fear that the waiters will get something wrong.

The waiters at Daniel made significant salaries. These were no part-time actors. This was a full-time, dedicated job. You had to know and taste everything. The wine list had more than sixteen hundred selections. You had to know the characteristics of each bottle and understand how they all paired with any given dish.

There were also three sommeliers on the floor at all times. The wine cellar was actually two floors below the dining room. We had the skinniest sommeliers in New York, because they had to run up and down two flights of stairs countless times a night.

. . . .

EVERYONE AT DANIEL was hands-on, especially the man himself. Even though it was an international company, it was family-owned and operated. Daniel lived in the apartment over the restaurant. He was there every night and noticed every detail.

The administrative offices, where I worked, lay deep in the recesses of that culinary oasis, through four immense kitchens, just above the twenty-five-thousand-bottle wine cellar. My official job title was special events manager under Georgette, the PR and marketing director for Daniel's restaurants and projects. Under her guidance, I handled all the events Daniel himself appeared at—for charity, for promotion, and for press. I worked on the marketing of all his restaurants, everything from the design of the Christmas card and business cards to the strategy for his line of knives and cast-iron pots.

There was a lot to keep me busy—three cookbooks already written, with three more on the way; another restaurant opening; and numerous TV, magazine, and charity appearances. My job wasn't my only challenge. If you think it's hard not to gain weight on *Top Chef,* you should have seen our workplace.

My goal was not to stay thin—an impossibility. It was basic survival: just trying to get through a day without making a total pig of myself, when the opportunities were endless. Each week presented a new set of obstacles for my willpower, and my stomach, while at the same time introducing me to a new batch of heavenly delights and what I called "educational research adventures." I actually kept a food diary one random October day in 2003. Here it is:

9:07 a.m.

Arrive at the office; walk through the vast prep kitchens, pastry station, and bakery to my desk. Stocks are simmering, butchers are butchering, and chocolate ganache is swirling in its bowl. I grab a piece of fruit from a walk-in refrigerator larger than my Greenwich Village apartment to start things off on a positive note. Fetch my morning coffee, with milk and sugar, from a half-empty, lukewarm urn tucked in between the ice machine and the vegetable prep area.

10:15 a.m.

The bakers are first to start work each morning, arriving as early as 4 a.m. to begin mixing, proofing, and finally baking the bread for all of Daniel's New York eateries. A waft of freshly baked goodness floats aimlessly across my desk from their bakery, just steps away . . . walnut raisin loaves, olive rosemary rolls, butter and garlic, hot Parmesan buns. I grab a fresh croissant from the cooling rack and run back to my desk undetected. It's all downhill from here. . . .

11:34 a.m.

Sandro, the pastry sous-chef, is experimenting with a new batter for citrus meringue cookies—I pass his workstation on my way to a meeting and look at him longingly. He lets me taste it.

12:15 p.m.

"Family Meal" is served. Since the restaurant has close to 150 employees, many of whom work tirelessly in twelve-hour shifts without much time for a break, we are provided with two meals daily (lunch and an early dinner before service begins). Today's lunch is paella with chicken, olives, and roasted red peppers; heirloom tomato salad with pea shoots and balsamic vinegar. I fill my plate with rice and salad and stand near the main counter of the service kitchen, an immaculate 1,750-square-foot space designed by the chef himself and used for the cooking, garnishing, and plating of all dishes during dinner.

This kitchen accounts for only a small portion of the total back-of-house—a term referring to the behind-the-scenes areas of a restaurant. Besides the kitchen, it includes the locker rooms, the massive wine cellar, storage for everything from printed material to dining room equipment, the administrative offices, and the stewards' offices. The stewards coordinate all ordering and deliveries in and out of the restaurant. All around me chefs are preparing for dinner: slicing, broiling, peeling, stirring. Chef de cuisine Alex Lee calls me over to where he is standing behind the counter and gently places something in my hand—a thin slice of white truffle from Alba, Italy, the first of the season. I love my job.

3:23 p.m.

My stomach is rumbling again. I take a short break from my computer and wander toward the Chocolate Room, a closetlike space behind our office, kept strictly at 60°F (15°C), which stores our fragile, handmade chocolates and sugar garnishes. Pastry chef Eric Bertoïa is coating a fresh batch of perfect truffles with the restaurant's insignia stenciled in edible gold leaf. These precious morsels are served as petits fours at the end of the meal—a last bite of sweetness before diners go on their way. He smiles knowingly and hands me two dark chocolate pieces: one filled with banana and one with praline. How can I resist?

4:30 p.m.

The second family meal is served: spaghetti and meatballs with salad. I take a pass reluctantly (unlike most people here, I leave work before midnight and can eat dinner out), but still manage to steal a bite from the general manager's plate as he dashes off to the waitstaff's predinner meeting. (The general manager is the top of the front-of-house brigade, the way that the chef de cuisine is the top of the back-of-house brigade.) Every demand is addressed, from birthday celebrations to favorite tables, strategic ring placement for marriage proposals, food allergies, and specific dining tastes—Bill Clinton likes frog's legs; Woody Allen enjoys the energy around him when he sits in the center of the room; while Whoopi Goldberg prefers to dine at our tented, more private corner tables.

5:12 p.m.

Walking past the dining room to the kitchen, I encounter Pascal, the fromager (our cheese expert, in charge of buying all the cheeses for the restaurant, as well as educating the staff on their rich, subtle differences). He is placing today's treasures on a rolling cart used for cheese selection during dinner. Guests may choose to include a cheese plate in their meal, between the savory and sweet courses. It is Pascal's job to always have at the ready a range of cheeses from around the world to present to them, paired with fresh and dried fruits, nuts, honey, or wines. He cuts off the edge of a soft, pungent Livarot from Normandy that we discreetly share. No one can deny that I'm getting an education!

6:52 p.m.

Katherine, the in-house recipe editor, tester, and jill-of-all-trades, is trying out a dish for Daniel's latest cookbook: Rocky Road ice-cream sandwiches! Not the ones wrapped in waxed paper either— these are thick and gooey, with a brownie on the bottom and a vanilla streusel cookie on top. I dive in, giddy with excitement. Upstairs the kitchen is in full swing and I can hear Chef Daniel making his rounds in the dining room. He's saying hello to his regular guests, greeting an out-of-town chef who is here for the first time, making sure everyone is blissfully satiated. Downstairs the Rocky Road ice cream is starting to drip from my hands onto the files on my desk.

7:25 p.m.

Home! And yes, I have managed to get some work done today—I have not spent all my time upsetting the company's food cost, as it may appear. Glancing at my watch, I wonder if I'll make it to my favorite class at the gym. The phone rings. A friend is in town from Toronto for the night and wants to go for dinner . . . that cute sushi place down the street from my apartment? Hmm, dinner. I almost forgot. My favorite meal of the day. . . .

Before striking out on his own, Daniel was the chef at the original Le Cirque, located at the time in the Mayfair Hotel. In 1993, Daniel left to open his own, eponymous restaurant on Seventy-sixth Street, in the Surrey Hotel. The Mayfair later became a condominium and Le Cirque moved to the Palace Hotel. When the Mayfair was renovated in 1998, Daniel relocated into what was originally that same Le Cirque space. So in a way, it was his homecoming. He bought a condo above the restaurant, turning the original Daniel space on Seventy-sixth Street into Café Boulud.

Daniel was one of the first restaurants reviewed by the *New York Times* critic William Grimes, who took over from legendary critic Ruth Reichl in 1999. Everyone expected Daniel to get four stars, but Grimes gave the restaurant only three. It was a terrible disappointment.

Leslie Brenner, a writer from the *LA Times*, spent a year following Daniel, chronicling his (successful) fight to reclaim that fourth star, which happened a year and a half later, when Grimes returned and re-reviewed the restaurant.

When I was working for Daniel Boulud, Anthony Bourdain's *Kitchen Confidential* would occasionally come up in conversation. A lot of chefs were frustrated by it, because it became the public's point of reference for life in a professional kitchen. They assumed every kitchen was the same: people fucking in the walk-in, doing lines of coke off the cooktop—cooking like douche bags, basically. They thought all chefs were these destructive, tattooed rebels. But let me assure you, that is not how a fine-dining restaurant like Daniel operates.

That's not to say there aren't chefs in any kitchens who are brutish or masculine or competitive, or that they don't smoke and drink. But most restaurants don't have the same aspirations as a restaurant like Daniel. Because of this, they don't require the same skill, artistry, quality of ingredients, equipment, and highly trained team that a high-end restaurant does. That's why it costs less than half the price to dine at them.

Everyone at Daniel was wholeheartedly dedicated. You would not last long on his team if you weren't. There are at least twenty great chefs leading incredible restaurants around this country at any given moment who are who they are because of him, who came up through his kitchens and went on to become the brightest stars in their field. But I knew that wasn't my calling—I took away something else entirely. From Daniel Boulud I learned about business.

The dining public, and even cooks themselves, often forget that restaurants are businesses. People visit restaurants with the notion they're warm, lovely, romantic places. But they are, first and foremost, moneymaking operations. People get upset when they realize it's about the bottom line, not just about the chef's whim and fancy. Until I worked at Daniel, I never knew the first thing about a bottom line.

I'd come from magazines, and not the accounting department. I was in editorial, doing fact-checking, editing, writing, and research. Then I was in culinary school, first learning how to cook and then on the line. In kitchens, when they gave me carrots to chop, I didn't ask where they came from, how much they cost, or how many plates they needed to sell to turn a profit. I just chopped the carrots.

Then I was working for Jeffrey, who had little budget to adhere to as the culinary czar of *Vogue*. It was the most amazing gig in New

York City. We worked out of his apartment. He had someone else paying for every meal he ate, his groceries, and all his travel. He flew to Thailand, to Paris, to Memphis for BBQ. He expensed everything. He'd order six porterhouse steaks a day from Lobel's on the Upper East Side. I never asked him how it all worked, how the cogs turned. I was living in an editorial fantasyland.

Daniel gave me a crash course in reality (albeit four-star reality). Sure, Daniel's kitchen was full of foie gras and caviar. But I was also working with the operations directors and CFO, and they had budgets. I learned how a restaurant is run at the highest level. I learned the vital importance of the waiters, sommeliers, and the rest of the front-of-house staff who sold the product. And, under Georgette Farkas, I learned the tangible value of press and marketing.

In January 2003, the New York restaurant community went to war and—for better or worse—I was on the front lines. I was one of the first to learn Daniel would be adding fresh black truffles to his already famous $29 DB Burger and charging an unprecedented $50 for it.

This may not sound like a reason to get out the battle armor, but this was no ordinary burger. It was filled with short ribs braised in red wine, plus foie gras, black truffles, and root vegetables. Its homemade bun was topped with toasted Parmesan and layered with fresh horseradish mayonnaise, tomato confit, fresh tomato, and frisée.

The extra layer of black truffles sliced and placed on top of the patty not only doubled its cost, but also its cachet. He called it the DB Burger Royale.

Within hours of the Burger Royale having been added to the menu, the *New York Post* published an article about it. What followed was a literal feeding frenzy.

Press from across the country and around the world descended on DB Bistro to taste the $50 burger. Never before had someone charged such a high amount for something usually so ubiquitous: a hamburger. It became the ultimate epicurean status symbol.

Enhancing the excitement, Old Homestead, a downtown land-mark steakhouse, added a $41 burger—made of Kobe beef—to its menu. The battle for the best and most expensive meat was on. Thus began the New York Burger War.

For weeks, all we could do to keep the press and public at bay was to make as many burgers as possible. We made that burger for every celebrity and every media outlet in town—no one could get enough of them. In fact, Georgette and I had to cook so many burgers our-selves to keep up with the numerous press requests—from David Letterman to the *Today* show—that we joked about calling our joint memoir *Flipping Burgers in Four-Inch Heels.*

．．．．．．．．．．．．．

I'M OFTEN ASKED if I would ever want to have a restaurant of my own. The public, and many young chefs, romanticize what it takes to run a successful restaurant. They think you only need to be a great cook to be rich and famous—if you just make beautiful food, people will come. You will shake hands in the dining room and ful-fill your purpose of making everyone happy.

But if those dining room seats aren't filled, it's not going to last. If no one knows about your restaurant, if no one knows where it is and no one eats there, you can make the best food in the world and never be successful.

Daniel taught me the importance of marketing for restaurants. He keeps things fresh and never rests on his laurels. He stays rele-vant and in the press. He's out there *working it* every day.

Eric Ripert, arguably another of the greatest chefs in the world, will swear by the power of marketing, too.

At the beginning of 2009, the financial world was imploding. Far fewer people were eating at restaurants like Daniel or Le Ber-nardin. And if they were, they were certainly not ordering the Dom Perignon and beluga caviar. Luxurious expense account meals were the first to go. Le Bernardin is an expensive restaurant to run. All the perishable food that gets delivered fresh each day! The wine cellar! The immense staff! The linen and florist bills! It's stressful, if the place is not full every night.

And then Eric's Season 5 guest judge episode of *Top Chef* aired. The next day, the phones lit up at Le Bernardin. It was packed again, and Eric was breathing a sigh of relief. Since then, he tells me, people stop him on the street all the time and say, not "Wow, you're one of the best chefs in the world!" but instead: "Hey! You're the guy from *Top Chef!*"

There's an irony there, of course. After all he's done for the food world, the thing that got him recognized on the street was a TV gig. But that's the reality of marketing. And who cares? If that's what it takes to get people eating out and eating well, I'm all for it.

I'm one of very few people I know who have moved from editorial to marketing. What I found fascinating in the transition from Jeffrey to Daniel was that I was no longer alone in an apartment or staring at a computer all day on my own. I was in a social universe. I loved working with people. I looked back and realized that while I was writing or doing research I was alone most of the time, with my thoughts and the occasional piece of chocolate or rooster thigh.

Daniel was a nurturing place for me. I got to know the line cooks but also the executive chefs. I was in on the book projects, the recipes, the new restaurant ideas, the ever-changing cocktail menu, private parties, and special events. I said hi to twenty-five people on the way to my desk every morning.

I was enamored of the nitty-gritty of running a restaurant and the people I met working there, especially the general manager, Michael Lawrence, who is now one of Daniel's directors of operations. He's from Monroe, Louisiana, and smart as can be, but he never loses his sense of humor. He would run around like a chicken with his head cut off most of the day spouting Southern sayings to get us all through the stress.

"Hey, Michael, have you seen Daniel?" I would ask.

"He's gone to Jersey to get a load of goats," Michael would jokingly respond without missing a beat.

"Michael, what's New Orleans like in July?" I once asked him. "Is that a good time to visit?"

"Girl," he said, "it's too damn hot. Louisiana in July is like a freshly fornicated fox in a forest fire."

Going into my third year at Daniel, I started to realize there wasn't a lot of room left for me to grow. I'd been through all our events and all four seasons twice. Certainly, there were still a lot of exciting things going on. We'd just opened a restaurant in Palm Beach and were starting to look at a space on the West Side that would later become Bar Boulud. Daniel was signing a contract for his first restaurant in Las Vegas, with Steve Wynn.

But there wasn't a lot of opportunity for me to move up. Georgette was my boss, but the only person above her was Daniel. There were probably four hundred people working for him across all his restaurants, but I wasn't going to move to Las Vegas to manage the restaurant or become a captain in the dining room. I wanted to keep learning. I wasn't actively pursuing other jobs. I didn't even know exactly what I wanted to do next. But I knew that sooner rather than later I would need to start thinking about the next step.

....

TEN

A Walk Through the Food & Wine Classic Tasting Tents

WELCOME TO THE *Food & Wine* Classic in Aspen. Enter the Grand Tasting Pavilion from the north at Wagner Park. To the south lies Aspen Mountain, looming behind the massive white tents. Green and ominous, with snowcapped peaks, against the cobalt sky. The air is thinner up here, and dry. Pace yourself. As you wander from table to table, there is a head-spinning abundance to sample: cheese from Denmark, Oregon, Greece, Tennessee, Ireland, Wisconsin, Alabama, France, Spain, Italy; beer the color of wheat, the color of sunshine, the color of earth; a whole roast pig that's been carried through the pavilion courtyard on a tray; Alaskan crab claws; American spit-roasted lamb; brisket sandwiches, prosciutto, bresiola, Iberico ham; spicy barbecued ribs; paella with shrimp and mussels; ceviche; olive oil that's grassy, spicy, fruity; bread with raisins, whole grains, olives; caviar both American and imported; tangy macaroni and cheese; paper-thin slices of smoked salmon; sushi of eel, crab, yellowtail tuna; potatoes, popcorn; white, milk, and dark chocolate; chocolate-covered cherries; chocolate with ginger, chocolate with orange; chocolate chip cookies; foie gras on toast points; strong coffee, delicate tea; grapes, strawberries; fish and seafood from Hawaii and Nova Scotia; meat from San Francisco ranches and Chicago stockyards; cheesecake; *bibimbap*; South African bunny chow (not real bunnies); jams, chutneys, spreads, relishes, sauces. Plastic tumblers filled with cocktails of vodka, absinthe, moonshine, brandy, bourbon, limoncello, cachaça, grappa, mescal, vermouth, gin, rum, scotch, tequila, agave; elderflower, grapefruit, and pear liqueurs. Flutes filled with Champagne from France, Cava from Spain, Prosecco from Italy, California sparkling wine. Glasses of port, sake, sherry. Dozens of bottles of Pinot Noir, Merlot, Cabernet, Granache, Syrah, Sangiovese, Riesling, Sauvignon Blanc, Pinot Grigio, Albariño, Gamay, Nebbiolo, Malbec, Grüner Veltliner, Tempranillo, Gewürztraminer, Falanghina, Viognier, Verdicchio. If you outdo yourself on the first day, you never quite recover. But first-time visitors never listen and are overwhelmed by smells and small bites. If you're not careful, the combination of too much food, too much wine, and high altitude wear you out before the sun goes down. And when the sun goes down, that's when the real party begins, with more delicious food and always more wine.

*I*N THE EARLY spring of 2004, Daniel threw a party to introduce his new chef de cuisine. His right hand and longtime chef de cuisine, the incredible, incomparable Alex Lee, had decided it was time to leave. He had four kids. He needed time with them and his wife, not to mention time with himself. Daniel decided to promote a young man named Jean François Bruel. We invited a hundred members of the press for lunch. We opened up the kitchen and let everyone meet the team and explore "backstage."

Among the invitees was a stylish guy named Kevin, who worked in marketing at *Food & Wine*. We had become friendly through my work at Daniel. I knew his title was special projects editor, but I didn't know what that meant. I knew he'd been to culinary school. We often chatted about food and restaurants when we saw each other at events around town. Once in a while I'd catch him on television lending his expertise on food and restaurants for a morning segment.

In the entrance of Daniel that day, Kevin turned to me and said: "I have two questions for you. First of all: Who is the gorgeous woman behind the reservation desk? I was out for dinner last night and she happened to be seated at the bar alone next to me. I couldn't take my eyes off her. I didn't get her name. And here she is. It's fate. And second: I'm leaving *Food & Wine*. I want to start my own business. Do you want my job?"

The first question was easily answered. The woman was my

friend Maite, our head reservationist. She had come to Daniel from San Sebastián. Her godfather is famed Spanish chef Juan Mari Arzak. Chef Arzak had called Daniel when she moved to New York and asked him to help her with a job. She was smart and beautiful. In no time, she had won the heart of everyone at the restaurant. It helped that she had an insanely sexy Spanish accent. She would go on to become the first female head maitre d' at Daniel, possibly at any four-star restaurant in New York. I happily introduced them.

The second question was slightly trickier. I wasn't entirely ready to leave Daniel, but I'd always wanted to work for a food magazine and perhaps get back to my original goal of writing. Here was my chance!

"Ummm, yes," I told Kevin impulsively, "I want your job."

We joke that he gave me my job and I gave him his wife. Kevin and Maite are now married and have a beautiful son, and I have the best job in the world. I'm still not sure who got the better deal.

. . . .

GOING TO WORK at *Food & Wine* made a lot of sense, and in a way it was still all in the family. Daniel and *Food & Wine* have had a long and happy relationship.

Daniel was in the first class of *Food & Wine*'s Best New Chefs, back in 1988. The award is given each year to ten chefs who have been running their own kitchen for less than five years and who *Food & Wine* believes will be the next great talents in the industry. That first year, along with Daniel, the award was given to a group of young culinary pioneers, including Thomas Keller, Rick Bayless, and Hubert Keller. *Food & Wine*'s goal has always been to get there first—to discover the trends, the people, and the places changing the way we all eat and drink every day. The magazine has a pretty staggering track record of finding these best new chefs very early in their careers.

It's fascinating to look back at the award winners from those first few years. At the time, they were relative unknowns, Nobu Matsuhisa, Tom Colicchio, Jean Joho, Gary Danko, Mark Peel and Nancy Silverton, Michael Romano, Michael Symon, and Todd English among them. They were all newbies, with their first restaurants, cooking exciting food. They were, and still are, the people who exemplify the industry at its most passionate, driven, and innovative.

It's safe to say *Food & Wine*, created by Ariane and Michael Batterberry, has been daring and influential ever since its first issue in 1978, when it appeared as an insert to *Playboy.* Its revolutionary goal was to speak equally to both men and women about food and wine. In 1980, it was sold to American Express. The magazine has always given equal time to delicious recipes for home cooks (no matter what their skill level) and to restaurants and chefs, wine and spirits. Travel was always a big part of it, too, but in a very accessible way, covering wine- and food-focused destinations from Maine to Shanghai.

For thirty years, *Food & Wine*'s biggest competitors were *Bon Appétit* and *Gourmet. Bon Appétit* was always a little more geared toward home cooks around the country, and a little more simplified. *Gourmet*, which sadly folded in 2009 after sixty years of publication, was much more about elaborate recipes, food essays, and aspirational destinations. Sure, there are plenty of other food magazines in existence. *Cooking Light*, for example, has a massive readership, but its whole focus is healthy recipes. *Saveur* takes a more academic approach, specializing in in-depth exploration of global cuisine.

Food & Wine has always been about inspiration rather than aspiration. The magazine tries to bring people of all cooking levels into the conversation. The ampersand has always been important to the brand. *Food & Wine* is all about the *and*: and travel, and design, and style. Great quality food *and* wine are at the core of its readers' active lifestyles.

While working for Daniel, I had come to know and admire

many people at the magazine. When Daniel did articles with them, I would help coordinate the details. I also helped arrange his appearances at several *Food & Wine* events, including the *Food & Wine* Classic in Aspen.

When I was still assisting Jeffrey, I'd even interviewed once at *Food & Wine*. My close friend Mindy introduced me to a woman at the magazine named Lily Barberio, who was an assistant editor. Lily and I went out for drinks a couple of times.

Lily, in turn, graciously introduced me to Tina Ujlaki, the executive food editor, who has been there for more than twenty-five years. Tina is the earth mother, soul, and all-around food guru of the magazine. She oversees every recipe and every piece of food that goes into it. I had a lovely meeting with her, but at the time magazines were still reeling after 9/11. As with so many other media outlets, there were no jobs available.

Tina kept in touch, and so did Lily, as she moved up the ranks to become a senior food editor. Tragically, Lily passed away a few years ago, of cancer. Thinking back to it now, it's unfathomable. She was so young. It happened so fast. I think of her often, and I will always be in her debt for first introducing me to the magazine.

When I told Kevin I was indeed interested in his job, he explained that the first step in the process was a meeting with *Food & Wine*'s VP of marketing, Christina Grdovic. I went in to talk with her and right away there was chemistry. Chris was my kind of woman—strong, smart, and intimidating. She talked a mile a minute.

She sold me on the magazine, which was not difficult to do, as I had been poring over its recipes and articles for years. But I still had no idea what the actual job was. I understood that it was in marketing. They needed someone with a culinary background who had a solid comprehension of the chef world and good connections. They produced a lot of large-scale events and needed more chef involvement on a number of projects. They also needed someone who could speak the language of their events department. We talked about Aspen because she knew that I'd helped Daniel there.

"Everyone gets their hands dirty here," Chris said. "You will be working hard, late, and long. You will be stuffing some gift bags, too. We all do. No one is too big or too small."

Chris built her marketing team around that chemistry. She has a knack for hiring and molding a group that works well together—and plays together even better.

"Everyone I hire has to be able to live in close quarters with everyone else on the team," she said. "Everyone has to be *in it.*"

It sounded good to me.

She explained that part of my job would be courting chefs, and why not start with my current boss?

"Can you ask Daniel to be in the cook-off at the Classic in Aspen?" she asked. They'd been trying to get Daniel to participate in it for years.

"I'm sorry, but no," I said, hoping this wouldn't make her question my ability to wrangle top talent. "He's a four-star French chef. His food is precise and exacting. So is his cooking style. He doesn't want to compromise himself in that setting. But I'm sure there are other ways in which he would love to participate."

"That makes sense," she said. "We'll stop asking."

She didn't seem too disappointed. At least I'd saved her a few phone calls pursuing him to no end. Maybe I could be useful when it came to this kind of planning: I was coming from the chef side. I knew who could—and would—do what.

They gave me a writing assignment. It was based on creating marketing programs that linked the message and capabilities of the magazine with some of their key brand partners and advertisers.

I had to create a proposal for what we could do with a car sponsor, for *x* number of pages of advertising, given their target audience and our assets. I'd only ever worked on the editorial side of media. I knew marketing for chefs, but I had no idea how integrated marketing—or magazine merchandising, as it was called back then—worked. I promptly panicked.

I called my friend Mindy, who had worked at *Saveur*.

"Call my dad," she suggested calmly.

Her father had been the head of marketing at a prominent Madison Avenue advertising agency for many years. He knew all about ad pages and media buying. I spoke to him for more than three hours. He gave me a crash course in publishing.

I learned that the $30,000 to $100,000 a page an advertiser pays a national monthly magazine is what basically underwrites the operation. If you don't have the advertising, you don't have a magazine. The number of pages of advertising determines how many pages of editorial you can create. It's no secret, but for me it was a revelation: courting advertisers was the same as filling seats at Daniel every night.

I scrambled to finish the proposal and went in for a second interview, then a third. I met with a woman named Sonia Zala. At the time, she was a marketing manager. Young and fierce, she was the team's secret weapon.

Finally, Kevin called with the offer I'd been waiting for.

"I'll take it!" I said. Then I delivered the news: "But . . . I need a visa. I'm Canadian." It would require some work on their part, but I said I would pay for the immigration lawyer or do whatever I needed to, if they were willing to take the chance on me.

"Stay put," Kevin said. "I'll call you back."

He took this information to Chris, who ran it up the chain of command. *Food & Wine*'s parent company, American Express, was not very interested in taking on my immigration issues.

But Chris fought for me. She didn't need to do it. She barely knew me, but I guess she had an instinct that it would work out well.

The visa process took six months. I was in limbo. I kept working at Daniel through it all, from April to September, wondering if *Food &*

Wine would ever come through. I couldn't tell Daniel. I couldn't get my hopes up. I couldn't leave, because I would lose my visa and be out of work for who knows how long if the magazine job didn't pan out. I refused to go back to my parents' basement.

Then in August of 2004, Chris called. "We got your visa. It's done. You start October first."

After all the anticipation, on my first day at the magazine I still wasn't totally sure what my position would entail. I knew I'd be working with chefs. I knew I'd be writing proposals for advertisers. I had to learn how to sell brands on partnering with *Food & Wine*. I kept staring at the job description, trying to make sense of it:

> The role of Merchandising Manager includes several key responsibilities that contribute and support the success of Advertising Sales. These responsibilities include high-concept program initiation and implementation of integrated marketing endeavors for advertisers as added value for media purchases. A marquis trait required in this role is an intimate working knowledge of the culinary industry, since most *Food & Wine* programs are directly related to talent sourcing (chefs, wine experts, restaurants, and epicurean destinations), being familiar with culinary trends, and experience in face-to-face hospitality management. Additional responsibilities include personnel, account, online, and onsite project management.

My direct boss, Frances, the merchandising director, had also just started. In that first week, she gave me examples of the style in which *Food & Wine* wrote proposals and assigned me one. I stayed late at the office every night trying to wrap my head around the assignment. But there I was alone at 8:30 p.m., staring blankly at my computer. I remember literally banging my head against the desk, wondering when I would adjust.

One of the emails Chris sent me that first week on the job read: "You're going to Wisconsin October 22–25 for the Kohler *Food & Wine* Experience. Please mark it on your calendar."

I'd been on two business trips in my life, once to Palm Beach for the opening of Café Boulud Palm Beach at the Brazilian Court Hotel, and once to Miami with the Café Boulud Palm Beach team to help at the South Beach Wine & Food Festival. Now, suddenly, I would be managing an event in an executive role?

It was less than one month away. Thankfully, before he left, Kevin had secured the chefs who would be appearing: Food Network's Tyler Florence, Chef Dean Fearing from Dallas, a wine expert named Anthony Giglio, and a cheese expert named Laura Werlin. I just had to coordinate their appearances, our sponsorship of the event, all the

With Café Boulud Palm Beach at the 2004 South Beach Wine & Food Festival

travel and cooking seminar logistics, and the integration of our advertisers. No problem!

Various coworkers would be coming with me, including my boss, Chris, and our intimidating and much-respected publisher, with the most outstanding shoe collection I had ever seen, Julie McGowan. So would our editor in chief, Dana Cowin. Up until this point, I'd only ever met Dana in passing. When I was in South Beach with Café Boulud, I was plating desserts at a barbecue when Dana came up to our table. "Hi, Dana," I said. "I'm Gail Simmons from Daniel."

"I know!" she said, smiling. "We've met before."

She thought I was introducing myself to her because I didn't remember meeting her. Of course I remembered meeting her! I just assumed she would never remember meeting me. Although a slightly awkward reintroduction, I was overjoyed to learn she knew who I was.

I was also elated to spend the weekend in Kohler, stuffed with fried cheese curds and sausages, at a fancy hotel and spa. I'd been to festivals with Daniel, but seeing one from the operations side was a thrill. To my coworkers it was just another event, but to me it was a whole new kind of fun.

Late one night, we ended up with the chefs at the hotel bar. This was the beginning of a close friendship with Anthony, one of the most hilarious and accessible wine writers and educators on the planet, and Laura, the Queen of Cheese. I was hanging out with wine and cheese geeks! I loved them!

We were hungry, so Tyler ran into the kitchen and made bratwurst, apple, and grilled cheese sandwiches for us. Anthony was busting out bottles of Amarone, Barolo, and Barbaresco. We all lifted our wineglasses and I cheerfully toasted with what I'd said twenty times a day at Daniel: "Bon appétit!"

A hush fell.

Chris gave me a murderous look.

"We don't really use that term at *Food & Wine*," she whispered.

"That's our biggest competitor. Instead we say: 'Enjoy your Food & Wine.'"

I promised myself I would never utter the phrase again.

....

KEVIN, MY PREDECESSOR at *Food & Wine*, had a background in both cooking and marketing. As part of his job he often represented the magazine to the media. When he left, a gap needed to be filled. Dana, our editor, couldn't do all the television and press for the magazine on her own. They needed more people with solid culinary and public speaking skills, who would be comfortable in front of a camera.

I had been the press contact for Daniel, behind the scenes, so I was familiar with a lot of the players in food media and how public relations worked. *Food & Wine* knew I had culinary training, so they suggested I take on some of the media for the magazine.

They put me through a few intensive days of media training, and then I started doing little appearances here and there. I did a *Fox & Friends* segment and a bunch of short stories on the local station, New York 1. I was on CBS's *The Early Show.* I would talk about "Best Wine Bargains," or "What to Cook for Easter," or "New Trends in Artisanal Ice Cream."

After a good deal of trial and error, I learned how to talk and cook at the same time. A year into the job, I was finally getting the hang of things.

Then the New York head of the Classic in Aspen at the time, Elizabeth (Biz) Deppisch, went on maternity leave. It was just after the three-day event had finished, in July of 2005. She worked on it all year round with a staff of three in our offices, in conjunction with four others on the ground in Aspen.

Whenever people talked about the Classic, they sounded as if they were in a cult. They got a glassy look in their eyes. Aspen in the summer is a staggeringly beautiful place, but I did not realize how special or massive the event was until I was there in person.

Food & Wine tents an entire soccer field in the center of town, leaving a courtyard in the middle. Close to three hundred stations are set up, where food, wine, travel, and other lifestyle brands create a gastronomic wonderland for consumers to taste and sample. When I had walked into the tented pavilion for the first time, just a month before, I was instantly amazed that it took only a year and a handful of full-time employees to assemble. The job was *enormous*.

And the tents are only one aspect of the whole event. In addition, there are more than eighty pieces of culinary programming throughout the weekend, including cooking demonstrations by the country's most accomplished chefs, from The Pleasures of Tuscany by Mario Batali to Paella Party with José Andrés, Secrets of the French Laundry with Thomas Keller, Giada De Laurentiis's Giada's Kitchen, and Bobby Flay's Spicy Grilling Tips. You also can attend seminars on every grape varietal from Riesling to Malbec, on every spirit from absinthe to mescal, hosted by wine and cocktail authorities from coast to coast. There's Pigs & Pinot with Danny Meyer and Dan Philips, Joshua Wesson's Fizzalicious: Great Sparkling Wines, American Craft Beers with Ray Isle, and a once in a lifetime vertical tasting of cult Napa Cabernet Screaming Eagle. It's all just waiting to be devoured, spread out across twenty-odd venues around the city center. There are celebrity chef photo opportunities for charity, cookbook signings, panel discussions, networking lunches, and pool parties. There are also events each evening for up to a thousand people where you eat, drink, and schmooze until the early hours.

The weekend culminates in my favorite event of all: the Classic Quickfire. In the early days of the Food Network, there was a show, hosted for most of its run by Sissy Biggers, called *Ready, Set, Cook*, which in some ways may have laid the groundwork for other competitive cooking shows, like *Top Chef*. It was the original food competition show.

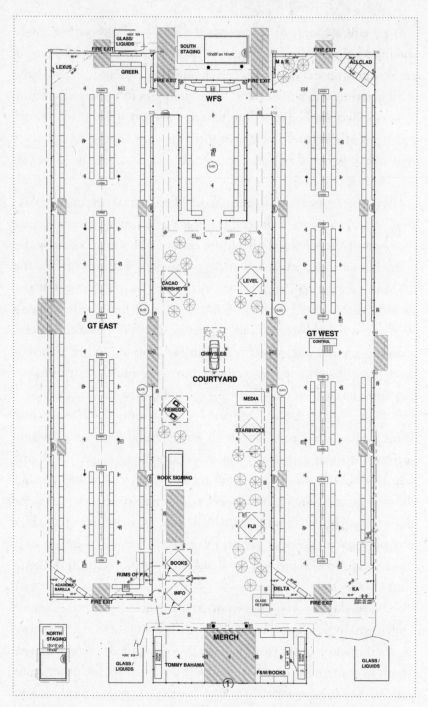

Blueprint for the 2007 *Food & Wine* Classic in Aspen Grand Tasting Tents

The concept was brilliantly simple: Two well-respected chefs went head-to-head on a kitchen set. They each got a mystery bag of ingredients and a sous-chef from the audience. They were only given twenty minutes and $10 worth of ingredients. Based on the dish's creativity and presentation, the audience chose the winner.

Ready, Set, Cook went off the air in 2001, but *Food & Wine* adopted the format for the Classic. For years we called it the Classic Cookoff. Sissy still hosts it. Two great chefs face off.

In recent years, the winner of *Top Chef*, who comes to the Classic as part of the show's prize package, has become one of the chefs in the game, facing off against an iconic chef like Jacques Pépin, the godfather of everything, or against the winner of *Top Chef Masters*, which is why we now call it the Classic Quickfire. Picture Season 6 winner Michael Voltaggio, with his tattoos and his liquid nitrogen canister, cooking against culinary heavyweight Rick Bayless, the Season 1 winner of *Top Chef Masters*. Throw in a couple of early morning cocktails, a few mystery ingredients, and an audience studded with star chefs. Hilarity and mayhem ensue.

Often Tom Colicchio and I judge, along with Dana Cowin. We often auction off a judging or sous-chef spot to an audience member, with the proceeds benefiting KitchenAid's Cook for the Cure and the Susan G. Komen Breast Cancer Foundation.

Now food festivals all over the country often stage a cook-off in some shape or form. At the Cayman Cookout, presented by *Food & Wine*, I recently hosted one such event in which two amateur cooks, a lawyer and a teacher, competed for a trip to New York. Judging were Eric Ripert, Anthony Bourdain, José Andrés, Susur Lee, and the governor general of the Cayman Islands. No pressure!

They had to make an original dish in a short amount of time using local Caymanian ingredients. As it turned out, they both picked spiny lobsters. In most of the United States, we are used to Atlantic lobsters, which have smooth black shells that turn red when you boil them, and large claws. Spiny lobsters, also known as rock lobsters, are found in more tropical climates. They don't have the big claws that Atlantic lobsters do, but they have bigger tails and a spiny exo-skeleton.

One of the contestants had a terrible time killing his lobster. We were all looking on from the judges' table in horror as he attacked the poor creature. He had it on its back and was hacking at it. The lobster slid all over his cutting board and kicked furiously. At one point it fell off the table.

To be fair, even a seasoned chef would probably panic at the thought of having to kill a lobster in front of Eric Ripert, possibly the greatest seafood chef in the country, if not the world. But it made me think about what we owe the animals we butcher and how it must be done respectfully. I actually really enjoy butchering. I've always found it methodical and contemplative, sort of Zen-like. It sounds grotesque, but I love the feeling of a sharp knife cutting through flesh.

So, a brief time-out here for a quick public service announce-ment about how to properly kill a lobster: People usually just drop it headfirst into rapidly boiling water. But if you want to be sure it's humanely killed before it hits the water, or if you want to remove the meat in order to cook it in parts, you need to kill the lobster first, preferably with a sharp, heavy chef's knife.

Hold the lobster stomach side down, flat against your cutting board. Plunge the tip of your knife deep into the back of its neck, right at the point at which the head connects to the body, and very quickly cut its head in half vertically, straight down the middle, right between its eyes. This is the fastest, most humane way to do the deed. Thank you.

Okay, back to the Classic. There is so much about the town of Aspen that's unique. The climate is so dry and the altitude is so high that alcohol affects you more easily. On the flip side, your hair always looks fantastic. Those were my first lessons in Aspen, and they sort of became my mantra. If all else fails, if the shit hits the fan, it's okay: your hair will always look great.

At the end of her maternity leave that fall, Biz told Chris she wasn't returning to *Food & Wine*. Chris and Frances called me into Chris's office one day and asked if I would consider the position. It would be a serious promotion. I would manage a large team and be the daily lead on the New York side for every aspect of the event, directing sponsors, handling programming, doing all the venue logistics and registration.

This was around the same time I interviewed to be a judge on *Top Chef* (much more on that later, of course). At the end of September 2005, within one week, I learned I had gotten the *Top Chef* job *and* the job of managing the Classic in Aspen.

It all seemed doable. We never anticipated that *Top Chef* would have the life that it has. Shooting the show would be a quick, three-week gig. The first season was shot in the fall of 2005, at the quietest time of the year for Classic planning, so I could go to San Francisco to shoot the show for Bravo, then come back and take over the event. I was simultaneously managing a few other events and projects for the magazine, but from February to June, I would focus exclusively on Aspen.

It occurred to me that I had never actually had a job where I could be promoted before, and it felt great to get the recognition. The Classic in Aspen was revered in culinary circles. It was a massive learning opportunity, and for the first time I would be the leader of a team.

I quickly realized that being a manager of people is deceptively difficult work. From Daniel and Georgette, as well as Chris and Frances, I learned that you need to take responsibility for your team's mistakes. Daniel's name is on the door. If a captain or chef screws up, it reflects badly on him. The same principle applied here. Their mistakes would be my mistakes. Errors happen, but if it was my department I had to take the blame, teach, direct, and correct it for next time. I also had to lead by example and support my staff in their tasks while still finding time for my own. Applauding and problem solving, celebrating their successes, and helping them to improve was all part of it too.

The Classic was heading into its twenty-fourth year when I took over the job. That's a long time in the life span of an event. There were deeply rooted, complicated relationships that I had to learn very quickly. Aspen has a complex mix of protective locals and luxury vacationers, multimillion-dollar real estate moguls and families going back generations.

Our job was to preserve the integrity of the town while also appeasing our consumers, sponsors, and advertisers, with whom we had long-term, loyal relationships as well. All the while, I was coordinating the needs of our culinary talent: finding an extra hotel room to accommodate Thomas Keller's lamber, confirming that José Andrés's Iberico ham had made it through customs, or that Giada De Laurentiis had enough security to not get mobbed by the hundreds of fans at her book signing.

It was like a polygon: the magazine, the sponsors, the talent, and the town—with our little team stuck in the middle, charged with figuring out how to make everyone happy.

Working in tandem with us was the team in Aspen. Devin Padgett, our special projects producer; his right hand, Mike Morgan; and a crew of more than twenty contracted crew members handled on-the-ground details, including but not limited to negotiating our city licenses, coordinating all the build-out and breakdown, creating and managing the programming schedule, and working to meet the needs of every wine distributor, every caterer, and every venue.

It's almost incomprehensible how hard they work and the minutiae of detail they tackle. Devin knows every microscopic detail of every facet of the event. He's been working on it almost since its inception. For me, Devin became a kind of Buddha, best friend, and consummate advisor. He is a trained chef. He knows everyone. Sort of like MacGyver; you want him in every situation. He makes you feel safe. He's unfazeable.

In addition to Devin's operations crew, there were two people at the Aspen Chamber Resort Association who worked with us almost year-round as well, Jennifer Albright Carney and Julie Hardman. They coordinated an enormous amount, too—from the details of every glass poured in every wine seminar, to our complex lodging needs, and of course our relationship to the town's retail and hospitality community, whom we relied on so heavily. They managed anywhere from five to seven hundred local volunteers who worked closely with us the week of the event to ensure that it all ran smoothly. They also happened to be the most calm and reliable friends to have at an event like this—equally adept at finding immediate solutions to a crisis and telling hysterical stories over sushi and too much sake after a long day of meetings.

When you factor in everyone's travel accommodations and transportation, the operations end of the festival becomes nearly endless. There was another team on the ground that organizes all our flights, attendee registration, and passes, and an extensive culinary crew who produced our cooking demonstrations. Finally, from *Food & Wine* alone there were more than one hundred staff members who come to Aspen to work on the event in some capacity over the weekend.

My favorite part of the job was when I went to Aspen at other times of the year for planning meetings. We'd sit around a conference table for three days and pound out the details, then, with luck, get an afternoon to ski. It was a chance to spend more time with the people who ran the hotels and restaurants, the shop owners, the caterers, and the people at the Aspen Chamber Resort Association.

For three years, I would leave my team without a boss for weeks at a time to shoot *Top Chef*. Going back and forth between the two worlds was disorienting. In the span of a single day, I would go from wearing a cocktail dress at a glamorous red carpet event to Crocs, cargo pants, a *Food & Wine* T-shirt, a fleece, a puffy vest, and a backpack. There would be times when I would be wired, with a headset, a walkie-talkie, a cell phone, and a BlackBerry all at once.

One year during the event, running out of the St. Regis Hotel with my headset on, yelling into a cell phone, putting out a fire, I ran into Nan Strait, then a supervising producer for *Top Chef* (she now runs the show as our co–executive producer). She was in Aspen shooting a video package for the Season 2 reunion show about winner Ilan Hall's prize. She and I were wearing the same uniform.

She loves to remind me of that moment, because until then she

Hanging with iconic chef Jacques Pépin at the 2011 *Food & Wine* Classic in Aspen

only knew me as the food critic at Judges' Table in full hair and makeup. When she saw me in all my gear, we realized we did the same job in a strange sort of way: we produced.

By the spring of 2009 I realized the juggling act between my two lives could no longer be sustained, so I handed the Classic reins over to a colleague in whose capable hands the event remains as exciting and relevant as ever. I have taken on a different role with the magazine: special projects director, which allows me to branch out more in the media and pursue other projects, both with *Food & Wine* and on my own. I do far less event producing now, but I miss it.

I came to feel like an honorary Aspen citizen, part of the fabric of that small town. I've been there more than sixteen times over the last seven years. Now, when I go back, to shoot the show or to participate in the Classic as part of the talent I once managed, it is a sort of homecoming—just without the headset.

ELEVEN

....

At the Judges' Table

WE ARE IN Singapore, on a crawl of hawker stands with a local chef. We have Kaya toast with runny eggs and buttered toast with strong coffee for breakfast. Slipper lobsters in garlic sauce with Chinese spinach. Crabs deep-fried in corn flakes. Rice with peanuts and mackerel presented on a banana leaf, made famous as the alleged obsession of the sultan of Brunei. White pepper crab (almost floral), black pepper crab (much more aggressive), and chili crab, soaked in a super-messy, spicy red sauce. We break open the shells, spoon the sauce over the crab, and sop up the rest with slices of white bread. And laksa! The famous Malaysian soup made with coconut milk, curry, ginger, shrimp, meat, pea shoots. Ten different people in the market serve laksa, but every one is different. You need to know which stall has the best. In this case, it's Katong Laksa, which uses evaporated milk and black clams. There's also "carrot cake," not made from carrots, but thick rice noodles with shredded daikon radish (locals call daikon "white carrot"), shredded fried egg, and chives. Hokkien prawn noodles with chili paste from the table bottle, calamansi squeezed on top. The chewiness of the two different kinds of noodles with the acid of the fruit, sautéed squid, shrimp, and fish is a perfect balance of tastes. Lard cracklings on top. What's better than lard cracklings? I could live on these noodles. And to drink, bright green palm sugar juice, so sweet and packed with ice, a miracle on a hot sultry night. No flavor, just sweetness.

OVER THE PAST nine seasons as a judge on *Top Chef*, I've had a dizzying array of meals and adventures. The show has changed the trajectory of my career, my life. When I think back now, I'm still amazed by how casual I was about the audition.

It was early September 2005. The powers that be at *Food & Wine* asked me to go to 30 Rockefeller Plaza with a few others to do a screen test for a new food-based reality show being developed by Bravo. I had done a number of TV appearances, so I suppose I was a logical candidate, but I still felt unprepared. First, I didn't even know what a screen test *was*. Second, I barely knew what this show was about. The only reason I wasn't nervous was that I didn't really understand why I was there to begin with.

Programming executive Dave Serwatka sat me in front of a camera in a tiny closet of a space. With the camera running, he fired question after question at me, and I did my best to answer him.

"What do you like to eat?" Dave asked.

"Just about anything except black beans," I said. "Oh, and veal, if given the choice."

"And where do you like to eat?"

"It depends on my mood and what I'm craving. But the adventure of restaurants always excites me, from the moment of being greeted at the door to that very last bite of dessert. Living in New York has given me the opportunity to explore it all."

"What are the hallmarks of a good chef?"

"A humble respect for food, knowledge of quality ingredients, and technique," I replied. "An understanding of its basic chemistry and science. Extreme focus, years of dedication—and comfortable shoes."

Dave then asked me to describe my worst restaurant experience. That was easy.

One recent morning, Jeremy and I had gone to a local diner for breakfast. I wanted an omelet. I'm obsessed with eggs in any form, especially omelets, but only if they're cooked as they should be—just until soft, pillowy, and still a bit runny in the center. I despise the dry, rubbery, overcooked versions that too often pass for breakfast in this country. If it's crispy and brown on the outside, it'll be chewy and hard on the inside, with a texture that reminds me of a flip-flop. Yuck.

Jeremy, all too aware of my high omelet standards, warned that this particular diner might not be the best place to order one. But that's what I was craving, so I told the waiter I wanted my omelet soft, with no brown crust on the top.

Several minutes later, a flip-flop arrived.

Very calmly, I explained to the waiter that I had ordered a *soft* omelet, and would he mind asking the kitchen if they could please make me another?

He snatched up my petrified omelet and soon returned with its replacement, probably spitting on it between the kitchen and our table. This time the eggs were completely raw and translucent. I considered trying to eat it anyway but the thought of salmonella poisoning made me think twice. I was frustrated and ravenous. My upper lip started to quiver and my eyes filled with tears. The tears started to puddle on the diner's faux-wood table. My lovely Jeremy paid the bill, grabbed my hand, and whisked me across the street for a perfectly cooked falafel.

"So you probably think I'm nuts, don't you?" I said to Dave. "Like, 'If you're that picky about your omelets, why not just stay home and make one yourself,' right?"

Dave didn't respond.

I rambled on to defend myself: "Well, *I* don't think there's anything wrong with ordering what I want the way I want it, whether I'm at a diner or a four-star restaurant. That's just how an omelet is *supposed* to be cooked. Besides, they're not paying for it—I am."

Dave nodded blankly. "Thanks, Gail," he said. "We'll be in touch."

Sure.

Flash-forward a few weeks. I was at my desk in the *Food & Wine* offices when an email popped up from Chris Grdovic. All it said in the subject line: "It's you!"

What's me?

Puzzled, I walked over to her office. Chris was on the phone, waving her arms wildly and motioning for me to come in. Finally she hung up and said, "You're going to San Francisco to tape the first season of Bravo's *Top Chef!*"

Really?!?

Wait—what will I tell my mother when she finds out I'll be appearing on reality television?

Compared to most people I grew up with, I haven't exactly taken a traditional career path. Until recently, my family and friends back home had little idea what I actually *did* for a living. (Until just a few years ago, my mother still joked that if things didn't work out in the food industry, there was still time for me to go to law school.) And now here I was, about to shoot a reality TV show. I felt I had to re-assure my mom that I wouldn't be tied to a tree in a bikini, escaping from a tank filled with snakes, or eating live spiders the size of din-ner plates.

In 2005, reality shows were still fairly new to television. *Fear Fac-tor* and *Survivor* had led the charge. They were enormously success-ful, but they were all I really knew of the genre.

With several successful reality shows under Bravo's belt—*Queer Eye for the Straight Guy* and *Project Runway* among them—the network's next idea was to create a reality show based on food and cooking. When *Food & Wine* had been approached by Bravo's marketing team about a partnership on the new series, Chris had had the foresight to give it a shot.

We learned during those negotiations that Tom Colicchio, the venerable chef and owner of Gramercy Tavern and Craft in New York City, had signed on as head judge, which made us more than a little enthusiastic. Tom was already a trusted member of the *Food & Wine* family; knowing he had agreed to take a chance on this pro-duction, we knew we could, too.

And so, within a month of landing the role, I found myself in San Francisco for a month of shooting, four suitcases packed with every piece of clothing I owned and no idea if this improbable en-deavor was going to work.

But work it did, and the winning formula has been pretty consis-tent since that first season. My husband affectionately describes my job as "I eat, I yap, I leave," but it's a *little* more involved than that.

It takes six weeks of almost-daily shooting—and a cast and crew of well over a hundred—to film a single season of *Top Chef.* The "chef-testants" are quarantined to keep the playing field even and fair, so we can't really break for weekends. Each episode consists of two challenges: the Quickfire Challenge, which tests basic skills (such as cooking with only canned products, or with one hand tied behind one's back), and the Elimination Challenge, a more elaborate scenario that requires contestants to cook over several hours or even days and serve their food to a larger group or at an event. Themes for Elimination Challenges range from fantastical and absurd to sophisticated and cerebral. Beaches, deserts, museums, campsites, boats, football-field parking lots, casinos, rodeos—no location is off-limits for our cast of talented young chefs. Dinner guests have ranged from three-Michelin-starred chefs to firemen, CIA agents to Natalie Portman, Cookie Monster to Buzz Aldrin— almost anyone with an appetite and an interesting point of view. Watching contestants fight it out in the kitchen is always exciting and full of drama—but above all else, *Top Chef* is about celebrating food, and the art and craft of professional cooking.

The bulk of the season—twelve to fourteen episodes—is shot over five consecutive weeks; several months later, we'll regroup for a week or so to shoot the finale. Each episode takes two to three days to shoot: one for the Quickfire and one or two days for the Elimination Challenge, depending on how much cooking time is needed. Although every day is different, a typical Elimination Challenge day goes something like this:

We start with hair, makeup, and wardrobe, at about 10 a.m, while the chefs finish their allotted cook time. In the first season, I wore most of my own clothes, but now I depend on the shopping expertise of the show's stylist. (Who has that many cocktail dresses in her closet? Plus, we shoot at picnics, at four-star restaurants, even at school gyms. That's a lot of outfits.)

While it may sound fabulous, the wardrobe process actually gives me a lot of anxiety. Since I'm neither supermodel-tall nor cover-girl-skinny, our long-suffering stylist usually has to shop for me, rather than just calling in sample sizes from designers. There are certain colors and styles I feel comfortable wearing. But there are many rules for what can and cannot be worn on TV: busy or tight patterns are out, as are whites and bright reds. I've learned that jewel tones and solids always work well on my skin, and a bit of plunge in the neckline and a belt gives me some shape. Sometimes I try on twenty outfits to find even one I really like. I've certainly made some questionable choices along the way, and heard about them to no end on blogs, Twitter, and Facebook, but I've learned to be a bit more discerning about what I wear—and a bit calmer about the criticisms.

Once we're dressed and ready, we travel to the challenge location. The hair, makeup, and wardrobe teams do a final touchup, and around 1 p.m. we'll start shooting the service and tasting, continuing until about 5 p.m.

The chefs, meanwhile, have been cooking all day, usually under extraordinarily difficult constraints. It's one thing to cook a great dish in one's own restaurant. It's another thing altogether to prepare a dish in an unfamiliar kitchen, with limited tools and ingredients, while eight cameras swarm around you (and sometimes in sixteen minutes flat!). Since air-conditioning interferes with the sound, we often have to go without, so the kitchen can be sweltering. Given the circumstances, when the chefs bring out their final dishes, I'm always impressed that they've managed to create anything at all.

When the service portion of the challenge is over—before moving back to the studio for Judges' Table—Padma, Tom, the guest judge, and I will talk through each dish on camera in what we call a "mini delib." We decide which plates were our most and least favorite. At this point the top three or four and bottom three or four contestants are selected.

While the crew moves everything to the *Top Chef* kitchen and sets up Judges' Table, we get a break. I'll usually grab a bite or drink with Tom and the guest judge, especially if we didn't eat well at the challenge. Around 7 p.m., after a quick makeup touch-up, we'll sit down at Judges' Table. (During the first few seasons, we sometimes didn't start until 11 p.m.!)

To kick things off, Padma usually calls in the top chefs of the challenge to see us—although once in a while we switch this up to keep the contestants on their toes. We stare them down a little, make them sweat, and ensure the cameras get those stress-provoking close-ups. (Cue the nerve-racking music.) The top chefs are then told they prepared our favorite dishes, and are questioned about their creative process. We'll tell them what we liked about their food and discuss what inspired them. Though we try to keep the conversation upbeat and positive, we do give chefs constructive criticism if it's warranted. At this point the guest judge announces the winner, and Padma asks that they send back the contestants who are up for elimination.

Out comes the next group. We stare them down even harder, so the cameras can capture all those uncomfortable moments. Padma tells the chefs that they're on the bottom. At this point, it's still anyone's game to lose.

We spend a good amount of time going through each dish, questioning every element. We're looking to discover if the chefs have any insight into their mistakes. Did they make errors in concept or in execution? If it was a team challenge, who was responsible for each component? Then we gauge who made the most egregious blunders.

In the "Out of the Lunch Box" episode in Season 7, contestants took over a Washington, D.C., school cafeteria, with instructions to prepare lunch for fifty kids. The budget for each child's full meal was a strict $2.68, which at the time was the government's reimbursement rate to schools for children eligible for free lunch.

Two chefs made extremely questionable decisions. For her chicken dish, Amanda bought an expensive bottle of sherry—an ingredient that wouldn't even be *allowed* in a school cafeteria. Jacqueline, meanwhile, used two pounds of sugar—almost two ounces per serving—to make her bland banana pudding more appealing.

We wanted to hear what was behind their thinking.

Amanda defended her choice by saying that she "liked cooking with sherry." She argued that the alcohol would burn off during the cooking process. Jacqueline, however, had no response when we pointed out the problem of adding so much sugar—and empty calories—to a child's meal. (To say nothing of her pudding's poor flavor and consistency.)

At this point the bottom-tier chefs head back to the "stew room," where they wait and wait and wait, while the crew resets the lighting and cameras for our deliberation. With the cameras running, the four of us spend an hour or more going over every dish again and again, factoring in the feedback we received from each chef, to see if our opinions have changed.

It's now time to decide who's going home.

Contestants—and viewers—often assume we make a quick decision. In all honesty, it's a long, drawn-out, deeply serious process, condensed into just a few quick minutes for the benefit of television. And trust me: we don't take the responsibility lightly.

Something a lot of viewers don't seem to believe: our decisions are based on what we eat, not on whom we like. Sometimes we're faced with more than one chef who made poor food and poor choices. Sometimes they've *all* made great food, and we'll have to go through each detail with a fine-toothed comb to decide which is the very best and who should go home. We ask ourselves which dishes had the most punishable flaws, and which combination of flavors and techniques fell flat. Usually we agree; sometimes we don't. The producers don't let us stop talking until our decision is unanimous.

At this point there's another break while the cameras are again rearranged. The anxious chefs are brought back to Judges' Table. Tom recaps our issues with each of their dishes—and finally, one unlucky chef has to hear Padma's dreaded words: "Please pack your knives and go."

. . . .

I'M ALWAYS SURPRISED that chefs take our criticism as calmly as they do, for the most part. If someone ever trashed *my* cooking, I think I'd toss a *"How DARE you?"* right back. I'd defend my choices and fight my hardest for another chance. And I confess: at times I wish more contestants challenged us on our decisions—if only so I'd know what is going through their heads. But I also can't imagine how hard it must be to think on your feet when you're nervous, stressed out, and intimidated, and you've been cooking since 4 a.m.

The only contestant who ever really talked back to us was Jennifer Carroll, on Season 8, our *All-Stars* season. We criticized her under-seasoned and poorly prepared bacon-and-egg dish, and without hesitation, Jen launched into a full-blown attack on us, vehemently disagreeing with our opinions. Many viewers—and Jen's fellow contestants—were shocked and appalled by her outburst, but I was secretly thrilled. Though her spirited defense didn't ultimately change our decision (she was eliminated), it certainly challenged us to evaluate her dish more closely.

After sending countless exasperated chefs packing, I find they usually fall into four types:

> *The Towering Egos.* Astonished to be on the losing end—it's totally beyond them as to why we didn't like their food—and ignoring our constructive feedback, they act as if they don't need any advice. They certainly don't listen to it.
>
> *The Confessors.* Instantly and completely defeated by the challenge, they can hardly wait to admit their mistakes. "My sauce didn't have enough salt." "The pâté was too grainy—I should have put it through a tamis." With these chefs, we barely have to say a

word: they can't stop talking, simply throwing themselves on
our mercy.

The Whiners and Blamers. They do nothing but complain. "My oven's
temp was off." "I cut my finger." "The milk curdled." "He
sabotaged me." Excuses, excuses, excuses.

The Learners. These are my favorites. No matter where they are in
the lineup, these chefs are most eager to improve. They know
what they did wrong, and will often try to defend their dishes,
but they also want to gain from the experience and advance
their cooking skills. They listen and take it all in. They're the
chefs who show the most evolution from the beginning of
the season to its end—think Carla Hall, Mike Isabella, Kelly
Leiken, Richard Blais, Kevin Sbraga.

That final confrontation is usually the end of our day with the
chefs. But more often than not, the four of us aren't going home yet.
We have to reshoot the lines that we blew or that the cameras didn't
catch (they call these "pickups"). We finish between midnight and
3 a.m.—sometimes later. We've seen the sun rise on too many occasions.

The shoot schedule is by far the most challenging part of working on *Top Chef.* It's hard being away from my "real" life—my home,
my routine, my husband—for such long stretches of time. The job is
physically demanding, not just for the long hours but for having to
sample up to forty-odd dishes each day. Living in a hotel for weeks
on end, while eating all my meals in restaurants, from room service,
or on the set wears thin pretty quickly, too.

For all the planning and orchestrating that goes into every episode, there are still countless unpredictable elements: this *is* "reality"
television, after all. Season 2 stands out in this respect. We'd filmed
the first ten episodes in Los Angeles. Already, it had been a rough
season: two contestants had quit (one because of a dispute over

stolen lychees, the other to defend a fellow chef—in the heat of competition, no less). Then there was an incident involving several
contestants ganging up on Marcel (one of our most controversial
contestants of all time) and attempting to shave his head; as a result,
we had to send another chef home prematurely.

A few months later, we flew to Hawaii to shoot the Season 2
finale. Taro fields in deep valleys full of emerald-green meadows
and savage forests. Mutant-sized flowers. Cattle and cowboys. Stop
signs reading "Whoa," for the horses. Volcanoes and helicopter
rides. Just weeks before we arrived, there had been an earthquake;
from the plane we could see the sides of the mountains that had
fallen off into the sea.

We'd voted off Sam Talbot, the fan favorite. (Sam tells me people still approach him all the time insisting he was robbed. I admit
he's talented, but neither of his dishes for that elimination employed
actual *cooking*—he made a mascarpone mousse and a kind of local
tartare called poke. As great as Sam is, that day he deserved to be
eliminated.)

It came down to Ilan, who was only twenty-four, and Marcel, who
was twenty-six. They were both so young. We had to resign ourselves
to the fact that we weren't looking for evidence of established greatness so much as potential.

The judges who came in for the finale were a blast, and among
the most lauded chefs in the country: Scott Conant, Wylie Dufresne,
Michelle Bernstein, Hubert Keller, and Roy Yamaguchi.

Ilan's meal was Spanish-inspired, starting with *angula* (baby eels)
and *pan con tomate*, but he did a great job including local Hawaiian ingredients, too—a gazpacho of native macadamia nuts and a fruit soup
with Surinam cherries, a species I had never seen before. His seared
squab with foie gras, shrimp, and lobster was simple and flavorful.
The Romesco sauce on his beef course was the best I'd tasted—coarse
and garlicky with just the right amount of smoky paprika.

Unwinding with guest judges and producers after our Season 2 finale in Hawaii

Our choice wasn't easy. Marcel worked hard at creating an experience we would never forget. He made sea urchin and Meyer lemon gelée with fennel cream, caviar, and kalamata oil; cucumber and radish salad with ouzo vinaigrette; hearts of palm and maitake mushrooms with sea beans and kaffir lime sauce; strip-line steak with garlic purée; blini with Kona coffee "caviar." It was ambitious. But Marcel ran before he could walk, so to speak. There were too many small flaws in his judgment, and too many bells and whistles. We left his meal unsatisfied.

There was a moment at the dinner table, as I sat with all these renowned chefs—having eaten this barrage of food—when they turned to me, seeking my opinion on who should win. The weight of my position, my personal opinion, *mattered* to them. I was now sitting at the table with the leaders of our industry—not just writing about them or eating in their restaurants, but literally breaking bread with the people I'd admired for years. And instead of being intimidated, I felt entirely, ecstatically, in the right place.

We picked Ilan, and then we all went home.

Cut to a few months later, when word hit that the winner's name had been leaked just two days before the final episode aired. An article about Ilan had been posted online for only a few minutes, but it was long enough to be all over the Internet. The blogs had a field day. We all scrambled to control the damage. Secrecy is essential to shows like ours, and the breach made us feel so vulnerable. What's more, now that the suspense was gone, we were convinced no one would watch the finale. I worried that everything we had worked so hard for would be wiped out with one ill-timed blog post.

I went to sleep the night before the finale aired and dreamed vividly that the headline on the front page of the *New York Times* Wednesday Dining Section the next morning would read: "Reality-TV Franchise Ruined." I woke up at four in the morning in a cold sweat, full of anxiety.

At six o'clock I got out of bed and picked up the paper. Sure enough, the front page of the Dining Section bore these words: "Under Pressure, That's Reality." The writer, Frank Bruni, was the formidable restaurant critic for the "paper of record," but he had never commented on reality television before—or *any* food show, for that matter. Now here he was, reviewing us, a show about restaurant critics. I took a deep breath and dug in.

The article was, to my surprise and immense relief, the most accurate, enthusiastic depiction of the show I'd read to date. Bruni articulated exactly what we were trying to do each week, praising the show's "surprising seriousness."

As it turned out, that night, our final episode's ratings were the highest they had ever been, with close to 4 million viewers, an astronomical number for a cable food show. People thought we'd staged the leak to boost the ratings!

The experience of Season 2—from the chaos in LA to the Hawaii finale, from the terror of the leak to the triumphant *Times* piece and the record-breaking finale ratings—made me realize: our little show was onto something. We weren't just a random cable reality series anymore. We were a cultural phenomenon. Frank Bruni, along with the world's most acclaimed chefs, journalists, and food bloggers—and, most important, the TV-watching public—actually cared what we were doing! They were all paying attention. And somehow I was part of it.

My life changed markedly. After Season 2 I was recognized on the street, in grocery stores, on the subway. Not because I'd exposed myself getting out of a limo or thrown a champagne glass at someone, but because I was part of a moment in pop culture that meant something to people.

....

AS MUCH AS I grumble about the amount of time we spend on the road, I have always loved to travel, and *Top Chef* has given me more opportunities than I ever could have imagined. Every season and every finale is filmed in a new destination, so I've been able to live and work in places that until now were largely unfamiliar to me: Las Vegas, Miami, San Francisco, Puerto Rico, Hawaii, Washington, D.C., Singapore, the Bahamas!

On my days off, I always take time to explore, take in the sights, spend time with distant friends I'd otherwise rarely get to see, and, of course, discover the local food scene. After six years on *Top Chef*, I have become a walking tour guide for friends and colleagues. (At the Atlantis resort in the Bahamas, for example, I recommend the highly refined and culturally significant water slides.)

What's more, I truly love the people I work with on the show.

Tom and I work most closely; he's like my big brother. And like my own brothers, he's never treated me with any condescension, even my first day on set, when he knew barely anything about me or my experience.

Regarding the seating arrangements at Judges' Table, Tom graciously says, "I'm most comfortable when Gail's sitting to my left." And I, too, feel most comfortable sitting next to him. On off-nights we hang out at the hotel bar. When we show up in a new city, we both have a list of restaurants we want to try together. Tom's always up for an adventure.

Tom has a puritanical stubbornness that can occasionally drive us all crazy, but it comes from a devout seriousness about food. He received three stars from the *New York Times* at the age of twenty-six and has stayed relevant as a chef ever since, with the scars to prove it. He's very active in the fight against hunger, donating to food banks and lobbying in Washington. And he still spends the vast majority of his time on the line at one of his restaurants, only taking time off to shoot *Top Chef*, to promote a good cause, or to spend quality time with his wife and three sons.

Padma, the Ginger to my Mary Ann, has become a good friend. She's like my sorority big sister, forever getting me into trouble, and always up for fun. It's great to have a girlfriend like her on the road, not to mention her uncanny ability to hone in on the best Thai food within minutes of landing in any location. She has a passion for food and travel that is sincere and curious, and an incredibly thorough knowledge of not just Asian herbs and spices but traditional Italian cooking (she speaks fluent Italian, along with Hindi, some French and Spanish), falafels, and cheeseburgers. If it weren't for the show's editing, you would hear her waxing poetic on any of these subjects at great length. She's an amazingly hard worker, having written two cookbooks and hosted several food shows of her own. Knowing her hours and the demanding nature of her role on the show, I don't think she gets enough credit for what she does.

Padma has embraced her new role as a single mother with bravery, passion, and utter adoration for her beautiful daughter. After suffering for years from endometriosis, she has become an integral advocate (she cofounded the Endometriosis Foundation of America in 2009) and a poster child for overcoming its odds.

Our crew is exceptional. We've had the same production team since our first season. We have a blast together on and off the set, descending on hotel bars and restaurants from city to city, celebrating milestones (births, birthdays, weddings, an Emmy), and supporting one another in moments of need (illnesses, accidents, family emergencies). I think of us as a traveling band of food gypsies.

Reality TV is an undertaking like no other. Our production company, Magical Elves, turns a barren warehouse in each city into a working television studio with a fully equipped professional kitchen, an art department, a culinary prep area, a video village of monitors and soundboards, production offices, the stew room for our contestants, and dressing rooms complete with makeup stations for us.

It's awe-inspiring what they accomplish in such a short amount of time. Once we've finished taping a season, and the flames and drama have subsided, the whole set is broken down and packed up, and the warehouse looks just as empty as the day we moved in.

In the beginning, the crew and producers held my hand, teaching me the internal lingo of production (chefs needing a "10-1"; "repo to one"; "OTF interviews") and *never* to assume that your microphone is off unless you turn it off yourself (for example, when you take a "10-1" and go to the bathroom).

My greatest fear has always been that the show will make me appear mean-spirited or overly critical. During the first few seasons I was occasionally labeled "the sinister judge" by the press. In the earlier days of reality TV, I think viewers and networks alike tried to fit all show judges into *American Idol*–style roles. It took me a while to understand that it was not Bravo's intention to make me look evil, and just as long for them to realize that only showing our most critical moments would not endear us to our audience either. Overall, I think they edit us more kindly now—and the show is better for it.

After all, if my fellow judges and I come across as passionate about the subject and well informed, viewers will trust our decisions and respect the show. We try the food on the audience's behalf. They need to believe us.

People often ask me what percentage of the food that I eat on the show is good. I would say 40 percent needs work in some way, 40 percent is great, and 20 percent is truly exceptional. There have certainly been bites I wanted to spit out, but I can say (gratefully) that not one of the countless dishes I've tasted on the show has ever made me sick. (I can't speak for the other judges, but so far I've been lucky. Knock on wood.)

Not that we haven't eaten some revolting dishes. *Top Chef* has required me to taste things I never dreamed of putting in my mouth, and hope never to again. There was Season 2's opening challenge, for instance, that required the chefs to combine escargots with processed cheese. Then there was the leathery rattlesnake in Season 3, and the huge, offensively phallic saltwater clams, called geoducks (pronounced, not for nothing, "gooey ducks"). It's hard to erase from my memory Emily's painfully over-salted surf & turf from Season 2, or the soggy ostrich-egg quiche with rice-pecan crust that Jill made in Season 5. I will forever associate the chewy chicken feet Casey made for us on *Top Chef: All-Stars* with a rubber tire.

Of course there are moments of eye-opening brilliance, when I am humbled and awed by the contestants' skill: dishes like Tiffani Faison's creamy artichoke risotto from the Season 1 finale, cut to the finest *brunoise*, with flecks of crispy pork; or Bryan Voltaggio's airy and inspired sweet-and-sour macaroons with guacamole, corn nuts, and fresh sweet corn purée. Some dishes stand out for the chef-testants' ability to capture the essence of a specific culture or locale, like Ed Cotton's piping-hot banana fritters with a spicy drop of chili paste and just the right amount of salt to bring it all together (for our Singapore finale in Season 7), or Carla Hall's New Orleans–style oyster stew, delicately sprinkled with bacon, celery, and potatoes (in Season 5). Kevin Gillespie's poached lamb loin with sherry-glazed golden beets and asparagus in sunchoke cream amazed a panel of the most intimidating and critical chefs to date, including Thomas Keller and Daniel Boulud, and won Kevin a spot in France's legendary culinary competition, the Bocuse d'Or. And I still find myself craving the dishes Richard Blais made the night he finally won his Top Chef title in Season 8—especially that raw hamachi with fried sweetbreads, Asian pear, and pickled radish—at once bright, ambitious, rich, and satisfying.

Sometimes at Judges' Table I learn more from the contestants' vast knowledge than they might learn from our critiques. One of the most insightful chefs we've had on the show was Kevin Gillespie. He was committed to bringing together soulful Southern food and modern technique. Though he didn't win, I will always feel that Kevin was the most articulate chef on the series to date. He could rationalize any technique he employed: why he chose to pan-roast instead of grill; why he chose to sear instead of poach; why he chose to combine two disparate flavors. After my six seasons as a judge on the show, Kevin gave me a new perspective on cooking.

Unfortunately, Kevin's finale dinner was not his best meal. It didn't go as planned, though he fought hard to sell us on it. During Judges' Table he broke into a soliloquy about his slow-roasted pork belly—and for twenty minutes, he had Tom, Padma, Toby Young, and me completely mesmerized. Kevin described the exact degree of doneness of his meat and explained exactly why (although it seemed too chewy to us) he preferred it that way. It was entirely convincing. When he finally stopped to take a breath, our producer cut the cameras and ran over to us.

"Guys: *three million people* just changed the channel!" Nan shouted, her eyes blazing. "*None* of this is getting on the show—it's boring! We need to move on. What's come over you?"

To us, this was the most fascinating conversation we'd had in the show's history—like a lecture by our favorite nutty professor. But, yes, we all had to agree, it would make for terrible television.

....

KEVIN GILLESPIE WASN'T the only man of intrigue who spent time on our set. The universal nature of our subject matter has lured stars of all types. One memorable episode included my introduction to several other of the country's brightest talents simultaneously.

Rock legends, food lovers, and enthusiastic *Top Chef* fans, the Foo Fighters agreed to do an episode with us for Season 5, which we shot in New York during the summer of 2008. They were on tour, performing in Rochester, so we decided to stage the Elimination Challenge there. The plan was to have the contestants cook Thanksgiving dinner for the band and their crew backstage before the show. The meal had to be ready by four o'clock, so the band could eat, digest, and go on at eight.

The episode's guest judge was none other than Grant Achatz, a young chef at the forefront of modernist cuisine. His Chicago restaurant, Alinea, is among the most ambitious in the country. Everything in the thirteen- to twenty-four-course tasting menu is a play on temperature, flavor, and the conventional dining experience. Grant was a *Food & Wine* Best New Chef in 2002, so I'd been following his career for years and was thrilled to finally have the chance to meet him in person.

He and I were supposed to fly up to Rochester around noon, but early that morning a summer storm grounded all commercial flights out of New York City. Tom was flying in from an event elsewhere. Padma was flying privately. So the producers arranged for a van to drive Grant and me up to Rochester together.

Grant's willingness to participate in the show was especially valued. Not only were we asking him to take four days away from his restaurant, but he had just endured an incomprehensibly difficult struggle. The year before, Grant had been diagnosed with tongue cancer; after months of aggressive treatment, one of America's pre-eminent chefs had lost his sense of taste. And yet he never let the disease deter him from his devotion to the craft of cooking. Through it all, Grant was constantly thinking up new combinations of ingredients, which he would execute through his sous-chefs. (He documents his remarkable story in his memoir, *Life, on the Line: A Chef's Story of Chasing Greatness, Facing Death, and Redefining the Way We Eat*.)

Fortunately, Grant made a full recovery, but he was still getting his strength back when we met that day for the first time. During the seven-hour drive to Rochester, he shared with me his incredible story. He talked about the ordeal with immense gratitude, as his temporary loss of taste ultimately allowed him to gain a new perspective on the nuances of food and flavor, let alone life itself. When you go through something as traumatic as that, I can only assume that the details become either more important or infinitely less so. In Grant's case they became vital. He embraced his work with newfound passion and realized, more than ever, the value of what he could contribute to the culinary world. We're all the richer for it. I keep Grant's story close to my heart not only because it's a moving account of how someone overcame enormous adversity, but also because it serves as a constant reminder to never take for granted even the simplest actions—like putting a piece of food on one's tongue—or the perpetual joy derived from tasting something new.

When we arrived on location, the production had set up a tented kitchen for the chefs outside the concert venue. In the middle of the shoot it started to rain, and we had to bring everything into the basement. It was a messy production, but the meal was impressive, all things considered.

Let me point out that I'm a serious Foo Fighters fan and have been for years. Lest we forget: Dave Grohl was in Nirvana, which for me defined the early 1990s. He and Kurt Cobain, Eddie Vedder, and

Chris Cornell were like gods to me. And here I was, chitchatting with Dave and his band about craft services and where to get the best tacos in LA.

I walked with Dave to dinner through the stadium hallway. He seemed nervous and excited.

"I can't believe I'm going to be on *Top Chef* right now!" he told me. "How cool is that?"

"Yeah," I said, teasing him. "I know perfectly well how cool it is that *you* are going to be on *Top Chef* right now."

It was surreal. Dave Grohl was about to play a concert in front of thirteen thousand screaming fans, and he seemed more anxious about being on *our* show.

Sure enough, he and the rest of the band loved the eating and judging process. During their show we sat backstage by the sound booth. At one point Padma jumped onstage and played the tambourine. It was all pretty awesome.

....

BEYOND MY OWN delight in doing the show, it's immensely gratifying to be part of something that's helped educate people around the world (the show now airs in dozens of countries, from the Philippines to Brazil) about food and cooking.

When *Top Chef* launched in 2006 on Bravo, it served as an antidote to the plethora of shows already in existence about fast, easy home cooking. *Top Chef* has always been about professional chefs. It's for people who are interested in a glimpse of that more rarefied world behind the kitchen door. It turns out, there are a lot of us. As I write this, *Top Chef* is the highest-rated food show on cable television.

I believe we're helping people talk about food in a smarter way. A friend tells me she keeps a food dictionary on the coffee table when she and her husband watch *Top Chef*. When they hear a word they don't know, they grab the book and look it up. They learn chef names and terms like *chiffonade* and *mise-en-place*, and it helps them understand the language of the kitchen.

College campuses around the country now have *Top Chef* parties on Wednesday nights. I am constantly stopped on the street by parents who claim their young children want to become chefs. They watch the show religiously, help their parents cook dinner, and would rather stage elaborate, make-believe Quickfire challenges than play videogames. The "cook-off" has become a phenomenon for a whole new generation, who are paying more attention to what they cook and what they put in their mouths, trying something new, or simply being more conscious of where their food comes from. It never fails to amaze me when people write in and tell me how we've stirred their imaginations, made them more food-curious, or changed how they look at an ingredient, whether they're dining out or cooking at home. *That* is a big deal. Everyone has to eat. Now there's a greater dialogue about it.

Spreading the gospel of good food was never a goal of mine, specifically, at least not until *Top Chef* came along. But doing so has been infinitely satisfying. Sometimes life's greatest rewards come down to serendipity. Several months after that first screen test, Dave Serwatka told me that part of the reason they decided to cast me was because of my ridiculous omelet story. They had never met anyone who could get *that* emotional over a meal. And to think, if I'd been served a decent omelet at that greasy-spoon diner, all this might never have happened. Perhaps the moral of the story is this: Be true to yourself, and know that sometimes it's okay—in fact well-advised—to cry over burned eggs.

....

TWELVE

Confessions of a Food Judge

IT'S THE FINALE of the first season of *Top Chef Masters*. The chefs are an inspired group: Hubert Keller, a classic French chef from Alsace and the chef and owner of Fleur de Lys in San Francisco, a bastion of haute cuisine; Michael Chiarello, established TV personality and lifestyle entrepreneur, chef of the rustic Italian restaurant Bottega in Napa Valley, a born showman; Rick Bayless, an American who's become the foremost authority on regional Mexican food in this country. Each one has been asked to serve dishes associated with his most cherished food memories. Each chef tells a story related to his love of cooking. A spare rib tastes better when you know why it's significant to the chef, as opposed to when you get it from a chain restaurant. Food is a window into a chef's culture and life. Hubert Keller's *baeckeoffe* is a stew of lamb, beef, pork, and potato cooked in a clay pot. It would cook on Sundays while he and his mother did the laundry. To Hubert, the braised meat and chunks of vegetables covered with pieces of roasted potato symbolize his home in Alsace. When he lifts the lid, he invites us into his childhood house, located over the family's bakery. It's a warm and comforting place to be. Michael Chiarello prepares two takes on his grandmother's gnocchi—one classic, one modernized—that are so different from each other it's hard to believe they're made from the same ingredients: one is light and delicate, bathed in a simple, vibrant tomato sauce; the other is rich, pan-seared, and laden with truffles. Rick Bayless's quail with hickory sauce takes us to his Oklahoma hometown, where his father works the grill at his family's barbecue joint. And Rick's remarkable pork *pibil* transports us to the table of his very first Mexican restaurant. In a mouthful, we understand why he fell in love with Mexico and its varied and ancient cooking methods. All three chefs cook with vulnerability and passion. They reveal themselves to us through the deeply personal nature of their food, giving us so much insight into what made them who they are. I'll never look at them the same way again.

WHEN WEIGHING THE merits of a dish, I ask chefs some pretty rough questions, like "What exactly were you thinking when you combined blue cheese and warm watermelon?" Or: "Was it your intention for this steak to have the texture of a tennis ball?" "Did you really think you could properly braise that pork belly in under fifteen minutes?" When I help vote off an audience favorite, fans no doubt have some questions of their own, starting with: "Who the hell are *you* to judge?"

Of course, if you've read this far, you know I have a fifteen-year background in the food industry, and I've made this my life's work. But it's a fair question, and one I continue to ask myself all the time: Who *am* I to judge?

For that matter, who is anyone to judge food, especially on national television? Why does our show even work in the first place? After all, the audience can't even taste the dishes. Watching *Project Runway* or *American Idol*, viewers can fairly assess the merits of the competitors, deciding for themselves, "Would I wear that dress?" or "Do I like how he sings?" But food television is one genre where the viewer can't fully participate in the judging process. (At least not until we invent a way to beam each dish right into your living room.)

Of course, we're not the first successful TV show about food— not by a long shot. People went crazy for Julia Child's *The French Chef* in the 1960s. You couldn't taste what she was making, nor were you necessarily ever going to make it yourself (although many people did, with the help of her cookbooks). Yet the show was a bona fide hit. For TV viewers, food programming has always been a blend of pragmatism and escapism, reality and fantasy. This was true even before Julia and Jacques Pépin. I recently learned that James Beard, the godfather of American gastronomy, was actually the first person to cook on U.S. television, in the 1940s—when TV was still in its infancy.

I like to tell people that watching *Top Chef* is like indulging in a lavish meal without the calories—*and* you don't have to do the dishes after. In that respect, our role as judges—and as "stand-ins" for the audience—is even more vital than it is on other shows. On *American Idol*, you get a say. You can call or text in to cast your vote. You can be your own judge, because you can hear the music and decide whether or not it resonates with you. But with food you can't. You can judge only based on what you see, which of course is only a small part of the final equation.

And so we the judges become the taste buds for our viewers. It's even more important for us to convey how everything tastes, so you get a true sense of the experience at home. What's good about it? What's bad about it? Why? Our descriptions and reactions to each dish become that much more crucial, as you see through our eyes and look to us to understand its value.

Because viewers can't physically taste the food alongside us, their reactions and judgments are mostly based on their relationship to the contestants, their investment in the chefs as personalities.

From where we sit, we experience the show from a completely different angle. The viewer sees the show fully edited, with the story lines cut together, and the on-the-fly interviews interspersed with cooking, tasting, and reacting. You see the chefs in the house, fighting with one another or talking with their families on speakerphone, working in the kitchen, strategizing and forming alliances.

We see none of these interactions when we're shooting the show. The judges only get to see the entire story line unfold many months later, at the same time viewers do. By then our decisions about the food have already been made, and the show's outcome has already been determined.

We don't ask about the chefs' personal lives or their relationships with one another, and we don't care. All we know is what we see when they're in front of us at Judges' Table or during challenges, when they're usually on their best behavior—and of course, what we taste of their food. Every decision we make is a singular judgment, exclusive unto itself.

Our refusal to "get personal" or to take into account the chefs' challenge history gives the show its integrity, but it also makes some viewers very upset. They see someone they hate moving forward. They see someone they love—because he's cute or because he did really well last time—serve one poor dish and get eliminated. It infuriates our devoted fans, who love to tell us how terrible and biased we are.

Actually it's quite the opposite. Remember: The viewers are the ones invested in these people as characters. We only care about their food. Of course, we do pick up on their cooking idiosyncrasies. Over time, we notice chefs' styles and habits: a tendency to use a lot of pickles, or to make an unreasonable number of dishes using scallops.

Still, I judge each dish as if I were a diner who has just been served it in a restaurant. If this were something I was paying for, would I be happy, or would I send it back to the kitchen like that flip-floppy omelet? When I go out for dinner, I don't care whether the chef has an outstanding reputation but just "had a bad day" so his food is off that night. I don't care if the sous-chef's wife left him that morning, or if he's hungover from a rowdy celebration the night before. If my meal is not good, I am not going back. On the other hand, if I have a wonderful meal, I will most certainly return and will tell all my friends to do the same. But even that doesn't guarantee I'll love everything I eat the next time I visit. The same thing holds true in the *Top Chef* kitchen. A chef rarely gets a second chance to please his customers. We can't judge these chefs based on their cumulative efforts over the season. They must be judged dish to dish.

Tom assesses the contestants as if they were working in his kitchen. He asks himself: "Would I be satisfied if this chef were on my crew? If he cooked this plate for diners at my restaurant, would I praise him or fire him?" The contestants need to cook to his standards. When Tom walks through the kitchen and inspects their *mise-en-place*, he asks questions of them as if he's their chef, checking in before a busy service.

Having a guest judge with us who is totally impartial to the process—someone who has never met the chefs or gotten to know their food—keeps us honest and even more objective. For each episode, the guest judge comes into our little world for only a few days, with no preconceived notions of how the chefs should be, how good their food is, or where they're from.

The guest judge is wholly responsible for choosing the Quickfire winner each week, usually less than two hours after meeting the contestants for the first time. The guest tastes a few bites from each chef as their introduction, then makes a split-second decision on whose food is best. For the Elimination Challenge the next day, they weigh in to the discussion as much as any of us.

To me, it's obvious how much we as the judges want the chefs to succeed. And yet we constantly hear: "You're so *mean* to the chefs!" Or: "Don't you have a hard time critiquing people to their faces?"

"Everyone gets reviewed," Tom smartly replies. "It's part of the process of working in hospitality." He's right. Whether you own a restaurant, write a book, or put on a Broadway musical, at some point in your career you will be critiqued. As a chef, you will be reviewed, whether it's by the *New York Times*, your local paper, or a thousand bloggers. That's part of being in a service-driven industry.

Tom has had to read countless reviews of his restaurants over the years, and while plenty of them have been glowing, they haven't always been perfect. *Top Chef* is, in a sense, a constant review process— one that, by the way, all the chefs actually signed up for in advance. As a rule, we try to be more constructive than newspaper reviews.

We allow the chefs to defend themselves on the spot. (Traditional restaurant critics visit anonymously; there's no dialogue.) We give our chefs the benefit of the doubt and the chance to prove us wrong. If they make it to the next challenge, they get to try again the very next day, with a completely clean slate.

....

TO BECOME A true chef takes a great deal of time. Though it may appear otherwise, there are no overnight successes in the culinary world. Some people see *Top Chef* and think, *This could be my golden ticket to fame and fortune!* They graduate from culinary school and expect to be in charge of a kitchen the very next day. But that's just not how it works. Have we perpetuated a falsehood that being a chef—a celebrity chef, no less—is easy?

What does "celebrity chef" even mean? I hate the term. I guess it means you're famous? And you cook, sort of?

Being a chef, being the head of a kitchen—being an expert of *any* kind, really—takes years of training and hard labor, keeping your head down and paying your dues. For chefs it typically takes ten to twelve years, maybe seven or eight if you're really ambitious. Many cooks will work a lifetime and never become a chef.

There is no single proven path to success. You don't necessarily have to go to culinary school, for example, but you do need to start at the bottom and rise up through the ranks, so you know how to work every angle of your craft fluently. You need to understand how to make creative decisions, financial decisions, staffing decisions, how to build purveyor relationships, and how to guide every single person on your team.

Mentorship plays an important role, too. There's luck and there's hard work, but there's also smart people to learn from, who set the standards and create climates in which others can thrive. I feel more than a little lucky that I've had people like Jeffrey, Daniel, and Georgette, my producers on *Top Chef,* and my bosses at *Food & Wine* to nurture and guide me. They took me in, taught me what they know, and of course allowed me to make many mistakes.

More and more, the role of a chef demands that you be out of the kitchen, too. Restaurant chefs can no longer hide behind the kitchen door—guests expect to see them. To market a restaurant you need to sell yourself and your product, which requires charisma. These days a chef has to be more multidimensional than ever: you need to be a manager, a host, an entrepreneur, and an innovator, oftentimes all at once. *Cooks* are in the kitchen all the time. But in 2012, to be a *chef* means doing a lot more than just cooking. Although cooking will always be at its core.

For years—back before it was sexy for chefs to be on television, and before they became fixtures in the media—chefs could be tyrants, because they were only ever talking to their cooks and waiters, and in the climate of a kitchen that behavior was tolerated, if not expected. Now everyone has a blog, including those same cooks and waiters. If you make enemies, plenty of people can do you a lot of damage. It's a lesson I see both chefs and aspiring chefs learn the hard way.

And it's not just industry people who have blogs. These days, everyone with a computer and a credit card thinks he can be a restaurant critic. From Wall Street bankers to the guy who sells me my morning coffee, they all want to play restaurant trivia with me. I can't tell you how many times I get asked questions like these:

"Speaking of April Bloomfield, have you been to her new place yet? I have. Twice."

"Did you ever eat at El Bulli in Spain? I did. Twice."

"Do you have the secret number for Balthazar? I do. Twice."

For a significant portion of diners, eating at the hottest new restaurants has become a status symbol, a notch on the belt. And some wind up blogging about their exploits. This definitely serves a purpose. Mainly, it democratizes things. Certain restaurants used to think they could get away with treating VIPs well and not caring for everyone else. Now you never know who could be watching, tweeting, photographing, blogging. It forces restaurants to devote more time and attention to every customer. And that's as it should be: every one of us is entitled to good food and good service.

The downside is that cowards can now hide behind their computer screens and write degrading, destructive criticism with no sense of the power they wield, or how damaging it can be. Too often I see the ethical code of journalism blurred in online reviews. Some people in the blogosphere have even given up their anonymity altogether, and will trade positive writeups for VIP service and free food. That's not just bad journalism; it's extortion.

....

ON A BROADER level, some people question what it means to critique food in the first place. I am asked all the time, "How can you be objective in food criticism? Eating is so personal! How do your own likes and dislikes not play into it?" (I get this last question from picky eaters, especially.)

Despite my personal aversion to black beans, pickled ginger, and veal, I'm still open to tasting them when I have to. If someone cooks with those ingredients on the show—or at a dinner party or at a restaurant as a gesture of generosity especially for me—I will eat them. But I won't choose to order black beans or veal or cook them for myself at home.

I'm not sure if my veal issue is a moral one or not. There are many other foods I will eat that are not much different, ethically speaking. Is lamb any different? It's baby sheep. What about foie gras? Those geese and ducks being force-fed for my foie gras should bother me, but for some reason they don't.

To me, veal always went under the category of unnecessary meat. As with tripe, I'm just not a huge fan. I'm not crazy about kidneys, either. But tongue, sweetbreads, and heart? Those hit the spot. Veal doesn't have a distinctive enough flavor to make me want to eat it. It's sort of meager beef. It doesn't satisfy me in a way I can be satisfied from eating chicken, or duck, or beef, or lamb, or turkey. To me, it falls into a gray area, literally and figuratively. I learned to cook with it in culinary school, but if given the choice, I have to say: it skeeves me out. That's a technical food term, by the way: "skeeves."

Of course, try refusing any food in my mother's home and see where that gets you. (Remember the zucchini incident?) When I was a kid and my mother would serve us veal, I would ask, "What is this?" "It's chicken," she'd always reply, just to get me to eat it. I'd take a bite. "No way, Mom. You are straight up *lying* to me." I was no dummy.

What's ironic is that my mother has her own irrational taste aversions. Recently, we were out for dinner and I was reviewing the wine list. I suggested a Spanish wine. (I love Spanish wines— Tempranillo, Albariño, I'll take them all!)

In unison, my parents said, "We don't drink Spanish wine."

"What are you talking about?" I said. "It's an entire country."

"We tried Spanish wine twenty years ago and we just didn't like it," my mother replied. "We prefer to drink American or French."

The truth is, my parents pretty much only drink sauvignon blanc. Yet my mother gets furious because I don't eat veal.

So, we all have our subjective eccentricities. It's no different from any other kind of criticism though. Book critics, music critics, and theater critics all bring their own preferences and personal contexts to bear. But all professional critics should have some training, in order to understand the foundations of what they're judging, and should be able to look beyond their own personal tastes. I take every decision I make seriously and try to give every bite the respect it deserves. I couldn't do my job if I had a long list of foods I dislike. The truth is, there are very few things I won't try.

Actually, food is far easier to judge than, say, visual art, music, or dance, because there are very strict rules to cooking. I would argue that judging food is based 80 percent on science and technique, and 20 percent on instinct and artistic flair. Taste may appear totally subjective, but there are scientific forces at work determining how food should be cooked and prepared. It's chemistry more than anything else.

Nonprofessionals tend to judge food based on their biases more than on science and proper technique. After years of paying close attention to other people's cooking, I think I now assess food based much more on fact than on feelings. It's not just about "I hate foie gras!" or "I'm not in the mood for duck today, so I don't like this dish." It's that I now understand and appreciate how one plus one equals two—regardless of how I feel about the number two. The only way to learn these things is by eating and cooking. A lot.

When it comes to cooking meat, for example, there is a mathematical formula to doneness. Correct meat temperature can be measured to the degree. Snooty food snobs didn't just make this stuff up. It's a scientific reaction of protein and heat, and knowing when to serve meat at its optimum degree for tenderness and flavor. When you're searing a steak, the pan needs to be very hot so that the natural sugars will caramelize and form a charred crust. This is also why you should never use olive oil to cook meat. Olive oil has a very low smoking point, as well as a very specific flavor. It burns easily and turns bitter, so you should use it only in dressings, as a finishing oil, or to lightly sauté or sweat quick-cooking vegetables. For higher heat or a longer cooking time, you need vegetable, canola, grape-seed, or peanut oil, which is also great for frying. Even better? Lard (yes, animal fat). The very best French fries are cooked in duck fat, which has a high smoking point and is a great heat conductor.

"Carryover cooking" is something chefs constantly refer to when discussing temperature. When you cook meat, the heat gets trapped inside the muscle. When you turn the heat off, the meat will continue to cook to a few more degrees. That's why you should take it off the heat just *before* it reaches your ideal temperature. Meat should also rest before it is served. If you cut into it as soon as you take it off the heat, when the meat is still tense, all of its delicious juices and moisture will pour right out, along with all the flavor they contain.

Temperature is crucial in almost every facet of eating. Take cheese: you want to keep it in the fridge to preserve it, but you should always let it come to room temperature before eating it, to bring out all those subtle cheesy nuances, or you'll be robbed of the gooey, runny pleasure of that creamy Brie de Meaux. In the same vein, there's nothing I loathe more than cold butter. My biggest pet peeve at restaurants is when butter is served right out of the fridge, making it useless and impossible to spread. People are always worried about food spoiling, but honestly, there's no reason not to leave a covered dish of butter out on the counter for a few hours before serving.

There is a science to knife skills, too. All foods have to be cut a certain way in order to cook properly and evenly. I'm a stickler for good knife work and can always tell when it's sloppy. (I could watch

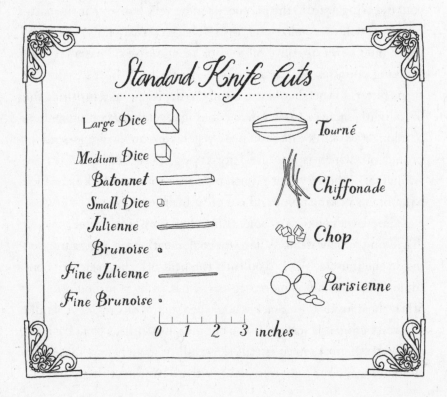

Standard Knife Cuts

Large Dice
Medium Dice
Batonnet
Small Dice
Julienne
Brunoise
Fine Julienne
Fine Brunoise

Tourné
Chiffonade
Chop
Parisienne

0   1   2   3 inches

the martial arts–like precision of a sushi master, as he wields a knife through fish, for hours on end.) Cutting ingredients correctly will bring out their best qualities, even after they're cooked. For example, you should always slice a hanger or flank steak against the grain; this makes it far tenderer and easier to eat.

Understanding the purpose of different cooking methods is also essential in order to bring out the best flavor and textural qualities of food. Brisket is best when braised for a long time, as it is tough and lacking in marbled fat. You need to break down the muscle to tenderize it. For me, there are few things more delicious than slow-cooked brisket that's been bathing in its own fragrant juices for hours on end. But other cuts of meat, like sirloin, are already tender and fatty to begin with. If you braise them, they'll toughen or seize. These cuts should be grilled or pan-seared—quicker, more direct cooking methods. A well-trained chef knows how to treat each specific cut based on this underlying science.

Moreover, there are classic flavor profiles that always work well together (excuse the use of the term "flavor profile"; it always seems kind of pretentious to me, but it gets my point across). These are the specific flavors that ground a dish. A classic Italian flavor profile, for instance, is tomato, basil, and olive oil. It's important for a cook to experiment and constantly look for new combinations, but there are proven standards at the foundation; as with color palettes in fashion and design, certain flavors simply make *sense* when they are eaten in unison. A good rule to keep in mind: if it grows together, it goes together—with respect to both season and geography.

The modernist cuisine movement (or molecular gastronomy, as it's more commonly called) is dedicated to exploring the science of food, down to the microgram and degree. Its practitioners study and apply the chemical and physical reactions of ingredients. They demystify cooking processes by breaking them down to their scientific roots, and use modern technology to make cooking more efficient and precise.

What most people associate with modernist cuisine is foam, which is made by using a siphon. These days, anyone can buy a siphon for about $50. It pumps nitrous oxide into any liquid and thickening agent, transforming it into an aerated substance. Think of a Reddi-Wip canister, but instead of cream, you're using Parmesan broth or tomato water, truffles or olive purée. The food comes out like Reddi-Wip, too, only lighter—more like spittle, or somewhere between spittle and Reddi-Wip. Foam allows you to add the essence of a flavor to a dish without adding texture or weight.

Of course, modernist cuisine isn't just about foam. It has contributed so much to our contemporary understanding of cooking and of how food works—not to mention our gadget collections.

We need chefs who push our industry forward, even if only three out of every fifty ideas they think up actually work. These innovations are what will save us from eating steak and potatoes for the rest of our lives. But there's a fine line between a new technique that enhances the way we cook and using a gimmick only for its cool factor. For me, the key question is: Does this innovation make food actually taste better, cook more efficiently, or look more beautiful? And if not, the next question is: Why bother?

With some modernist cooking, I can't help but think something is lost—something that made me fall in love with cooking in my mother's kitchen, watching those eggs turn from a liquid to a solid as I applied heat the old-fashioned way. I still love standing over a stove, seasoning meat, adding a bit of fat to a scorching hot pan, placing the meat in it, then touching it to gauge its doneness.

As a result of all this new equipment, are young chefs ever going to learn how to feel a piece of meat with their fingers to test if it's done? With techniques like sous-vide—by which food is cooked in airtight plastic bags, immersed in water that can be adjusted to a fraction of a degree—you lose the immediacy of standing over a fire, and the expression of individuality in your food. On the other hand, you gain precision and consistency. It's sort of like cloning. Efficient? Yes. Soulful? Not really.

Part of the pleasure and point of eating is realizing the emotional side to food. If eating were just pure science, it wouldn't be so deeply satisfying. There is so much about food that triggers emotion and memory. Most of it is actually about smell. The tongue itself only detects five things: salty, sweet, sour, bitter, and savory (what the Japanese refer to as *umami*). The rest is interpreted in coordination with our other senses.

In addition, the *ritual* of cooking is so vital to the preservation of culture, to what separates us from animals. The preparation of food is one of the greatest accomplishments of human civilization. (And here you thought my anthropology degree wasn't useful!)

Just as I see the scientific and the personal elements of cooking at play in professional kitchens, I find there are also two kinds of home

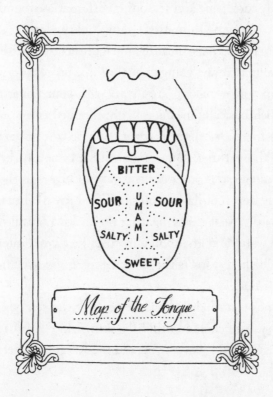

Map of the Tongue

cooks: the methodical ones and the improvisational ones, those who follow recipes and those who prefer to just "throw stuff together."

I meet so many people who tell me they love to cook but who feel they need a recipe to do so. They're not confident enough to feel as they go, so they follow instructions to the letter.

If these cooks simply paid closer attention to the steps and the order of techniques they use in each recipe, they would start to see patterns, which they could then use with other ingredients and other dishes. If you know how to sauté a piece of chicken, you don't need a whole new recipe to sauté a piece of fish: you use the exact same technique. The timing might change, but the basic method doesn't. If you know the foundation behind the science of cooking, you can apply it in endless combinations. Baking is a little more exacting, because of all the subtle chemical reactions required. But a braise is a braise is a braise, whether it's a slab of pork belly, the tail of a monkfish, or an old rooster. Only cook time and seasoning differentiate them.

An easy technique to master at any cooking level is soup. I love making soup. It's fast, easy, healthy, and it often tastes better over time. Building a soup is always going to be the same process, no matter what kind of soup you're making. You start with your flavor foundation: *mirepoix*, which basically means roughly chopped celery, onions, and carrots. It's the classic French trinity. There can be variations, but usually it's those three, sometimes with a bunch of herbs added, called a *bouquet garni*. If you want the natural sugars in the vegetables to have more depth of flavor, you sauté (or brown) them first. Otherwise you just sweat them, heating them slowly until they soften. Or just add water and let it boil to infuse the flavor—presto, vegetable stock. Chicken stock is the same thing, but with chicken bones (browned or not).

Sometimes you might add garlic or omit the celery, but it's usually that easy. You can add other flavorings, like bay leaf or tomato paste, beans or grains, before you add the water or other vegetables.

Maybe you want to roast butternut squash in the oven before you add it to your soup. Or you can sauté meat and add it in at this point too. Sometimes you puree the soup, or just puree a few cups of it to add more body and thicken it, or you can leave it all chunky. Once you know how to make a simple stock, you can make any soup, using the same basic method.

The opposite of the recipe-followers are the improvisers. They prefer to experiment, with little guidance. They often make simple mistakes that could have been avoided if they'd only read a recipe. For example, they might not realize that you should deglaze a pan with wine before you add the stock when making a sauce, so the alcohol has time to burn off and you're left with just its flavor.

Mixing up the order of ingredients and steps in a recipe is a mistake so many of us make. One of the first things they teach you in culinary school is to read a recipe all the way through before starting. Who hasn't been burned by this? You're cooking dinner an hour before guests arrive and suddenly you come to an instruction in a recipe like "Refrigerate for twenty-four hours."

There are always reasons why you cook in a specific order. It's about building flavor. You put in the carrots before the tomatoes because they take longer to cook. If you put the tomatoes in first, they will burn or turn to mush before the carrots are done. And no one likes mushy, burned tomatoes.

That's where the term "*mise-en-place*" comes in. It means having everything in its place; gathering all your ingredients in the exact portions required, prepped and ready to go, before you start the actual cooking. If my recipe for Chickpea, Artichoke, and Spinach Stew (page 255) calls for a large onion, finely sliced, don't just take out an onion and set it on the counter. Peel it, slice it finely, and set it alongside the rest of the ingredients needed, in the order they're listed in the recipe. Preparation and organization make cooking so much simpler.

I was one of those kids who would always ask "Why?" when

someone said, "Put your coat on." "Why?" "Because it's cold out." "Why?" That's what you have to do when you're cooking. Often there are really good answers.

. . . .

FOR ANY RECIPE to be a success, whether cooked by Daniel Boulud or my mother-in-law, all of its elements need to be harmonious. That's what I'm looking for when I taste and judge food. When discussing dishes on *Top Chef*, we tend to use words like "acid" or "heat" or "proper seasoning." This is because we are always trying to create balance for our taste buds, and adding acid cuts fat, which helps achieve this. When eating rich food, you always need a counterpoint. I wouldn't want to eat a piece of foie gras with butter and cream alone. Or maybe I would.

But certainly it would be monochromatic. That's why food as fatty as foie gras is usually served with some preparation of tart fruit or paired with sweet wine. It creates contrast to the fat. There's acid in fruit, and acid equals brightness, balance.

It's why Americans put ketchup on their fries. Ketchup is basically sugar and tomato paste. And it provides acid to cut the fat and brighten the carbs. Europeans use mayo, which may be rich and fatty, but good quality mayo has brightness, too, as it's made with lemon and mustard. Hooray for acid!

In Southeast Asian cooking, achieving balance between spicy, sweet, sour, and bitter all in one bite is the constant goal. Acid, in the form of vinegar or citrus, creates a sense of harmony on your palate.

When all of these elements come together—temperature, texture, knife skills, cooking method, and seasoning—it's like sunshine in your mouth. I'm joking, but really: that perfect balance makes me want to hold hands and sing "Kumbaya." It just feels so right.

And maybe that's why I'm the right person to judge food after all. I have a basic understanding of the science of food, but I'm also able to break into song over a little lemon juice.

....

THIRTEEN

Wedding Pickles

GIDDILY, WE SPREAD out our banquet on the living room floor. Welsh rarebit. A frittata with olive oil–cured tuna and shishito peppers. A bottle of ice-cold cava that tastes of apples and citrus. A puffy, eggy German pancake with blueberries. A Scotch egg. A rustic peach tart, fresh and fragrant. A big bag of unpeeled lychees, mild and sweet, just like my mother would buy in Chinatown when I was small, or like the ones I would eat in Israel, under the avocado trees. It's luxurious not to go outside, not even to get dressed, just to sit in our living room and peel and eat lychee after lychee.

BOUT TWO YEARS into our relationship, Jeremy and I decided to go to Italy.

My parents were renting a villa in Tuscany for a month and invited us to join them. Who could resist a dreamy Italian vacation? Jer and I planned to stay with them for a few days, then spend a week on our own visiting wineries and Tuscan hill towns.

From the very start, just about everything went wrong.

First of all, my mother had come down with a middle-ear virus. She probably shouldn't have made the trip in the first place, but my father was insistent. She went even though she felt miserable.

Then the airline lost our luggage. Adding insult to injury, we had made a reservation at an elegant and well-known restaurant for lunch that first day, and now we had to show up in the grubby sweatpants we had worn on the plane.

Then we got to the villa my parents had rented. It was not as advertised. It smelled terrible, the rooms were dark, and it was in the middle of nowhere. The owner was actually there doing renovations on the bottom floor all day, so there was hammering and drilling at all hours, and loud Bollywood ballads blaring late into the night. My father later told me that the owner was drunk when we arrived.

My father is, shall we say, an impulsive traveler. He has been known to make quick decisions before thinking them through. It's his one flaw—that, and a refusal to admit defeat. But he finally acknowledged he'd made a mistake with the villa, and went to the rental office to insist they find us something better. They offered to move us to a new house, a short distance away.

We set out that evening for the new place, with my parents in one car (along with our family friend Frances) and Jeremy and I following in the second car. It soon became clear that my father had no idea where he was going. He had just been given an address, with vague directions and no map. We took turn after turn, barreled down road after dusty road, driving in circles in the Tuscan countryside. The sun had long since set and it was becoming difficult to see the road. My mother grew so furious with my father that she demanded he pull over, and she got into our car instead.

"Where is he going?!?" she screamed. "He doesn't even know where we are! This is ridiculous!"

This continued for several hours. Midnight approached. There was not a light, a signpost, or a human to be found. The situation reached a boiling point when we were halted by a herd of cattle in the road and were forced to turn around. My mother insisted we give up and find a hotel back in Cortona.

It was around this time that Jeremy, who had been a true stoic up until this point, leaned over to me and whispered: "I am never traveling with your family again."

The only place open at that hour in Cortona was a fleabag flophouse on the edge of town that probably rented rooms by the hour. We were afraid to touch anything. We checked in, but we were so riled up that Jeremy and I went down to the bar for a drink. There we found Frances nursing a scotch. We joined her for a few cocktails, until we all had calmed down enough to sleep.

The next morning we decided to give up on the villa idea, and Jeremy and I went off on our own. The rest of our trip was glorious. We ambled through Montepulciano, Siena, and San Gimignano, devouring every wild boar ragu in sight and drinking copious bottles of Chianti and Vino Nobile. Meanwhile, my mother forced my father to take her back to Florence, where she punished him by insisting they stay at the most expensive and luxurious hotel available.

Over the years since, Jeremy and I have traveled a lot together—from Guatemala to London, Spain to Japan, France, Bali, and beyond. But we haven't taken any more road trips with my parents. I think it's best for everyone.

. . . .

JEREMY AND I were together for three years before I moved in. Through it all, we did what we came to call "the walk" back and forth between my quirky one-bedroom in the West Village (which my mother lovingly referred to as "tenement chic") and Jeremy's apartment in Chelsea. We grew so tired of that damn walk, which we did every other day, carrying bags of clothes.

Finally, it seemed crazy to be carrying two rents, especially after his roommate moved out. New Yorkers tend to move in together more quickly because of the high rent. But we were really ready. Well, at least I was—Jeremy has since confessed that he had a panic attack the night before I moved in. But from the first day, it's been like a sleepover party every night. I slowly feminized his apartment, and gradually it became ours.

Still, we were together for seven years before he proposed.

About a year into our relationship, I knew this was the person I would be with forever. He had already become my best friend. In other relationships, I'd tried to please men and avoided showing them the less-than-perfect parts of myself. I've noticed this pattern in myself and in my friends, in young women in general: by trying to please boys, we tend to give up a bit of ourselves. We start to like their music, to root for their sports teams. We dress the way we think they want us to. We think they'll like us more if we do every-thing their way. And so we lose our sense of self.

With Jeremy, I never did that. I never had to. He always liked who I was to begin with. He knew all of me and still stuck around. I think we gave each other a welcome sense of peace in a frantic city where it was often difficult to find any.

"Why aren't you guys married yet?" my friends would ask. My parents would ask. My parents' friends would ask. I wanted to get married. I wanted to marry him.

And yet: I loved our life. I wasn't in a rush. I never felt like I was waiting around. Maybe other people thought I was. But I knew we would always be together. I never thought of it as a decision he had to make—or else.

I had a friend who refused to move in with her boyfriend because she said he would think, *Why buy the cow if you can get the milk for free?*

I couldn't relate to that. I knew one day I would be Jeremy's wife. I also knew that he was worried about the wedding itself more than the actual marriage. Unlike me, Jeremy loathes being the center of attention. Besides, the thought of all that coordinating and organization petrified him, even though there was no question that I would be the one doing most of the planning. I was working in the event and food world; naturally I was prepared to deal with a wedding. It was the marriage that we were most excited about. As soon as we were married, we both realized it only made things better, in ways we could have never appreciated before.

Now the pressure is on to have children. You always assume it's the mothers who will be clamoring for grandchildren, but in our case our parents are pretty laid back about it. Instead, it's friends and even strangers who are asking us about children all the time.

Ironically, many people think we already have kids. Perhaps it's because *Top Chef* threw a bridal shower challenge for me during Season 5 and then I left, halfway through the season, to get married—compounded by the fact that both Tom and Padma have had children recently. Surely somewhere in there I had children too, right?

I get stopped on the street or asked in press interviews all the time, "How's your baby?" or "How did you lose the baby weight?" My personal favorite: "You look so great, considering you just had a baby!" Oh, yeah? So how do I look considering I have never had a baby?

. . . .

BEING AWAY FROM Jeremy is the hardest part of my job. Our friends will call him when I'm out of town to see if he needs someone to play with. But he has his own life, and his own successful music programming and marketing company. He creates music programs for businesses all over the world—restaurants, hotels, events, and retail stores. He actually works with a lot of chefs and restaurants that I know well, so our jobs occasionally overlap.

In a way, being apart several weeks a year has helped us appreciate each other more. But there are times when my constant traveling exasperates him. He'll call when I'm on set and, just to get me riled up, tell me there's no food in the house and that he had a frozen hot dog for dinner. Making sure Jeremy is fed is one way I show him how much I care about him. Feeding friends and family is about nurturing and sustaining them. If he tells me he's been eating Chinese takeout leftovers for days, it signals to me that we need more time together.

When I'm in New York, I still eat out a lot for events and for work, but I try to cook at home at least two or three nights a week. I eat so richly in the rest of my life that at home I try to keep things simple. We don't eat very much meat. I make big salads and lots of roasted vegetables, inspired by weekend trips to our local farmers' market: roasted asparagus with poached eggs, quinoa salad with roasted tomatoes, fennel and feta, whole-wheat pizza with roasted cauliflower, chilies, and pecorino. I'll sauté fish with herbs and lemon or roast chicken with harissa and spices.

In the winter months, I make huge vats of chicken and barley stew from my mother-in-law's recipe, or kale and white bean soup with kielbasa, or squash or lentil stew.

For breakfast I often bake eggs with mushrooms, potatoes, and chives, or use that whole-wheat pizza dough with a fried egg, cheese, and lots of caramelized onions.

Jeremy definitely has his limits when it comes to how much I am away, and he does occasionally lose patience with the fact that I'm more of a public person now. I've been with him far longer than I've been on television. For the most part, he thinks it's fantastic, and often hilarious. He's genuinely happy about how this adventure has unfolded. And though Jeremy is along for the ride, he can also sit back and watch it with a little more distance. My career has afforded us so many opportunities to travel and eat extraordinary meals around the world. He's supportive, protective, and in every way my partner. We have a ritual of sharing our life at the end of the day. He gives me a sense of safety and security. My work requires me to do a lot of smiling and being "on," at events or on camera. With him I can completely let go. And no, we will never have a reality show about our marriage. That's ours and ours alone.

I also appreciate having a home life that is arm's length from the industry. It gives me needed perspective. When I become too concerned with what people think of me or what I should be doing next, if I should be working harder or going out more, he's always there to help me detach from it and refocus my priorities.

Jeremy also helps me keep food in perspective. I'm often asked if I ever get sick of food. The answer is no. But there are times when I'm saturated and can't think about eating for a while, or when I'm tired of going out and just want to eat something simple. Jeremy reminds me that every meal doesn't have to matter so much. Sometimes the best thing you can do is have a bowl of soup and go to bed.

Luckily, we have very similar palates. His fervor for food is just like his grandfather's, Papa Benjamin, who always is up for a good *nosh*, a good snack. Papa is the only person on Earth who loves pickles even more than I do. Until recently, he drank shots of pickle juice on a regular basis, including on his ninetieth birthday. I believe it is

A birthday card for Papa's ninetieth—pickles and all!

the elixir that has kept him alive for so long. He's now ninety-five years old, and still sharp as a tack.

Like Papa, Jeremy's tastes tend toward the traditional foods of our ancestry. He loves nothing more than kasha (cooked buckwheat grains) and bowtie pasta (also known as farfalle), known in Yiddish as kasha varnishkes. Anything beige and soft gets his vote (slow-cooked helps, too). Brisket. Short ribs. Matzo balls. He'll take a pastrami sandwich or a potato knish any day of the week, at any and every possible meal. I married an old Jew.

I never liked kasha before I met Jeremy. As a child, I thought it was bland and tasted like cardboard. But I've come to love it, because it's Jeremy's favorite, especially loaded with caramelized onions and rich mushroom gravy.

Perhaps the most important food-related fact about Jeremy is that he's the first man who could keep up with my eating. I can't outeat him and he can't outeat me. The result: we fight over every last bite. He and I always order the same things. We have the same sensibility.

We joke sometimes when we are eating a particularly delicious meal that he wishes he'd married the girl who just ate salad. He'll say: "Just once can't you be one of those girls who only eats a bite out of her food and lets her husband finish the rest?"

He insists we should not split food 50-50, but instead 60-40, because he is a big person and I am a medium-sized person. I suppose he's right. But I'm hungry.

Given how my mother raised me, it should be no surprise that I married a man who is my gustatory equal. When I was about six, artist Judy Chicago's famous exhibit *The Dinner Party*, an installation featuring a banquet table with settings designed to represent important women in history, was touring and my mother went to see it in Toronto. She was greatly moved.

Afterward, she came to pick me up from school. She was so inspired that she asked me a question she'd always said she wouldn't ask her daughter: "What do you want to be when you grow up?"

"I want to be a dental hygienist," I said proudly.

"Why not a dentist?" she asked.

"*Mom*, men are dentists," I explained to her as though she was being ridiculous. "Women are dental hygienists."

Well, as you can imagine, she lost her mind. I got the lecture of my life. She made it clear to me that I could do anything I wanted to do, including become a dentist. And that my career options should never be limited by my gender. Whether or not that was or ever will be completely true remains to be seen, but it is an important dream to instill in young women.

My mother was fiercely independent, and she instilled in me that same drive. She wasn't preachy, but she always insisted that women needed to make their own money, especially because her own mother was so dependent on her husband. If my mother hadn't had children, maybe her career would have gone in a different direction. I don't know what she sacrificed to have us. She worked my whole life, but she certainly made specific decisions that allowed her to work from home and raise her family.

I never did become a dentist, although I did go into a field that's male-dominated. I credit my mother with giving me the courage to strive for both a career and a fulfilling personal life.

....

MY PARENTS HAVE been married for more than forty-five years. So you can imagine how overjoyed they were when Jeremy eventually proposed.

One of Jeremy's and my favorite neighborhood restaurants in August 2007 was, appropriately enough, called August and was located around the corner from our apartment. The chef at the time was a young guy named Tony Liu. In the tiny universe that is the culinary world, he'd worked for Daniel Boulud just before I was there, and then for Mario Batali at Babbo.

We ate dinner at August on occasion, but it was their weekend brunch that we especially loved. Jeremy and I would sit in the glassed-in courtyard and linger over coffee on lazy Saturdays, eating whatever creation Tony and his wood-fired oven would dream up for us. There was always some sort of baked eggs with chorizo, or basil and fresh tomato sauce, fluffy German pancakes with black currants, delicate gravlax with soft scrambled eggs and dill. Tony would make golden hash browns the size of hockey pucks that would sit up in the window of the kitchen, and it was all I could do not to grab them as I was walking to our table. Tony's menu highlighted regional specialties from all over Europe, from house-made Irish corned beef to

Spanish *calçots* (wild spring onions often blackened on an open fire and served with romesco sauce).

My favorite was his Welsh rarebit: hearty dark rye toast slathered with a sauce made from cheddar, strong mustard, and ale, served with a fried egg on top and a side of cornichons.

How could it not be? Mustard is my favorite condiment. Eggs are my favorite food. Cheese—obviously. Beer—adds bite. It's in my personal Food Hall of Fame.

I'd been traveling through California for ten days—from LA to San Francisco, and for several days to Sonoma for an event with the *Top Chef* Season 2 winner, Ilan Hall—and returned home on a Friday night exhausted. We had dinner with Sonia, who still worked with me at *Food & Wine*, and drank a bottle or two of wine. I was so tired that I collapsed into bed without washing the makeup off my face.

I woke up the next morning and remember feeling so grateful that I had nothing to do for a whole weekend. In my half sleep, I rolled over to nuzzle under Jer's arm and I hit something. I thought it was the phone or the TV remote, and I batted it away. Then I opened my eyes.

Jeremy was wide awake. His eyes were huge and alert. I looked down and saw that in the bed beside me was a small box. He started talking nervously. Words were falling out of his mouth. I barely even heard what he said. I opened the box and there was a ring. I was in such shock, I blurted, "No!" from surprise.

"No?" he said, startled.

"No! I mean, yes!" I said. "Yes! Yes!" I cried, still disoriented from sleep, and put the ring on my finger. It was so beautiful and feminine and perfect. I looked up at him, happy, and he started to laugh.

"What?"

"You might want to look at yourself."

I went to the bathroom and saw black streaks of mascara running down my face; my hair was sticking up at all angles.

I cleaned myself up, went back to bed, and he said, "Don't move. Just stay here."

We lay in bed, beaming, for a little while and then the doorbell rang.

"I'll get it," I insisted, putting on my bathrobe.

When I opened the door, there was a man standing outside with a huge box. I took it from him and it almost knocked me down, it was so heavy.

Inside was a full breakfast delivery straight from Tony at August. Since they have a wood-burning stove, they cook everything in cast-iron skillets. They hadn't transferred anything into to-go containers. Instead, they had just piled the skillets into this box and had it couriered over. There was my beloved Welsh rarebit, and so many other treats, enough food for at least three meals. We made it last the whole day, laid out like a picnic on our living room floor.

Twenty minutes later, the doorbell rang again. Two deliverymen arrived bearing vases full of flowers; huge peonies, dahlias, roses, and hydrangeas. They lasted for days.

....

IT OCCURRED TO us that now we had to actually get married. We had a lot of anxiety about the wedding, partially because both of our mothers had strong feelings about the subject. Jeremy's mother hated the cookie-cutter traditions of a formal wedding. She also hated how much they cost and thought it was frivolous to spend huge amounts of money to get married. My mother, too, would go on and on about how huge weddings were unnecessary. She often said she wished we would just elope.

For the most part, we agreed. We didn't want a gratuitously over-the-top affair. It was overwhelming to conceive of dealing with the seemingly endless details a wedding required, the politics, the invitations, the family drama. We wanted none of it. Just a small, personal ceremony. But we also realized we really wanted to celebrate with all the people we loved. In the end, our wedding was a celebration, a great party that we made our own, but it did take some doing.

First, there was the matter of the dress. Throughout the years Jeremy and I were living together, Aunt Linda was impatient. She wanted a wedding! From the moment I was born, she was looking forward to shopping for my wedding dress. When the time finally came, she was over the moon, and my mother was happy to hand over the job.

By contrast, my mother never cared much for fashion or frills. I actually didn't care for them either until I moved to New York and discovered that the city was basically a glorified shopping mall.

So, this was Linda's moment. She said to my mother, "Renée, don't say a thing. This is my job." They came to New York together, with my mother-in-law in tow, to pick out the dress with me.

I wanted the simplest design, nothing strappy or poufy. We had decided to get married the following August, in New York. It was going to be excruciatingly hot. I tried on maybe fifty dresses. The one I picked—we found it at Carolina Herrera—was the only one that came remotely close to what I had envisioned. It had a delicate grosgrain ribbon at the plunging neckline and the bodice was made from flowing layers of silk in a summery Swiss dot pattern, but otherwise, it was the simplest possible dress. Most importantly, it got Linda's approval.

The wedding itself, for all our internal stress leading up to it, was informal and comfortable. We held the ceremony and reception at The Foundry, a restored metal foundry in Long Island City, Queens, right across the Queensboro Bridge from Manhattan. It had a lush back garden and views of the New York City skyline.

We had a traditional Jewish ceremony, more or less, but many other aspects of the typical American wedding didn't feel quite right for us. We didn't have bridesmaids and groomsmen, although my nieces and nephew did the most incredible job as our flower girls and ring bearer. Never, I'm convinced, has a ring been carried so

Jeremy and me with my parents, on our wedding day

well. We didn't have a first dance. Ironically, considering my job, we didn't even have a cake!

It will come as no surprise that food was the most important detail. For our rehearsal dinner, we served barbecue from Daisy May's, a take-out spot in Hell's Kitchen. The owner is an alumnus of Daniel. It's my father's absolute favorite, and ours, too. The meal was casual, a buffet of sticky ribs, Texas-style brisket, fresh corn smothered in sharp cheddar, mashed sweet potatoes and collard greens, beer-can chicken, and smoky beans.

For the wedding reception itself, Jeremy and I spent a lot of time thinking about what we wanted to serve. There's a lot of bad wedding food out there. We wanted it to be personal and unconventional. Most of all, we wanted it to be good. We felt it fitting to take advantage of the abundance of local summer ingredients, so the food could speak for itself. Of course, the best person for this job was Daniel Boulud.

Jeremy, Daniel, his catering manager, and I sat down to craft the menu in the bar at his flagship restaurant. Jeremy and I already had in our heads an idea of what we wanted. But I knew you could not tell Daniel what to do. The truth is: he will figure out how to do what you think you want better than you could ever imagine yourself.

It is true that if given the opportunity, Daniel would put foie gras and caviar on everything. He has a penchant for rich French ingredients, but he is a genius, and I was ready to suspend any doubts.

This took some explaining to Jeremy. He was worried about all the ingredients Daniel was suggesting. He was concerned it would be too fussy for some of our guests and argued that several of our family members and friends weren't as ambitious in the culinary department as we were.

"Figs with fish?" Jeremy balked at this incongruous-sounding suggestion from Daniel. "Our friends will freak out!"

"The man is a master," I explained. "We need to trust him."

Jeremy relented, and we wisely gave ourselves over to Daniel's vision.

The menu was the most colorful and plentiful I'd ever seen. I'm biased, of course, but I think it was objectively spectacular. It achieved all we had hoped for, indulged our beloved guests, and celebrated our appreciation for the summer bounty.

We seated everyone at long communal tables in the garden courtyard. We designed the meal to be eaten family style, with people sharing and tasting food off one another's plate.

The four-course meal began with three chilled soups, alternating on the table so everyone could sample to the left and right: minted pea velouté with rosemary cream, corn puree with sautéed zucchini, and tomato gazpacho with basil oil and cucumber.

This was followed by a feast of seven fresh summer salads: sucrine lettuce with shaved crudités and lemon olive dressing; traditional ratatouille with grated Parmesan; artichokes *barigoule* with basil; Satur Farm red, golden, and candy baby beets; Hawaiian hearts

A TASTE OF
CHILLED SOUP
MINTED PEA VELOUTÉ WITH
ROSEMARY CREAM
CORN PURÉE WITH
SAUTÉED ZUCCHINI
TOMATO GAZPACHO WITH BASIL, OIL & CUCUMBER
CREAMY RICOTTA WITH GARLIC CROSTINI

FEAST
OF FRESH
SUMMER SALADS
SUCRINE LETTUCE WITH SHAVED
CRUDITÉS & LEMON OLIVE DRESSING
TRADITIONAL RATATOUILLE WITH GRATED PARMESAN
ARTICHOKE BARIGOULE WITH BASIL
SATUR FARM RED, GOLDEN & CANDY BABY BEETS
HAWAIIAN HEARTS OF PALM WITH AVOCADO
COLORFUL HEIRLOOM TOMATOES WITH PISTOU

MENU

GRILLED
STRIPED BASS *with*
RED WINE
ROASTED FIGS
YOUNG TURNIPS
BRAISED ROMAINE
POLENTA

DELECTABLE
DESSERT
BITES
TO FOLLOW
GAIL & JEREMY 08.17.08

Our wedding menu

of palm with avocado; heirloom tomatoes with *pistou*; creamy ricotta with garlic crostini. The salads were paraded out on large platters and placed in the center of each group of six.

The next course was fish: grilled striped bass with red wine, roasted figs, young turnips, braised romaine, and polenta. Even Jeremy agreed that it was sensational.

Due to noise regulations, we needed to be back inside the space by 10 p.m. We wanted to be quick about finishing dinner and a few short speeches, so we opted not to do a plated dessert, which meant no wedding cake. Instead, we served small bites of sweets that were easy to pick up and eat while dancing, even with a drink in the other hand.

The desserts included mini fruit tarts (peach, strawberry, and raspberry), French macaroons in vanilla and coffee, bite-sized banana marshmallows on sticks, strawberry sorbet bars dipped in dark chocolate.

To top it off, we asked City Bakery (a New York City institution we've been eating at for well over a decade) to make us a few hundred of their chocolate chip cookies. Their cookies are famously decadent, golden brown and crumbly around the edges, chewy and buttery in the center, with large chunks of semisweet chocolate scattered throughout. We set them out in giant glass jars, a nod to my mother's kitchen counter.

It felt like the perfect summer feast: simple, fresh, and festive, with plenty of cocktails and lots of good wine.

I dreamed of having jars of my father's famous homemade pickles for guests to take away. But I realized that shipping two hundred jars of kosher dills through U.S. Customs would be no easy task. Instead, we convinced Gus's Pickles, one of New York's oldest pickle merchants on the Lower East Side, to specially jar a batch for us, and we created a special label that read: "New York Pickles! They're not as good as Ivor's, but they're pretty darn close!"

....

THEN JEREMY AND I went on our greatest trip to date: a honeymoon in Vietnam and Japan. Friends who knew the country well told us to start in Hanoi, the culturally rich capital, because it was quieter and we could acclimate before we made our way to Saigon, in the south, which they explained was much more intense.

As you can imagine, I did an enormous amount of research on where to go for all our meals. Through the course of my life, I seem to have developed a kind of food-related OCD, and can put a lot of pressure on myself about where and what I eat. The one place on the top of my list was a well-known family-run shop called Cha Ca La Vong in Hanoi's old quarter. Cha Ca is a traditional Northern Vietnamese dish made with snake-head fish, turmeric, dill, salt-roasted peanuts, and yellow chili peppers on a bed of rice noodles. This little spot was said to make the ultimate version.

We landed in Hanoi and spent three glorious days exploring the city's historic sites, and strategically planned that on our last full day we would go to Cha Ca La Vong for lunch. We spent the morning at the Temple of Literature (the country's first university, founded in 1070) and Ho Chi Minh's mausoleum, where his embalmed body lies. We lost track of time. In a panic we jumped into a cyclo (those bicycle-drawn rickshaws) and raced across town. When we arrived, they were already closing the shop and shut their door in our faces. There was no pretense of hospitality or charm. We pleaded, but they weren't interested in listening.

I was determined to eat there before we left, so we decided to rearrange our schedule and go back for dinner. That night, we got roped into seeing a water puppet show—a ridiculously touristy performance we didn't really need to attend. The show ended at nine, and I knew if we moved fast, we could make it to Cha Ca La Vong in time. We ran through the dizzying streets of the old quarter, navigating our way past chickens and children, old ladies aggressively prodding us to purchase their wares, souvenir vendors clamoring for our attention. Again, the moment we finally arrived, for the second time that day no less, they slammed the doors in front of us.

That was my limit. Maybe it was the combination of exhaustion from jet lag, the time change, the foreign locale, the claustrophobia of the heaving city, and the general culture shock, but it all just suddenly overwhelmed me and I broke down, sobbing loudly right there in the street. I was inconsolable. It was now getting late and everything was closing. There was nowhere else to eat dinner. Jeremy, God bless him, tried to calm me down. He put me in a cab and finally found us a badly lit buffet, where he made me a plate of tepid vegetables and unidentifiable meats. I sobbed harder.

"What's wrong?" Jeremy kept asking. "What can I do?"

It was obviously about more than not getting to eat this one dish. I knew it wasn't rational, but I couldn't control myself. I cried all the way back to the hotel and was still weeping when we got into bed. Jeremy's gentle attempt at consolation turned to frustration, and finally exhaustion. He rolled over and went to sleep. This, on the third day of our honeymoon. It's a wonder he stayed married to me!

I woke up the next morning, my eyes puffy and swollen. I walked out onto our terrace and watched the city slowly wake from its slumber. It looked so much less menacing in the daylight and I was able come to terms with the events from the night before.

As I sat there, I came to realize that I don't always have to check everything off my list or always clean my plate. My life is incredibly fortunate, in that there are still a million extraordinary experiences waiting to be had. There will always be another meal. Not every one has to count so much.

Jeremy woke up shortly after me and asked if everything was okay. He started to tell me how I needed to learn to let go. But, by then, I already had.

The rest of our trip was extraordinary. We flew to Hoi An and spent three days exploring its markets and ancient architecture. From there, we went to a small island in the South China Sea, off the coast of Nha Trang, where we hiked, lounged on the beach, and took boat trips to the daily market and a nearby lobster farm.

We ended the Vietnam portion of our trip in Saigon, which was just as intense and chaotic as we had been told. But the food there was truly outstanding. We relished the chance to sit on red plastic stools in front of stalls on the street where they meticulously cooked crab a hundred different ways. At the Ben Thanh night market, we feasted on whole grilled fish with chilies and lemongrass, and large river prawns poached in coconut milk and dill, then dipped in salt ground with chilies and lime. We ravenously consumed pâté-filled Banh Mi sandwiches, sugary sweet mangosteens, rich, earthy *pho*, and countless Vietnamese iced coffees.

Then we flew to Tokyo, armed with a list of restaurants that Jean-Georges Vongerichten had recommended through our friend Dorie Greenspan, the cookbook author I had befriended when first interviewing with Daniel. My most highly anticipated of these was a tiny restaurant run by a revered sushi chef, described to us only as the Yoda of sushi.

The streets of Tokyo create a labyrinth, and this restaurant was down a tiny, unmarked alley, in the heart of Shinjuku. The taxi couldn't even find it. Eventually we set out on foot and were able to locate its unremarkable entrance. There were only eight seats. We were the only Caucasians in the room.

No one there spoke English. (In my experience there is little English spoken in Japan, unlike many other Asian countries, where you can get around pretty easily speaking English and perhaps a few words in the local vernacular, like "hello," "sorry," "please," and "thank you.") We were at their mercy. So we ordered the *omakase*, or tasting menu, and we just nodded and smiled as they started bringing us food.

We didn't recognize half of what we were ingesting, endless bites of raw fish and meticulously sliced seafood, carefully constructed vegetable dishes, hot dumplings, immaculate sushi, seaweed that looked like tiny green fish eggs, which I later learned are called "sea grapes" or "sea caviar."

At one point, the sushi chef passed us what looked like a large white mussel in a delicate broth. It tasted salty and soft, a little bit sweet.

"I wonder what this is."

We shrugged our shoulders and kept eating. The sake flowed freely. We felt like we were in an alternate universe. We could only understand each other and could not get over how lucky we were that we had found ourselves in this master's hands.

By the end of the night, it was just Jeremy, me, and two other patrons at the other end of the sushi bar. Eventually, the chef turned to us and in broken English asked what we were doing there. We gathered they rarely saw foreigners. We threw out the name Jean-Georges Vongerichten, hoping it would spark some recognition. He shrugged and went back to his work.

Suddenly, the man at the end of the bar piped up. "Jean-Georges? I sell him fish!"

It turned out this man was one of Tokyo's leading fish distributors. He'd been working at the Tsukiji Fish Market since he was fourteen and supplied some of the greatest restaurants in the world. I asked if there was any way for us to get into the private and prized bluefin tuna auctions that happened each morning. I had been hoping to see them ever since I learned about the market so many years ago while working for Jeffrey. We'd been trying to find a guide, because you need special authorization to get in.

"Of course," he said. "I'll take you. Meet me there tomorrow at five a.m."

We went went back to our hotel, slept for two hours, then headed out. We realized we didn't even know this man's name, but we showed up that morning, and sure enough, there he was.

This extraordinary gentleman put passes around our necks and took us through the fresh and frozen tuna auctions, where all the bluefin tuna for the whole world is rated and sold.

"Stay close," he told us. Then he pointed at a bag of soft white mounds. "That's what you ate last night."

"Oh, right," I said. "What is it?"

"Cod sperm," he replied, giggling.

Jeremy gulped. While at first I found it slightly shocking, perhaps it's not that different from eating caviar, if you think about it.

The market was organized chaos. Everywhere we turned, men were hauling massive flats of fish in all shapes and sizes. The tuna themselves were moved around on the floor with giant hooks in their mouths. Each weighed hundreds of pounds. Dozens of people gathered, bells rang out around us, and the furious haggling of the auction began.

Afterward, our guide took us to the live section of the market, where they keep enormous tanks with creatures from the deep—octopi, eels, rays, blowfish. It was a sight to behold. Around 7 a.m. he took us for breakfast to a sushi restaurant just outside the main

Morning at the Tsukiji Fish Market's bluefin
tuna auctions

market building, the perfect end to our adventure. We flew home
the next day to start our married life.

....

THERE'S A BOOKSTORE in the West Village that sells vintage,
hard-to-find, and first-edition cookbooks. The owner, Bonnie Slotnick, will hunt down special editions for you. My mother and I used
to go there together every time she was in town. One day Bonnie
called to say, "The book your mother ordered for you is in."

I didn't know what she was talking about, but I went in and

picked it up. It was an old Jewish cookbook called *A Treasure for My Daughter*, first published in 1950 and written by the Montreal chapter of Hadassah (a Jewish charitable organization) to which my grandmother belonged. It was a collection of traditional Jewish recipes and marital advice meant to include everything a good Jewish wife would need to know to nurture her household.

Plenty of the advice and recipes in it are outdated and hilarious: Prune whip. Baked gefilte fish molds. Giblet fricassee. Potato and liver blintzes. Haleshkes. Liver varenikes. Brain latkes (yes, brain latkes). Yeast delights. What did they find delightful about yeast?

Ironically, this kind of nose-to-tail (although in the Jewish version, not with a pig!) cooking has come back in fashion lately. Chefs love cooking giblets, liver, and brains these days.

The trend makes a lot of sense. These dishes were born out of the need to stretch the dollar by using more inexpensive parts of the animal along with basic ingredients that could go a long way, too, like potatoes, onions, and cabbage. This is what my people ate in the old country, in the ghettos of Eastern Europe.

These working-class recipes born from necessity have become the hearty, ambitious food that chefs now praise and crave. You have to work hard to make these cuts tasty. It's not an already-delicious piece like a New York strip. With knowledge and aptitude, though, the less popular cuts become exemplary, both in flavor and in affordability.

While I had no intention of making brain latkes for Jeremy, I was touched that my mother thought to find me that book. It's a link to Jewish women before me and a direct connection to my grandmother. Besides, I'm happy for all the marriage advice I can get. It's a struggle to find enough time with my husband while keeping a hectic work schedule, and we don't even have children yet.

Now that I'm married, I also feel like I have a better answer to that clichéd question: Why are there so few female chefs with restaurant empires?

It's definitely not because women don't cook as well as men. But there are some logistical hurdles.

I never wanted to be a chef. I wanted to be a food writer and work in the media. Obviously, I have a deep respect for chefs and their work ethic. But as a career path, cooking can be very trying on your personal life.

Consider this: If becoming a true chef, meaning to be in charge of a kitchen, takes about ten years and you start when you're as young as, say, eighteen or twenty, you come into your own when you're around thirty, right? At around thirty, what do women have to start thinking about very seriously? Children.

It's no great coincidence that there are still so few female chefs in the United States. The difference between the chef world and the corporate world, for example, is that not only do you have the long hours away from your family, but being a chef is also manual labor. You have the hours of a banker and the physical demands of a construction worker. You are on your feet surrounded by knives and fire twelve hours a day, six days a week or more. Period.

Can you name five women in New York with more than one restaurant? I can name a dozen male chefs who have at least five! Gabrielle Hamilton, award-winning chef, owner of the critically acclaimed restaurant Prune, and best-selling author of the memoir *Blood, Bones & Butter: The Inadvertent Education of a Reluctant Chef*, is very honest about her experience working in the food world. Her book touches on the issue of how difficult it can be for women in the industry. Women are often doing double duty: working just as hard and fast as men, but also constantly trying to create a secure identity for themselves within the context of such a male-dominated sphere.

For some reason, women tend to fare better on the West Coast. Maybe it's less cutthroat. The quality of life is a little better. That's not to say that the chefs don't work just as hard. In Los Angeles, Suzanne Goin has three restaurants with her partner Caroline Styne, and three more with her husband, who's also a chef. Elizabeth Faulkner has three; she's on the West Coast, too. As does San Francisco's Traci des Jardins.

Few women on the East Coast that I can think of, with the exception of April Bloomfield and Lidia Bastianich in New York, Barbara Lynch in Boston, and Michelle Bernstein in Miami, are empire builders in the same way their male counterparts are. Why?

Maybe it's because women prefer to maintain more control, to do one thing well and not stretch themselves as thin. And it's more difficult to pawn the care of children off on their partners, especially in the early years. Generally speaking, no one else is going to carry, deliver, or nurse that baby but you.

To be a full-time, working chef, you have to be there when the shop is open. For restaurants that means evenings, weekends, and holidays. That's when people eat. Sure, you can own a restaurant and find some balance. I know plenty of chefs who take two days off a week, but it's not easy. Most of my friends who are married to chefs are alone at least five nights a week and most days.

That's why plenty of chefs, both male and female, have chosen a different path in the food world, at the risk of never having that same kind of large-scale, celebrity success. I've already told you about Daniel's chef de cuisine, Alex Lee. The husband of another friend of mine was Daniel's sous-chef for years. He is incredibly talented and could have easily gone out on his own to wild acclaim. But he loves to paint and he wanted time to have a family. He took a job running the corporate dining room at a major bank. It's a great gig. He serves breakfast and lunch only and has full control over a state-of-the-art kitchen, with a budget to match. He leaves by three. Now he has time to paint and has recently become a sculptor, too. He picks his son up from school.

He's never going to be renowned in the restaurant world like Daniel, but he's chosen the reward of family and balance instead of fame and glory. Even for men, it's rare to be able to do it all; you can have both, but not mega-both.

I, too, might make more money and be more successful if I weren't married and didn't want a family. I could travel twice as much, work the room at more parties and events, and not worry about spending time at home. But I'd rather have more balance in my life. I have to believe I'm not alone.

There are plenty of women in the food industry—food writers, editors, recipe testers, food stylists, publicists, event planners, and caterers—who have made this same choice of quality of life over empire building. Life experience has always come before material possessions for me. It's how I was raised.

My father is one of the most frugal men I have ever known. He saves every bottle cap and recycles everything he can. He deplores waste of any kind and has always been an environmentalist. He's a great advocate for the planet. But he rarely spends money on himself or indulges in anything that is not entirely necessary. He will stand in line for six hours in the freezing cold to buy $2 cheese knives on sale. At the same time, he has an appreciation for high-quality, artisanal cheese.

In a way, this sent me mixed messages. It taught me not to be frivolous, to save money and be responsible and independent, which I believe was one of the best lessons I ever learned. But it also set up this mentality of martyrdom and guilt at any thought of extraneous luxury or occasional splurge, even if rightfully earned. That's part of the way my father was raised, too, I guess.

I'm all for frugality. I went to school with a lot of wealthy kids who wore fancy clothes and drove expensive cars, and I envied them. We never wanted for anything, but our parents never let us spend large amounts on frivolous things. My father drove the same Honda Civic hatchback for twenty years, which we referred to affectionately as "the shit box." It was filthy all the time. He didn't care.

When I became an adult, I realized my parents had so much

more than so many of the people around us. Not just financially. My parents spent their money on travel, not on designer brands. That was something they could give us as a family, something more valuable than a BMW on your sixteenth birthday. This, I came to understand only years later, was true wealth.

Because of my parents' financial prudence, we were all able to go to college, and then I was able to go to culinary school, debt-free. No student loans (even the best universities in Canada are government subsidized and significantly less expensive, so we don't typically carry the student loans that Americans do, but still).

Partially because of what I do for a living, I often don't question spending money on food. It's my job, but it's also my passion. I love the act of sitting down with friends to enjoy a special meal, whether cooked at home or in a restaurant. So a $500 bill for dinner doesn't bother me, but it's hard for me to wrap my head around a $500 bill for a sweater or shoes. It's counterintuitive. At least with the shoes, you get to wear them for a while. No matter how good the meal, you still have to eat again in a few hours.

Not a day passes without a reminder of how fortunate I am. And the gross dichotomy between the extraordinary access I have to food and the fact that so many others, even in my own city, go hungry. Approximately 3 million people in New York alone have trouble affording food for their families, and as a member of the culinary community, I feel a strong responsibility to be active in the fight against hunger, both here in the United States and abroad. I make a point of spending as much time, energy, and money as I can on the problem. I sit on the board of several anti-hunger organizations, including City Harvest and Common Threads. I donate to the Food Bank for New York City, Share Our Strength, Oxfam, and the Red Cross on a regular basis. And I hope using my voice to this end will help others do the same.

My parents set a strong example for me with their activism. My mother helps run a winter soup kitchen and does a lot of work with an anti-hunger organization in Canada. My father spends countless hours volunteering every week for wildlife and environmental conservancy groups. They made it clear that giving back starts at home. Part of raising us was preparing us to go out into the world and do our best to make a difference.

Finding the time and budget for causes other than those that affect my own daily life takes a bit of effort and the constant checking of priorities. It makes me reexamine just how complicated it must have been for my own mother. When you're young, you don't see the pressures. You take for granted that your parents' lives revolve around you, around making sure your needs are met. My mother made it look easy. Now that I'm creating a foundation for my own family, I can't help but think back to the way my mother balanced her multifaceted life. She found a way to take care of herself, her family, and her community. I only hope I can one day set the same example.

....

FOURTEEN

Sugared Up on Just Desserts

THE PANTRY BUILT for *Top Chef: Just Desserts* is packed with every gadget and confection I've ever dreamed of. It looks like a science lab, but for unicorns. There are edible colored paints, glues, glitters—and, of course, "disco dust." An endless array of flours: all-purpose, bread, whole-wheat, cake, buckwheat, self-rising, hazelnut, rice, almond, semolina, pastry. Polenta and cornmeal. Barley malt powder. Chocolate with every ratio of cocoa from 40 all the way to 85 percent. Extra-dark, extra-bitter, manjara, guanaja, couverture, modeling; in every possible shape: callets, blocks, pearls, flakes, chips, shavings. Gelatin in sheets and powder, edible lacquer spray, edible color sprays, edible gold flakes. Pastillage, gum paste mixes, meringue powder, coconut oil, peanut oil, olive oil, white balsamic vinegar, buttermilk, yogurt. Dextrose, sorbitol, citric acid, tartaric acid, silica gel, active dry yeast, instant yeast, fondant, isomalt crystals. Calvados, dark rum, amaretto. Filo dough. Rose water. Puffed rice, sodium alginate, sodium citrate, calcium chloride. Colored sugars, silver and gold dragées, regular and Dutch processed cocoa. Taro, baby fennel, and rhubarb. Smoked paprika. Marshmallow fluff. Tapioca maltodextrin. Sugars: brown, white, muscovado, turbinado, demerara, confectioners' (10X). Acetate sheets, airbrushes, food colorings, piping gels, liquid nitrogen. Pop Rocks, Phizzy, agar, lecithin, baking powder, baking soda. Lavender, key limes. Chewing gum base. Guar gum. Carrageenan. Xanthan. A blast chiller that freezes anything in seconds, and a $30,000 ice-cream machine flown in from Italy. A sugar-pulling station with special lamps that keep everything warm. A big marble countertop for rolling out dough that stays cold. The walls are bright and pink and shimmering, just waiting to be dusted in flour.

AFTER I HAD completed six seasons on *Top Chef* and two seasons of *Masters*, having eaten somewhere in the vicinity of a hundred meals on camera, Bravo asked me to consider hosting a spin-off series. It would be called *Top Chef: Just Desserts*.

I'd never particularly thought of myself as a "dessert girl," but who wouldn't get excited by the prospect of eating chocolate every day? And I do adore desserts. Every kind. At culinary school I did my mandatory six-week stint in bread and pastry, so I comprehend the basics. And at Daniel I spent endless hours in the bread and pastry kitchens, watching the chefs work their magic.

But I still considered dessert-making a sort of wizardry. I knew enough about the field to appreciate how incredibly difficult it is—but not enough to be able to do it myself, at least not on a professional level. Perhaps this had something to do with why they asked me to host the show. I speak the language, but the science of pastry still mystifies me.

We'd always felt there was a void on *Top Chef* when it came to dessert. Savory chefs usually aren't that competent in the pastry kitchen. They have a totally different set of skills and training. Pastry is a whole different science, much more precise and exacting. I liken it to the difference between a psychiatrist and a surgeon. They may both be doctors, but you don't want them to do each other's job.

We never had high expectations of desserts on the original show, but the public didn't quite understand that. Desserts became a stigma. At best, we were served what's often called a "chef's dessert." All savory chefs should have in their back pocket a few basic desserts, like a simple tart, molten chocolate cake, basic ice cream, poached fruit, or bread pudding—things that aren't complicated in pastry technique and can be made quickly. There are very few chefs who have a mastery of more complex pastry. That's why, on the dessert menus of small restaurants with no pastry kitchen, you often see the same few offerings: crème brûlée, panna cotta, chocolate cake, apple tart, rice pudding, sundaes. All delicious, but not very original.

Top Chef viewers started to complain: "They're supposed to be chefs! Why can't they make a good dessert?" Or: "Pastry is so much more beautiful. Since we can't taste the food, give us some architectural creations we can look at!"

Pastry chefs groaned about it, too: "You're giving our craft a bad name. Give *us* a chance to shine!"

Thankfully, Bravo decided to take a chance on the show.

....

ONCE I AGREED to host, the next step was finding our judging panel. The producers wanted to keep the same basic format as *Top Chef.* The head judge would be a professional heavyweight—in this case, an acclaimed pastry chef. The third seat would alternate between two passionate industry insiders. The fourth spot would be filled by a different guest each week.

Johnny Iuzzini had been the pastry sous-chef at Daniel for several years and was practically Daniel's adopted son. He had left right around the time I started, accepting a prestigious job as the executive pastry chef at Jean-Georges. At the time, he was only in his mid-twenties—a prodigy, to say the least.

In between jobs, Johnny came back to Daniel to work on a friend's wedding cake. The pastry team did their chocolate and sugar work in a small, temperature- and humidity-controlled room near the pastry kitchen. Georgette and I used part of that room to store our printed materials. One day I walked in to grab some press kits, and there was Johnny. He was handsome and had great energy, not to mention an exhaustive knowledge of cocktail mixology. We've been friends ever since.

With his experience and charm, Johnny was a natural choice as our head judge. I can only imagine that Daniel loves seeing two of his surrogate offspring hosting a show together so many years later.

I met Hubert Keller on the very first episode of *Top Chef,* Season I. He was our inaugural guest judge. The producers brought all our chef-testants to Fleur de Lys, his restaurant in San Francisco, to work the line during dinner service until they messed up. The next day Hubert joined us to judge the Elimination Challenge, where the chefs had to cook their signature dishes. He's very regal and soft-spoken, with an Alsatian accent and a mane of long silver hair—a true gentleman.

We were shooting in an industrial part of Emoryville, over the Bay Bridge from San Francisco. The makeup artist, wardrobe stylist, and I decided to go for a drink during our two-hour break. We invited Hubert to come along. Suddenly we were having a cocktail with one of the greatest French chefs in the country, in the middle of nowhere. *Maybe this show won't be so bad after all,* I remember thinking.

The feedback Bravo received from viewers that first season was that *everyone* loved Hubert Keller. How could you not? He was everything people thought a chef should be: authoritative, charming, and French.

He came back as our guest judge for the Season 1 finale in Las Vegas, where he owns Fleur Restaurant and Burger Bar, as well as to Hawaii and the Bahamas for finales that followed. Then of course he was a finalist on the first season of *Top Chef Masters*.

When the producers were putting together the original cast for *Just Desserts*, they learned that Hubert had a background in pastry. His parents owned a bakery in Alsace, and he had a strong emotional connection to desserts. With Johnny as the head judge, Hubert was the perfect complement: a sage savory chef with a love of sweets.

It was trickier to pinpoint who should alternate with Hubert at our Judges' Table. Bravo wanted a woman, if possible, for balance. They didn't need a trained pastry technician, since they had our two professional chefs.

"Do you have any ideas?" Dave Serwatka asked me. "We need a woman who's fun, funny, and extremely enthusiastic about dessert. If she has TV training that would help, too."

I gave it some thought, put together a list, and reached out to my food-industry network for additional ideas.

Back at the *Food & Wine* offices, Chris Grdovic—who was now the magazine's publisher—suggested Dannielle Kyrillos, a close friend and the wife of J. P. Kyrillos, the publisher of *Travel + Leisure* magazine, our sister publication. Dannielle was the editor-at-large of *Daily Candy* at the time, and had been there since its inception. She'd made frequent appearances on TV as their brand ambassador. Aside from being witty, smart, and beautiful, she was an accomplished home baker and an aficionado of all things sweet. I suggested her to Dave and they screen-tested her.

Dannielle emailed me shortly afterward. "Thank you so much for connecting me to the team at Bravo!" she wrote. "I *bombed*. It was horrible, but I was thrilled to just be considered. Good luck with the show!"

Simultaneously, I received an email from Dave. "Dannielle is amazing! Thank you so much for sending her our way. We're going to offer her the job."

Hubert, me, Dannielle, and Johnny on the set of *Top Chef: Just Desserts*

So our little group of sugar addicts was set, and it was even better than I could have imagined. I just had a little more say in things, a little more pressure, and a lot more standing around in high heels.

....

OUR FIRST SEASON was a roller coaster, to say the least. Wolfgang Puck's longtime pastry chef at Spago in Los Angeles, the venerable Sherry Yard, consulted on the building of the pantry and the kitchen, and it was a hall of marvels. We were pretty confident going into production. We had the same extraordinary team from Magical Elves, the same director and crew, and we figured we all knew exactly how it would all work. This was just *Top Chef* with whipped cream and more ovens, right?

Wrong. As it turned out, this was not like *Top Chef* at all.

First of all, the insanely tight time constraints we were so used to for Quickfires and Elimination Challenges were not applicable to pastry.

To make professional-caliber desserts, you need to preheat, mix, cook, cool, glaze or frost, garnish or decorate, slice, and serve. In pastry kitchens, the schedule works much differently from on the hot line. You simply can't bake most pastry *à la minute* the way you cook savory food in a restaurant. You can't bake an apple pie from scratch in fifteen minutes, between the time you serve your guests their main course and the time they expect their dessert. The baking alone takes forty-five minutes or more. That's why bakers start early in the morning. They make all their cakes, ice creams, and cookies in advance. They cut and fashion all their petits fours, glaze their candies, and coat their truffles long before dinner service begins.

If we wanted our pastry chefs to produce high-quality, elaborate dishes on *Just Desserts*, we would need to exponentially increase their cook times or find ways to work around it. We learned this the hard way. In a wedding-cake Quickfire challenge, for example, we gave the chefs an hour and prebaked basic sponge cake, called *génoise*, in vanilla and chocolate, so all they had to do was assembly, layering and fillings, and decoration. If they'd had to bake their own cake layers from scratch, it would have added anywhere from three to ten more hours to the challenge. It can take days to make a wedding cake when you factor in baking the base and creating intricate designs and details in sugar, chocolate, fruit, buttercream, fondant, and even flowers.

"Your time starts now," I announced.

Forty-five minutes later, we were watching the monitors and noticing that barely any of them had made a dent in their cakes.

It was like asking them to run a marathon in twenty minutes.

I went into the kitchen and gave the chefs another hour, but by that point it was hard for them to readjust their plans. From then on, we knew we had to be more generous with time.

Then there was the recipe question. That first season, we gave the chefs a constraint that wound up throwing them for a major loop: they couldn't bring any recipes with them. We modified this rule for Season 2.

Taking away a recipe from a contestant on *Top Chef* makes sense. As I've explained, if you know how to sauté, you can sauté anything, from broccoli to chicken livers. You need far fewer exact recipes if you are a professional chef who cooks every day and truly understands the savory kitchen. You can taste as you go, touch and feel your food, add or temper or change direction to adjust the seasoning.

But pastry doesn't work that way. You mix a batter and put it in an oven. When it comes out, it's done, and there's no way to go back and fix it if it didn't turn out as planned. If you're even a single gram off in your formula, the cake may well be ruined, and you don't have time to bake another. Basic recipes are vital, at the very least, so pastry chefs get their ratios right.

Pâte à choux, for example—the dough with which you make éclairs, gougères, and profiteroles—is always the same basic ratio. It's made with one cup of water, one cup of flour, one cup of eggs (four large), and half a cup of butter. It's always 1:1:1:½. You can memorize the ratio and apply it as needed, so a cake for one hundred is the same as a cake for twenty. Pastry recipes are usually written in ratios like these, and a chef is never without his or her recipes. It's all about *exactitude* (or the more serious-sounding, made-up word "exactillation").

Putting pastry chefs under time pressure upsets them; putting them under time pressure *and* taking away their recipes makes them utterly volatile.

When chocolate guru Jacques Torres, M.O.F. (the highest honor bestowed on pastry masters in France), came on the show as our very first guest judge, we mentioned that we'd taken the contestants' recipes away.

"Are you out of your *minds*?" he asked. "Why have them stumbling through the basics? They'll revolt, and you'll be stuck eating the same four pastries all season long!"

Jacques's argument, which we came to see as true, was that providing the chefs with a foundation of recipes would allow for a greatly expanded repertoire of desserts on the show and many more creative flourishes. But by the time we realized this, it was mid-season, and too late to change our no-recipe policy. All things considered, it's astounding how many fantastic dishes our chefs composed under such huge limitations.

. . . .

WE WERE ALL learning together. I, for one, became so much more conscious of texture, temperature, and what a huge role they play in the dessert experience, more so in some ways than in savory cooking. You want smoothness in your whipped cream and chewiness or a crispy crunch in your chocolate chip cookie. You want your popsicles to be ice cold and your gooey chocolate sauce to be warm. It changes how you perceive the dish entirely.

The responsibility of being the show's host was another big challenge. I'm a quick study. I had a basic understanding of what it entailed, having watched other people do it from my seat at Judges' Table for so many years. But until I did it myself, I never quite fathomed the scope of the job.

Padma tried to prepare me. The month before I left to shoot the show, Padma was toward the end of her pregnancy. I would bring her lunch, whatever she craved, and we would sit on her bed while she gave me hosting advice. "The hours are the most challenging thing," she explained. "Hosting the show takes twice as many days and hours as judging."

We shot the first season in Los Angeles, in exactly thirty-four days. During that time I had a whopping two days off, plus a fast and furious seventy-two-hour break in which I had to fly to Miami to host a dinner honoring Daniel Boulud at the South Beach *Wine & Food* festival, then to Chicago to host a charity gala for Chef Art Smith's Common Threads foundation.

As with *Top Chef*, workdays were usually twelve to fourteen hours, but often longer. Some days we started at 11 a.m. and went until three in the morning. The next day I might start at eight or nine and go until 9 p.m. The following day, we'd start at 6 a.m. Sometimes I had less than eight hours between shoot days. I quickly understood just what Padma had meant.

What's more, the host has to keep the plot moving forward and serve as a go-between for the chefs and the judges. You have to moderate the conversation, making sure each judge gets the chance to express an opinion, and ask the appropriate questions to ensure everyone has all the information needed to make an informed decision. You're like an umpire. And when someone is eliminated, you're the one delivering the bad news.

The host also has to handle all the business. It's not like I made up those challenges on the spot. (I didn't invent the Dawn Hand

Renewal challenge!) I had to memorize challenge guidelines that, for legal reasons, I had to deliver in a specific way. I'll be the first to admit that I didn't sound natural those first few days. The first time I had to say, "Your dessert just didn't measure up. Please pack your tools and go," I felt terribly awkward. I tried to be empathetic but also say it with conviction.

My producer asked me to stay late to work on my delivery and to figure out exactly how we wanted it to sound. I said it maybe fifty times, until the words didn't mean anything anymore. Finally, we got the line close enough to sounding like something a real person would say, and I went back to my apartment, with a heightened respect for Padma.

"How was your first day on set?" Jeremy asked excitedly over the phone from New York.

My cracking voice said it all. I was so disappointed in myself.

Though I'd had the advantage of watching *Top Chef* from the inside for so many years, it was also in some ways a disadvantage. Padma was always there in my head, and let me assure you, she casts a long, thin, beautiful shadow. I didn't want to come across like a cheap version of her. But how do you own something that you're not writing yourself, something that's been said by someone else so many times before? There are only so many ways to say, "Pack your tools and go"!

After a while, I learned to riff and improvise, to make the role my own. I developed a comfortable rapport with the chefs, and I think it was clear how much I respected them. We became more relaxed together on the set.

Our contestants that first season were a very sensitive bunch. There was a lot of drama. Seth had a breakdown on episodes 3 and 4 and had to be excused from the competition. Malika quit. Heather C. was voted off, returned to replace Malika, and then was voted off again.

When I saw the edited show, I was shocked by how much tension there was between some of the contestants. We never saw that side of them at Judges' Table or during the challenges. Just like on *Top Chef*, we typically only see chefs on their best behavior. Our cast revealed their true—if somewhat exaggerated—selves in the house and in their interviews.

I was mesmerized by Erika's voice. I wanted her to sing me to sleep every night. She was graceful and lovely under pressure and always seemed so calm and collected. I adored Danielle's quirkiness. She was like a cartoon character with her expressions. Someone nicknamed her "Olive Oyl," and I thought that was perfect.

Zac, with his disco dust and his obsession with my Jimmy Choos, was smart and confident, if just a little sassy. Eric was a sensitive, earnest baker. He had never plated a dessert in his life before he came on the show. The winner, Yigit, was truly gifted at pastry and had an extraordinarily positive outlook on life. At the tender age of twenty-nine, he was such an old soul, wise beyond his years.

At least that's how I perceived our motley crew. I suppose the truth lies somewhere between what I knew before the show aired and what I learned afterward.

Within the dessert genre, there are many distinct skill sets. The restaurant pastry chef focuses on single-serving, plated desserts. Hotel pastry chefs do much of that, too, plus buffets, whole cakes, amenities, and catered banquets; they usually work a lot more with chocolate showpieces and sugar sculptures. Bread bakers make bread and savory baked goods; for them, dessert generally means cakes and sweets that come out of the oven complete unto themselves—cakes, cookies, brownies, and single-serving pastries. They may have to employ decorations, but they don't plate individual dishes with ice cream, garnishes, and sauce.

Learning the subtle intricacies of the dessert and baking worlds was a real education for me and, I think, for our viewers. In this way, *Just Desserts* has fulfilled its mission, which was to finally give dessert chefs their due.

....

EVERY JULY, JEREMY and I spend a week in Gloucester, Massachusetts, where his family has been vacationing for almost forty years. It's become one of my favorite corners of the world. One July morning in 2007 we were fast asleep at the house in Gloucester when my cell phone rang. I answered in a fog.

"*Mazel! Mazel!*" came the voice from the other end. It was Andy Cohen, executive vice president at Bravo and one of *Top Chef*'s executive producers.

"What happened?" I said blearily.

"*Top Chef* just got nominated for an Emmy for Outstanding Reality Series!"

I jolted out of bed, waking up Jeremy, then woke up everyone in the house. I called my family. I called *Food & Wine*. I called Tom and Padma. I was elated. Until the hunt for my dress began.

I go to cocktail parties and events all the time, but it's rare that I attend anything truly formal. The only other time I'd worn a long gown in recent memory was at my wedding.

Luckily, *Food & Wine* offered to help. We engaged the styling services of Mimi Lombardo, the fashion director for *Travel + Leisure* magazine, who has since become a trusted friend.

To be honest, I didn't think it was going to be that complicated: People call in dresses all the time. Dresses appear. One of them is magnificent, and you wear it.

Alas, it wasn't that simple.

First of all, there are many parts to an Emmy outfit: not just the dress, but the undergarments, the shoes, the jewelry, the bag. (This is when I curse all men on television, who can wear the same basic tuxedo to the Emmys every year, just changing their tie or adding a different set of cuff links.)

Second, on the long list of celebrities attending the Emmys, rest assured I am close to last. That's not me being self-deprecating; that's just a simple fact. I'm a judge on a food reality show, not a breakout ingénue from the season's biggest network drama.

The other issue was sizing. Even if a designer agrees to provide you with dresses to try, you're typically only sent samples. Samples are usually a size 2 or a size 0. I'm not overweight—but not even *one* boob of mine would fit into those sample dresses!

Trying on dress after dress for days on end, and finding most of them too small or just not attractive on me, definitely takes an emotional toll. In most ready-to-wear, I wear a size 6 or 8, but in certain high-end designer brands, I may need to go up a size or two. All of this adds up to a lot of reasons to feel bad about myself. But not so bad that I stay home, of course, and I have always arrived at the Emmys fully dressed, in a designer gown at that.

When we actually won the Outstanding Reality-Competition Emmy in 2010, usurping the award from seven-year category domination by *Amazing Race*, I was so overjoyed to be there in the first place, so completely dumbfounded and elated to be on stage with our production team and small heap of gold statues, in front of tens of millions of people, that it really didn't matter what I was wearing anyway.

．．．．．．．．．．．．．

I'M STILL NOT entirely used to being recognized and scrutinized in public. And I struggle with how much energy to put into all these superficial things like clothing, hair, and makeup. When I first started working in television, I thought: *I can't ever imagine being one of those women who needs hours of primping just to get the paper.*

And I'm not. I really don't devote a lot of time or thought to it. But part of me now understands why people do.

The number one question I'm asked by viewers and by the press, whether it's on the street or in an interview, is: "How do you eat so much and not gain weight?"

Padma is a pro at answering this question. She talks about how it's a real struggle for her, and how her stylist has to buy her different sizes depending on where we are in the season, because she usually goes up a dress size or two during shooting, then has to lose it all again when the show is over. (Nevertheless, Padma managed to rock a bikini on our *All-Stars* season finale. I guarantee you will *never* catch me on the show in a bikini.)

My answer to the question is this: Yes, I exercise. I stress about it. I do my best to stay in shape. I really am taking in an enormous amount of extra calories, especially on *Just Desserts*. I need to burn off some of the energy from all that sugar. I have ramped up my workout, and I try to keep it up throughout the year. I run consistently and get outside whenever I can, but I am no marathoner. Running four miles or so a few times a week, going to the gym, taking a spin class or simply taking a long walk or a hike whenever I get the chance is a small price to pay for getting to do what I do. I refuse to let these concerns consume me. Some of it is genetic, I guess, and I try to make the healthiest food choices I can when I am not on set or working.

I have also learned to *taste*, which is different from eating. When we're served eighteen dishes in one sitting, we only need a bite or two from each to determine its success or failure. We certainly don't need to finish the plate. As my Vietnam adventures taught me, because I am so lucky in this life, there will always be another meal.

Keep in mind that although I work on a competitive cooking show, I'm not in the business of competitive consumption. Seeing how many hot dogs or burgers I can stuff in my stomach in one sitting is not the end goal. I work in quality, not quantity. On one recent occasion I was asked to judge a contest where I was required to taste in the realm of twenty-four meatballs in one night to determine a winner. While having a chance to sample such a wide variety, made by the country's best restaurants, may sound exciting, rest assured that by the end of the night I was sufficiently nauseous and happy to retire my meatball judging title for the foreseeable future.

It can be exasperating, though, to be constantly reminded of the issue. Google my name, and you'll find that one of the top auto-fills after "Gail Simmons" is "weight." Now Google Tom Colicchio. I assure you that "weight" is *not* one of the top suggested fill-ins. No one interrogates Tom on how *he* stays trim—and Tom's not exactly a small guy. Sure, he exercises, but he's no Calvin Klein model.

And yet, Tom is a heartthrob—one of *People*'s Sexiest Men Alive. I can't count the number of women (and men!) who tell me they have a crush on Tom. There are certainly no blogs obsessively considering his workout schedule. And he's immune from the perennial "Is she pregnant?"

Find me a woman in America who doesn't wish she could lose five pounds. I stand in front of the mirror like anyone else and poke at my stomach or analyze my hips. We all struggle with that desire to be a little more perfect. Combine typical female insecurity with the fact that I have to spend most of my days gorging myself on national television while viewers study every bite, and you can see why the issue can be stressful.

I know so many women who let their weight define them, until it becomes all they talk about. There is nothing more boring and painful to me than talking about one's diet at the dinner table. It breaks my heart when people can't appreciate good food because eating triggers issues of control or fear. It's obviously a complex and emotionally fraught topic, but I want people to know that food is not the enemy. Moderation is vital, but so is pleasure.

I promised myself early on never to let my weight take up that much breath or time. So far I've been able to keep things in relative perspective. Somehow I managed to find a partner who loves me, and a livelihood that lets me use my brain and my passion. This gives me confidence and sustains me—both emotionally and intellectually. Thankfully, there's more to my life than how I look. On my deathbed, will I regret not being five pounds lighter? No. Will I regret eating that double chocolate chunk brownie with salted caramel? No—because it was mind-blowingly delicious and added a little something sweet to my life.

In fact, maybe I'll regret not having had two.

Which brings me seamlessly, respectfully, to the best part of it all: without even that much scheming or groveling, I not only found a way to eat for a living, but more specifically, *eat dessert*. It's an extraordinary truth. Most days I cannot help but think I have been handed the proverbial golden ticket.

And unlike with savory food, desserts are rarely inedible. The expanse between good and bad on the dessert spectrum is arguably smaller than when you are considering poorly cooked or poor quality meat, fish, or vegetables. Desserts can be undercooked or overcooked, too sweet or too dry, but all things considered, a bite or two of even the most disappointing pudding is nowhere near as stomach-churning as chewing on raw chicken or swallowing a mouthful of grit from improperly washed mollusks. Even my most trying days on the set of *Top Chef: Just Desserts* bring reasons to thank karma for whatever I did in my last life. Sure, I had to endure some things I didn't love—for example, in Season 1, Erika's poppy seed and lavender ice cream, which tasted vaguely of soap, or the soupy mess that was poor Tim's Basil Pudding with Orange, Kumquat, and Lime Granita. In the second season, Craig's syrupy, sickly sweet lemonade with pink rock sugar rim and Rebecca's garlicky falafel panna cotta were also a far cry from delectable. But for every failed mousse or crumble, misguided cake concoction or cloying candy coating, there has been a triumph of soul-stirring proportions for us to enjoy: In Season 1 there was Eric's Peanut Butter Krispy Bar, created for a high school bake sale, or Danielle's Pistachio Shortcake with Lemon Cream and Strawberries on our Dessert Shop Wars episode. Yigit's

Season 1 finale tasting started with subtle Cucumber Lime Sorbet with Straus Yogurt and Caviar Pearls, and ended with Hazelnut Dacquoise, Milk Jam, and Salted Caramel Ice Cream. Yes, Milk Jam! It's more or less the English translation for *dolce de leche* (sweetened condensed milk cooked until caramelized). So good was Yigit's version that when he sent me my own personal stash a few months later, I greedily gobbled it up with a spoon and didn't share. Not even a dollop.

All of our wildest childhood fantasies were fully realized in Season 2, when the original cast of *Willy Wonka & the Chocolate Factory* joined us to celebrate the film's fortieth anniversary. We created a challenge in which our talented contestants had to build their own version of Wonka's "world of pure imagination," complete with fruit leather wallpaper, a carrot cake garden patch, chocolate flower cups filled with cream, and an edible beehive dripping with honey. It was as close as I can imagine to the rapture of heaven, and easily my favorite day working in television to date.

But the pleasure of dessert is not only derived from a complex list of plated ingredients like manjari caramel mousse, passion fruit gelée, and pineapple sauce or a carefully constructed mille-feuille with layers of mocha cream and spun sugar. It can come in the form of the humblest scoop of ice cream, roasted fruit, or chocolate chip cookie. No matter how you slice it, dessert's purpose is not to sustain us. It doesn't fulfill any biological need; it is not a requirement for health or nourishment by any medical authority. Dessert is a simple splendor, craved and rhapsodized for its ability to uplift and comfort. In short: to make us happy.

And a little happiness is never a bad thing. It shouldn't be something we have to earn or deserve. It's about relishing a moment of joy and satiety in our hectic, complicated lives. If a few bites of chocolate help along the way, so be it.

Epilogue

....

Petits Fours

IN EVERY PANEL discussion or interview I do, people try to suggest that food television is the demise of sophisticated dining.

"Hasn't food TV ruined food for foodies?" someone always asks.

"No," I reply. If anything, it's broadened the country's interest and savvy about how to read a menu and shop for ingredients. This education has raised everyone's standards and expectations. The result: now we can get *pluots*, organic soy, and Meyer lemons at our local grocery stores. How can that be bad?

Maybe it makes me cowardly: that I don't fully come down on the side of either what I like to call the simplifiers, with their quick-and-easy recipes for budget-friendly meatloaf, or those who proudly call themselves food snobs or "foodies," insisting as they do on eating only organic micro-greens handpicked by locally raised nuns. Certainly, the simplifiers have a broader reach. But the snobs are the ones moving the industry forward by discovering new trends and funding or supporting the chefs and artisans who are creating cutting-edge cuisine. When it comes to this fight, I'm Switzerland (or Canada?). I'm just happy we're having the conversation in the first place.

Of course, I'm a product of the times I live in. My education in the food industry coincided, serendipitously, with a widespread boom in enthusiasm about the culinary world. My job didn't even exist when I started unconsciously working toward it. Without meaning to, I stumbled into a career full of smart, interesting, wonderful people, and lots of delicious food. I certainly couldn't have planned it, but I am so happy to have arrived at this moment just in time.

About two years ago, I was sitting with Dave Serwatka, talking about a decision we had to make about the show. I disagreed with him and was pushing for our producers to approach the issue from another angle, but he wouldn't relent.

"Fine," I responded. "You would know more about these things than I do anyway. I'm just a magazine person."

"Gail, get over yourself," he laughed. "You're a TV person now. It's time to face the facts."

As reluctant as I am to admit it, it's true. I've chosen this path. No one forced me to be on TV. With it comes great privilege, but also the knowledge that I'm being scrutinized by the people who watch me. That's human nature. We all do it. It's a gift that I'm able to be part of a very public conversation and have an impact on the world in a larger way, thanks to the magical reach of television.

Having had the opportunity to work in so many different parts of the industry over the past fifteen years has also made me realize that I don't have to be just one thing. I can be a Canadian and a New Yorker, a magazine person and a TV personality, a wife and a businesswoman, a fan of four-star restaurants and an avid lover of street stalls. The Internet trolls who post their nasty commentary, having to go to the gym a little more, getting asked in interviews if a loose dress means I'm pregnant—they're all occupational hazards.

In the ever-expanding food universe, I like to think of myself as a sort of cheerleader, or perhaps a translator. My job, as I see it, is to help everyone access, understand, and enjoy exciting food and adventurous cooking as much as I do and to spread the good word on how it can enrich all of our lives. I appreciate that what chefs do at all levels takes great skill, craftsmanship, talent, and patience, and I admire the farmers, purveyors, restaurant owners, and servers who play a large role in the way we all eat today. Everyone who cares about food, whether making a Toll House cookie or an elaborate petit four, is okay with me—as long as I get to lick the bowl.

Recipes

....

My Life in One Day of Meals

Breakfast

Scrambled Eggs with Chives and Parmesan Cheese

....

YIELD: 2 SERVINGS

Teenage heartbreak may have clouded my summer spent in Israel, but at least I learned how to make great scrambled eggs.

5 large eggs

1 tablespoon unsalted butter

½ small onion, thinly sliced

¼ teaspoon coarse salt

⅛ teaspoon freshly ground pepper

1½ tablespoons heavy cream

3 tablespoons Parmigiano-Reggiano, finely grated, divided

2 tablespoons chives, finely chopped, divided

In a medium mixing bowl, whisk the eggs until just beginning to foam. Set aside.

Melt the butter in a medium non-stick skillet over medium-low heat. When butter is foaming, add the onions and cook until very soft and translucent, about 3 minutes.

Season eggs with salt and pepper, add cream, and whisk to evenly combine. Add egg mixture to onions; cook over low heat, stirring continuously with a rubber spatula. When eggs are almost set, stir in 2 tablespoons Parmigiano-Reggiano and 1 tablespoon chives. Continue stirring until eggs are fully set, but still soft. Sprinkle with remaining Parmesan-Reggiano and chives for serving.

Brunch

Welsh Rarebit

YIELD: 4 SERVINGS

The perfect dish to accompany a marriage proposal, or any other late-morning event.

2 tablespoons unsalted butter, divided

1 tablespoon all-purpose flour

1 1/2 teaspoons mustard powder

1/4 teaspoon cayenne

1/2 cup Guinness Stout

1 tablespoon Worcestershire sauce

4 ounces extra-sharp cheddar cheese, coarsely grated

4 pieces lightly toasted pumpernickel bread, sliced about 1/2-inch thick

4 large eggs

Coarse salt

Freshly ground black pepper

Cornichons or pickled vegetables, for serving

Place rack in the middle of the oven and preheat broiler.

Melt 1 tablespoon butter in a small saucepan over medium heat, then stir in flour with a rubber spatula. Cook, stirring often to ensure no lumps form, until mixture is golden brown and very fragrant, about 3 to

5 minutes. Stir in mustard powder and cayenne, followed by beer and Worcestershire sauce.

When mixture is well combined, turn heat to low and whisk in cheese until very smooth. Spread a thick layer of the mixture on toasted bread slices. Place on a sheet tray under the broiler, until cheese is bubbly and edges of toast are crisp and golden, about 4 minutes. Meanwhile, melt remaining 1 tablespoon butter in medium skillet over medium heat. When butter begins to foam, reduce heat to medium-low, crack eggs into butter, and fry until whites are set and yolks are still runny. Place one egg on top of each slice of bread and season to taste with salt and pepper. Serve immediately with cornichons or other pickled vegetables. Leftover cheese mixture may be refrigerated up to 1 day.

Lunch

Chickpea, Artichoke, and Spinach Stew

YIELD: 4 SERVINGS

The family I lived with in Spain tortured their vegetables. Here, I redeem them.

2 cups dried chickpeas, soaked overnight and drained

¼ cup plus 2 tablespoons extra-virgin olive oil

1 large onion, finely diced

2 garlic cloves, minced

½ pound soft cooked chorizo, sliced ¼-inch thick

One 28-ounce can diced Italian tomatoes, juices reserved

3 large artichokes, trimmed, hearts quartered and reserved in lemon water

2 teaspoons sweet pimenton

1 bay leaf

2 cups chicken stock

Coarse salt

Freshly ground pepper

1 pound spinach, thick stems discarded

In a medium saucepan, cover the chickpeas with 2 inches of water and bring to a boil. Reduce the heat to low and simmer until the chickpeas are tender, about 2 hours. Add water as necessary to maintain level. Drain the chickpeas and set aside.

In a medium, heavy pot, heat the olive oil. Add the onion and garlic and cook over medium-low heat until onion is translucent, about 7 minutes. Add the chorizo and cook until just beginning to brown and oils have been released, about 10 minutes. Add the tomatoes and cook until sizzling, about 4 minutes. Add the artichoke hearts, pimenton, and bay leaf; cook for 5 minutes. Add chickpeas, then reduce heat to low and pour in reserved tomato juices and chicken stock.

Bring stew to a boil, adjust seasonings as desired with salt and pepper, and simmer until artichoke hearts are cooked through, about 30 minutes.

Just before serving, stir in the spinach and cook until wilted, about 5 to 7 minutes. Serve with slices of pan con tomate (recipe below).

Pan con Tomate

YIELD: 4 SERVINGS

8 slices thickly cut country bread

4 garlic cloves, peeled and slightly crushed

2 ripe tomatoes, quartered

Extra-virgin olive oil

Coarse salt

Freshly ground black pepper

Toast or grill bread. Rub garlic over warm bread. Grate the tomatoes on a box grater, then spread the grated pulp evenly over the bread. Drizzle lightly with olive oil and season with salt and pepper.

Afternoon Snacks

From My Culinary School Kitchen

YIELD: 1 SERVING

This is what I ate every day while I was in culinary school. Two ingredients that kept us all going for hours.

Tear off a hunk of French baguette.

Cut a piece of Gruyère cheese.

Combine.

Serve alongside strong coffee, with whole milk and a heaping teaspoon of sugar.

Zucchini Bread

YIELD: TWO LOAVES

My mother made this spiced bread often when we were little. Despite its description, I assure you it is delicious. I wouldn't normally choose to put raisins in a recipe like this, but they add great texture and needed moisture, which is part of the reason it is so addictive.

2 cups whole wheat flour	1 ½ cups sugar
1 ½ teaspoons ground cinnamon	1 cup vegetable oil
2 teaspoons baking soda	2 teaspoons pure vanilla extract
1 teaspoon table salt	2 cups shredded zucchini, drained
¼ teaspoon baking powder	1 cup chopped, toasted walnuts
3 large eggs, room temperature	1 cup raisins

Preheat the oven to 350 F. Brush two standard loaf pans with softened butter.

In a large mixing bowl, whisk together the flour, cinnamon, baking soda, salt, and baking powder. Set aside. In a large mixing bowl, beat the eggs with a fork until frothy. Add the sugar, oil, and vanilla extract, stirring well to combine. Stir in the zucchini, then add the flour mixture, walnuts, and raisins. Using a rubber spatula, fold ingredients until just combined. Do not overmix.

Divide the batter evenly between the prepared loaf pans. Bake until golden and a toothpick inserted in the center comes out clean, about 45 minutes. Let the bread cool in the pans on a wire rack. When they are cool enough to handle, run a knife around the edges of the pans, invert, and release the loaves.

Dad's Full Sour Pickles

YIELD: FOUR 1-QUART JARS

These are the pickles of my dreams. Make sure to store them in a cool, dark place or they will not pickle properly.

8 garlic cloves, peeled and lightly crushed	4 tablespoons kosher salt
2 bunches fresh dill	4 teaspoons pickling spice
16 Kirby cucumbers, scrubbed with a brush to remove any dirt	

Sterilize four 1-quart jars by running them through the dishwasher or boil them in water. Place lids in a large mixing bowl. When jars are sterilized, pour boiling water over lids. The bands do not need to be sterilized.

Place a garlic clove and a quarter of one bunch of dill in each jar. Tightly pack 4 cucumbers in each jar. Add another garlic clove and another quarter of one bunch of dill, 1 tablespoon salt, and 1 teaspoon pickling spice to each jar.

Fill the jars with cold water. Using tongs, remove the lids from the hot water, then put on the bands, turning so they are as tight as possible. Turn the jars upside down and leave for 24 hours. The next day, turn the jars upright and store in a cool, dark place. For half sour pickles, let them pickle for one week. For full sour pickles, let them pickle for one month. Once opened, keep the pickles in the refrigerator.

Dinner

Kasha and Bowties with Mushroom Gravy

YIELD: 6 SERVINGS

My husband loves "old Jewish" food, and you'll see why when you try this recipe. Serve it with your favorite meatballs and a side salad.

5 tablespoons unsalted butter, divided

2 large yellow onions, thinly sliced

Coarse salt

1 large egg

1 cup medium kasha, washed

Freshly ground black pepper

2 cups chicken stock

1 pound farfalle pasta

1 garlic clove, minced

1 pound mushrooms, mix of cremini, white, and shiitake, sliced

2 tablespoons flour

¼ cup red wine

2 cups water

1 tablespoon thyme

Melt 2 tablespoons of butter in large sauté pan over medium heat. Reduce heat to low and sauté onions until fully caramelized, about 1 hour. Sprinkle 1 teaspoon of coarse salt over the onions and begin scraping brown bits off the bottom of the pan. Remove onions to a bowl and set aside.

In a medium mixing bowl, whisk the egg until just beginning to foam. Add the kasha and stir to ensure the egg evenly coats all the grains. Melt 1 tablespoon butter in the same pan, then add the kasha. Sauté for 5 minutes, then season with salt and pepper. Pour chicken stock over the kasha, cover, and cook over low heat until all the stock has been absorbed and the kasha is tender, 15 to 25 minutes.

Meanwhile, bring a large pot of salted water to boil. Cook the farfalle to al dente according to package instructions. Reserve a cup of the water before draining the pasta.

When the kasha is tender, combine with the noodles and onions in a large bowl, and set aside. In the kasha pan, melt the remaining 2 tablespoons of butter. When butter is foaming, add garlic and mushrooms, and sauté until well-cooked and soft. Add flour and stir until no lumps remain, about 2 minutes. Deglaze the pan with red wine. When three-quarters of the liquid has evaporated from the pan, pour water into pan and cook until gravy thickens, about 15 minutes, then add thyme to finish.

Portion kasha and bowties into bowls, ladle mushroom gravy over the top.

Desserts

Blackberry Soufflé

YIELD: 4 SERVINGS

At the end of a rough night on the line, this soufflé made it all worth it. Years later, while attempting to re-create the recipe, I went straight to the source and spent a magical afternoon making soufflés and reminiscing about Le Cirque 2000 with the master himself—pastry and chocolate wizard Chef Jacques Torres. His quick way of moving about the kitchen and producing batch upon batch of beautiful soufflés was awe-inspiring. The results were just as breathtaking and satisfying as I remembered.

¾ cup fresh blackberries
10 tablespoons sugar, divided
4 large egg whites, room temperature
1 lemon, cut into thirds

1 cup blueberries, raspberries, and/or additional blackberries, if desired
Vanilla ice cream, for serving

Preheat oven to 400°F. Brush four 10-ounce ramekins with softened butter and coat with granulated sugar, tapping them well to make sure the sugar is evenly distributed. Set aside.

In a medium saucepan, combine blackberries and 5 tablespoons sugar, smashing the blackberries with a spatula. Cook mixture over medium-high heat, reducing until berries have completely broken down and liquids thicken, about 4 minutes. Turn off heat and set puree aside.

In a clean mixing bowl, whisk egg whites until foamy, then squeeze in juice from the top third of the lemon. Slowly add the remaining 5 tablespoons sugar to the whites, then whip until stiff, glossy peaks form. Very gently, fold the blackberry puree into the egg whites, just until the two mixtures are combined. Scoop soufflé batter into a large piping bag or large sealable plastic bag and snip a large opening off the corner of the bag. Pipe half of the batter evenly among the four prepared ramekins. If desired, place a few fresh berries on top of this initial layer and then pipe the remaining batter over the berries to fill.

Place ramekins in the oven and immediately reduce the temperature to 375°F. Bake until well-risen and tops are just beginning to brown, 10 to 12 minutes. The center of the soufflé should be just barely set. Serve immediately with a scoop of vanilla ice cream right on top.

Frozen Chocolate, Peanut Butter, and Banana Bar with Toasted Coconut

YIELD: 16 SERVINGS

My husband, Jeremy, adores chocolate, peanut butter, and banana in any combination. This recipe is one of his favorites.

½ cup unsweetened coconut, divided

½ cup roasted, salted peanuts, chopped

2 cups (12 ounces) semisweet chocolate

¾ cup creamy peanut butter

1 cup heavy cream, divided

2 ½ ripe bananas

⅓ cup whole-milk Greek yogurt

¼ cup coconut milk

2 tablespoons honey

Preheat oven to 350°F. Prepare a standard loaf pan with non-stick spray and line with parchment paper. Allow the ends of the parchment paper to hang over the sides of the pan.

On a baking sheet lined with parchment paper, toast coconut until lightly golden and fragrant, about 10 minutes. Set aside. When cool, combine 2 tablespoons toasted coconut with peanuts and sprinkle over the bottom of the prepared loaf pan, forming an even layer.

Fill a medium saucepan with about 2 inches of water and bring to a simmer over medium heat. Place the chocolate in a large heat-proof mixing bowl that will rest securely in the rim of the saucepan over the water. The bottom of the bowl should not touch the simmering water. Stir chocolate occasionally until completely melted and shiny. Remove bowl of chocolate from the water and set aside. When chocolate has cooled slightly, fold in the peanut butter, stirring until smooth and fully combined.

In a medium mixing bowl, whip $2/3$ cup heavy cream until it holds stiff, glossy peaks. Fold half of the whipped cream into the chocolate–peanut butter mixture until lightened, and then fold in the remaining whipped cream until completely combined. Pour half of the mixture into the prepared loaf pan, smoothing the top with an offset spatula to ensure a smooth, even layer is created; set aside remaining chocolate mixture.

In a blender, puree the bananas, Greek yogurt, coconut milk, and honey. Pour the pureed mixture into a medium mixing bowl and fold in remaining toasted coconut. In a separate mixing bowl, whip the remaining $1/3$ cup heavy cream until it holds stiff, glossy peaks, then fold into the banana-coconut mixture. Pour mixture on top of the chocolate layer, smoothing the top with an offset spatula. Freeze until just beginning to harden, about 1 hour.

When banana-coconut layer is ready, pour the remaining half of the chocolate–peanut butter mixture into the loaf pan. Run your offset spatula flush across the edges of the loaf pan to create a flat bottom for the bar. Wrap the loaf pan tightly with plastic wrap and freeze until firm, about 1 hour.

Remove the pan from the freezer, run a paring knife along the inside edges, and place a cutting board on top of the bar. Invert the board onto a countertop so the loaf pan is upside down on top of the board. Lift the pan, remove the parchment paper, slice, and serve immediately.

Just Before Bed

Dark Chocolate Hot Cocoa

YIELD: 4 SERVINGS

My father could subsist easily on hot chocolate alone. I don't blame him.

3 cups whole milk   *1 cup bittersweet chocolate,*
cut into shavings

Over low heat, warm milk in a large saucepan until just beginning to simmer. Whisk chocolate into warmed milk until smooth and velvety. Divide evenly among four mugs. Sweeten with a little sugar if desired.

Midnight Snack

Plum Tart

....

YIELD: ONE 9-INCH TART

This tart is deceptively simple, and my childhood memories are filled with the intoxicating smell of vanilla released while it was baking. It is really more of a cake and it's best in late summer, when plums are at their peak. Feel free to substitute other stone fruit, apples, or pears and use the recipe year-round.

1 cup all-purpose flour

1 teaspoon baking powder

Pinch table salt

1 stick unsalted butter, room temperature, plus more for coating pan

1 cup sugar

2 large eggs, room temperature

1 teaspoon vanilla extract

1 pound red plums, pitted and sliced ½-inch thick

Half of a lemon

Cinnamon-sugar (2 tablespoons sugar, plus ½ teaspoon cinnamon, mixed together)

Preheat the oven to 375° F. Lightly brush a 9-inch springform pan with butter.

In a small mixing bowl, whisk together the flour, baking powder, and salt. Set aside.

In a stand mixer fitted with the paddle attachment, cream the butter and sugar on medium speed until light and fluffy, about 3 minutes. Add the eggs one at a time, allowing to fully incorporate before the next addition, then mix in vanilla. Reduce to low speed and incorporate the flour mixture just until the batter comes together. Do not overmix the batter or pastry will be tough. Pour batter into the springform pan and spread evenly with an offset spatula; wrap the pan in plastic and chill at least 20 minutes or overnight.

Remove the dough from the refrigerator. Arrange the plums in a concentric circle on top of the dough. Squeeze the juice from the lemon half evenly over the plums, ensuring no lemon seeds escape. Sprinkle the cinnamon-sugar mixture over the plums. Bake tart until edges are golden and center is set, 45 minutes to 1 hour.

Allow tart to cool in pan. Run a sharp paring knife around the edge and then remove the springform. Serve warm.

ACKNOWLEDGMENTS

The task of properly thanking everyone involved in bringing this book to fruition is almost as daunting as the process of writing the book itself. What started as a list of questions from my agent almost three years ago, about the world of food and chefs, as well as how I saw my place within it, took many twists and turns before it morphed into these pages. I am forever indebted to so many individuals who gently coaxed it out of me, often despite my growing neuroses. My narrative has never been straightforward, but instead has wound itself through the lives of so many extraordinary people. It is due to these countless, cherished friendships that I have been able to accomplish anything at all.

First, infinite thanks to Andy McNicol, my tireless champion and literary agent, who always knows just what to say, when to push me, and how to handle any situation, with the perfect combo of brutal honesty and amazing grace. Serendipitously, our journeys both started as assistants at *Vogue*, and I am so grateful the universe put us together again so many years later.

It was through Andy that I met the remarkable Ada Calhoun, my partner in crime and consummate articulator, kitchen table thera-pist, and confidante. Ada's guidance and expert hand in this project have been immeasurable, and I will always be thankful for the op-portunity to learn from and collaborate with her.

Finding my way to my editor Jill Schwartzman at Hyperion was equally fortuitous. From the moment I set foot in her office, I felt at home and at ease. Jill's eagle eye, empathetic shoulder, patience, and knowledge were used in equal portions, allowing me to write the book I dreamed of but had no idea how to approach. Many thanks to the whole Hyperion family, especially Ellen Archer, Elisabeth Dyssegaard, Kristin Kiser, Sarah Rucker, Mindy Stockfield, Bryan Christian, Marie Coolman, Christine Ragasa, Claire McKean, Karen Minster, Cassandra Pappas, and Sam O'Brien.

Thank you to Jeff Googel and Kenny Slotnick, the other two-thirds of my team at William Morris Endeavor Entertainment, for agreeing to take me under the wings of their well-tailored suits. Their business savvy, humor, and constant encouragement is always accu-rate and appreciated.

Shana Faust, creative director, style guru, and college roomie, has remained the pillar on which I lean at every weak moment, and I assure you those moments are plentiful. Her calm, creative nature and advice were integral and infinitely valued. I am certain Jer and I would not survive if she, Steven, and sweet Bea were not in New York to share it all with us.

A very special thank-you to Allison Veinote, who came into my life, and this project, at just the right time, and put so many dispa-rate pieces of both together, keeping me on track and, when I let her, on time.

For making this book look so much better than I could have alone: Melanie Dunea, Seton Hurson Rossini, Peter Lindberg, Alexa Mulvihill, Julia Rothman, the brilliant team of THUSS + FARRELL, Kimberly Fusaro, Bradley Wayne Tischler, Allan Zepeda, Mikey Katz, Tara Donne, and Zone 4 Architects.

Of course, a story about my life so far is only as strong as the people who fill its pages, and I am beyond lucky to have many families, who let me move between them seamlessly and call them my own:

Thank you, Mom, Dad, Alan, Eric and Kim, Tyler, Elle, and Brooke for giving me more love and support than I could ever imagine, through every twist, turn, and tumble. I love you so much.

I do not take for granted how blessed I am that Noreen, Herb, Jodie, Karen, Rena, and the entire Abrams/Gold contingent, my family-through-marriage, have welcomed and embraced me since we first met. Each and every one of them is, to borrow a phrase from my exceptional mother-in-law, *the best.*

To the friends who have been at my side from the start and whose smarts, generosity, and clarity I cherish beyond words: Vanessa Comisarow, Stacey Grill, Jessica Goldberg, Mia Brown, Mindy Fox, and your valiant husbands, I admire and adore you.

My mentors, Jeffrey Steingarten and Chef Daniel Boulud, along with the amazing Georgette Farkas, Katherine Yang, Celia Laurent, Kathryn Kellinger, Jeanne Koenig, and Elizabeth Alsop, all must take credit for teaching me how to cook, how to eat, how to write, and, well, just about everything important in between.

I also owe so much to my family at *Food & Wine*: Christina Grdovic Baltz, Dana Cowin, Devin Padgett, Wendy Mure, Jay Meyer, Sonia Zala, Diella Koberstein, Francesca Andreani, Rory Tischler, Jodisue Rosen, and so many others. Thank you for betting on the Canadian kid, who seemed more trouble than she was worth, and, most of all, for allowing me a seat at your ever abundant table. Love this job. Love this team.

And of course, thank you to my TV family: Tom Colicchio, Padma Lakshmi, Johnny Iuzzini, Dannielle Kyrillos, and Hubert Keller, who have all taught me so much and made me laugh so hard, always when I needed it most.

Thank you to Lauren Zalaznick, Frances Berwick, Andy Cohen, Dave Serwatka, Tory Brody, Ellen Stone, Suzanne Park, and Monica

Reyhani at Bravo, along with my beloved traveling band of hooligans at Magical Elves: Dan Cutforth, Jane Lipsitz, Nan Strait, Liz Cook, Steve Hryniewicz, Paul Starkman, Paul Hogan, Michelle Brown, Darshan Gress, Jason Duffy, Kristen Kiyan, Megan Ray, and the dozens of others who work tirelessly behind the scenes and who make my day (and often long-into-the-night) job the most fun I have ever had.

I am indebted to a few others along the way for their random acts of kindness and constant support, including Nilou Motamed, Jay Takefman, Stevie Devor, Brandon Creed, Chef Jacques Torres, Harriet Bell, Samantha Hanks, and Marcy Blum. Superheroes all.

Foremost and finally, thank you to Jeremy: my home and the infallible love of my life.